NINE LIES ABOUT WORK

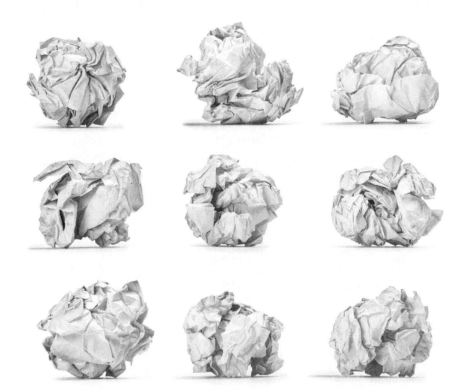

Freethinking
A Leader's Guide to the Real World
^

NINE LIES ABOUT WORK

MARCUS BUCKINGHAM
ASHLEY GOODALL

Harvard Business Review Press
Boston, Massachusetts

10 9 8 7 6 5

No part of this publication may be reproduced, stored in or introduced into a retrieval system, or transmitted, in any form, or by any means (electronic, mechanical, photocopying, recording, or otherwise), without the prior permission of the publisher. Requests for permission should be directed to permissions@hbsp.harvard.edu, or mailed to Permissions, Harvard Business School Publishing, 60 Harvard Way, Boston, Massachusetts 02163.

The web addresses referenced in this book were live and correct at the time of the book's publication but may be subject to change.

Library of Congress Cataloging-in-Publication Data

Names: Buckingham, Marcus, author. | Goodall, Ashley (Author of Nine lies About work), author.
Title: Nine lies about work : a freethinking leader's guide to the real world / Marcus Buckingham, Ashley Goodall.
Description: Boston, Massachusetts : Harvard Business Review Press, 2019.
Identifiers: LCCN 2018046989 | ISBN 9781633696303 (hardcover)
Subjects: LCSH: Organizational effectiveness. | Industrial management. | Organizational change.
Classification: LCC HD58.9 .B84 2019 | DDC 650--dc23 LC record available at https://lccn.loc.gov/2018046989

Hardcover ISBN: 978-1-63369-630-3
Paperback ISBN: 978-1-63369-803-1
eISBN: 978-1-63369-631-0

The paper used in this publication meets the requirements of the American National Standard for Permanence of Paper for Publications and Documents in Libraries and Archives Z39.48-1992.

To Chris and Graeme, who taught us to
start with what's knowable.

Contents

NINE LIES ABOUT WORK

Introduction

It ain't what you don't know that gets you into trouble.
It's what you know for sure, that just ain't so.*

—MARK TWAIN

Here's who we are.

Marcus is a data geek. He loves figuring out how to measure things you can't count, such as personality, performance, and engagement. He spent much of his career doing this at the Gallup Organization. He then built his own coaching and software company devoted to helping people do their best work, and he now leads the ADP Research Institute's investigations into all things people and performance. He's a transplanted Brit.

Ashley lives in the world of big companies. After an early stint designing the acoustics for concert halls, he dedicated his career to helping the likes of Deloitte and Cisco get the most from all their people. He's the kind of practitioner who loves to pressure test every innovative

---

*Ironically, one thing we know for sure that just ain't so is that this quotation is from Mark Twain: though it is most often attributed to him, the truth is that no one is sure who coined it. In this way it serves as a sort of double reminder of the dangers of misplaced certainty.

idea against the messy realities of the world of work. Currently he's doing this for Cisco's hundred and forty thousand employees and contractors around the world. He's also a transplanted Brit.

A couple of years ago, the *Harvard Business Review* asked us to combine Marcus's reliable data angle with Ashley's real-world-leader angle and write an article about the most effective, reliable, and valid way to do that uniformly unpopular ritual, the performance appraisal. The article was bluntly damning of existing practices, and stirred up the field to such an extent that HBR came back to us and asked whether we could take this same rigorous and realistic approach and apply it to the entire world of work. We said yes, and the book you're holding is the result.

We began the book with a paradox: Why do so many of the ideas and practices that are held as settled truths at work wind up being so deeply frustrating to, and unpopular with, the very people they are supposed to serve? Why, for example, is it a settled truth that having your goals cascaded down upon you from above is the best way to align and evaluate your work, when those of us in the trenches feel the yearly goal-setting process to be meaningless rigmarole with little connection to our actual work? Why is it a settled truth that you need critical feedback, when, in the real world, most of us lean away from such feedback, and feel more inclined to give it to the other guy than to get it ourselves? Why is it a settled truth that your manager can reliably rate you on your performance, when, on actual teams, none of us has ever met a team leader blessed with perfect objectivity? Why is it a settled truth that all the best leaders possess a defined list of attributes that you should aspire to acquire, when, in our everyday lives, none of us has ever met a leader with all of these attributes?

This paradox led to the core idea and audience of the book. The idea is this: the world of work today is overflowing with systems, processes, tools, and assumptions that are deeply flawed and that push directly against our ability to express what is unique about each of us in the work we do every day. Workplace data buttresses this idea. Global worker engagement is weak, with less than 20 percent of workers reporting that they are fully engaged at work.* And economists, in seeking to explain the global decline in productivity growth since the mid-seventies, have suggested that "the technological advances and management strategies that worked to propel productivity in the past have been fully implemented and are no longer contributing to productivity."[1] In other words, whatever our current practices may be, they are no longer giving us much lift.

These practices are by now so commonplace and ingrained that they are hard to see for what they really are. Some of them we encounter as the necessary but frustrating things that large organizations just do and have always done. Some of them, though, are born of convictions held firmly by those who run our companies and who then impose these convictions on the rest of us. Together they form the backdrop and justification for almost everything that happens to us at work—how we are selected for jobs and how we are then evaluated, trained, paid, promoted, and fired.

And yet, look more closely and you'll discover that they "just ain't so."

We could call these things "misconceptions," or "myths," or even "misunderstandings," but because they are pushed at us so hard, almost as if they're being used to steer us away from the world as it truly is, we'll call them "lies."

There are nine of them in this book. And since, in Picasso's framing, "every act of creation is first an act of destruction," before we can build something strong and fine with our teams we need to deconstruct each lie—to discern how it begins life as a truth in one small set of cases and then spreads into a lie applied to all cases—and then push on to uncover the broader truths hidden behind.

The first three chapters, after asking why culture, plans, and goals are imposed on us so resolutely, reveal better ways for getting us all to

---

*See appendix A.

pull together. Chapters 4, 5, 6, and 7 each address a particular aspect of our human nature, and then reveal how we can best grow ourselves and our people when each of us is so glaringly and enduringly different. Chapter 8 questions why "balance" is held up to each of us as the ideal, and then presents a very different aspiration. And finally, the last chapter takes on our reverence for all things "leadership," and offers up a new window into what really happens when we, as followers, give our breath and our passion to the vision of another.

As you read, you'll realize that these Nine Lies have taken hold because each satisfies the organization's need for control. Large organizations are complex places, and a strong and understandable instinct of their leaders is to seek simplicity and order—not least because this makes it easier to persuade themselves and their stakeholders that they are moving toward their objectives. But the desire for simplicity easily shades into a desire for conformity, and before long this conformity threatens to extinguish individuality. Before we know it, the particular talents and interests of each person are seen as inconveniences, and the organization comes to treat its people as essentially interchangeable.

This is why you are told that your organization's culture is monolithic, that the plan must be adhered to, that work must be aligned through cascaded goals, that humans must be molded into well-roundedness and given constant feedback until they become so, and that each one of us must rate the others so as to conform most closely to the prescribed models of leadership, performance, and potential.

You'll see, as well, that the strongest force pushing back against the lies, and the force that we all seek to harness in our lives, is the power of our own individuality—that the true power of human nature is that each human's nature is unique, and that expressing this through our work is an act, ultimately, of love.

The audience we imagined at the outset was someone leading a team for the first time—someone who is facing a glorious but challenging world, and someone who wants to do something extraordinary with his or her team, to achieve greatness with them, to enable greatness for them, to become the kind of leader they talk about for years to come. We imagined leaders who are asking themselves how they will get the most from each team member; how they will keep them all focused when each seems to have their own personal goals; how they will prevent them from making mistakes that will hurt the team, yet allow them room to experiment and learn; how they will be fair judges of their performance, yet still build relationships with them that are real and caring; and how they will do all this while remaining true to who they are as people. We imagined someone who, in attempting to do all this, would be confounded and stymied by the Nine Lies—by all the things we know for sure but just ain't so.

But as we wrote, our sense of who we were writing for grew. We realized that we weren't writing just for a first-time team leader but for any leader frustrated by the (sometimes benign) attempts of his or her organization to exert control and impose uniformity. We came to think of our audience not as the new leader but as the *freethinking leader.* A leader who embraces a world in which the weird uniqueness of each individual is seen not as a flaw to be ground down but as a mess worth engaging with, the raw material for all healthy, ethical, thriving organizations; a leader who rejects dogma and instead seeks out evidence; who values emergent patterns above received wisdom; who thrills to the power of teams; who puts faith in findings, not philosophy; and above all, a leader who knows that the only way to make the world better tomorrow is to have the courage and the wit to face up to how it really is today.

If this sounds like you, then you are a freethinking leader. We don't know you personally, of course, but over the last six months we've thought a lot about you—who you might be, how you might be feeling, and what you might need to thrive. This book is for you.

LIE #1

People care which company they work for

Meet Lisa. She works in the field of corporate communications and marketing, and has done so for more than twenty years. We spoke to her the other day about her recent experiences at work, in the same way that we speak to hundreds of people every year about their experiences at work. Lisa told us that she'd recently moved from one company to another and then back again, and we wanted to understand more. Here's what she said.

> *Marcus and Ashley:* Why did you leave Company A* after eighteen years?
>
> *Lisa:* I'd moved from a role focused on events—the big events we put on for our customers and partners—to a role focused more on marketing. I found I couldn't be creative in the marketing role, and

*Obviously, we've disguised the names of the companies.

then my prior events role had been filled and I had nowhere to go. So the only way I could get back into events was to go elsewhere.

Us: That's what led you to look at Company B?

Lisa: Yes. And anyway, after all this time at Company A, I felt like exploring something new, and a new environment.

Us: As you considered working for Company B, what was most important to you about the company?

Lisa: The brand—whether it was seen to be a name-brand company in a market-leading position; innovation and the pace of innovation; whether I could build something new; where the job was located and whether I could work remotely; how cool the place was; whether I would learn there; and whether I could try new things easily. Those were some of the things I remember thinking about.

Us: And how did you try to evaluate each of those?

Lisa: Obviously, through the interviews I did for the job. But I'd also done my research beforehand—I spent six months researching the company and the job, on Google, on Glassdoor. I spent two months prepping for my interviews, and at the same time I talked to as many people there as I could find.

Us: What did you conclude at the end of this?

Lisa: I thought Company B probably wasn't a perfect place, but it had checked enough of my boxes for me to feel comfortable going there.

Us: So you went to Company B. How long did you stay there for?

Lisa: Two years.

Us: Given you'd spent eighteen years at Company A, were you expecting to be at Company B longer than two years?

Lisa: Yes, for sure.

Us: So can you explain why you were only there for two years, given how thorough you'd been in your research about the job? What happened?

Lisa: What happened is that I met my manager. I mean, I'd met her during the interview process, obviously, and there were a few things that bothered me—but when I started I saw her true colors, and that's when things started to go wrong.

Us: What bothered you during the interview process?

Lisa: Her style struck me as severe, and formal, and a bit hierarchical. But I figured that was just her game face—how she was to the outside world—and that if I joined her team it would be different. But it wasn't.

Us: And when did you realize that?

Lisa: It was on Day Thirteen.

Us: Day Thirteen? How can you be so precise?

Lisa: I wrote it down in my calendar. I wrote down all the key dates during my time at Company B—it was my way of documenting what was a really tough experience for me. On Day Thirteen I was in a meeting with my manager and a more senior executive, and the senior person asked what I thought was a simple question about booking hotel rooms, and I answered, and my manager looked shocked. As soon as the meeting finished, she took me to one side and said, "We don't share that sort of thing with senior people here. Next time run it by me." And from that point on she micromanaged me, and I realized that she was fear-based, both in how she thought of her bosses and in terms of how she ran her team.

Us: Were there any other days you noted in your calendar?

Lisa: On Day Fifteen I wrote down, "Possible last day at Company B" for my two-year anniversary, and "Last day at Company B" for my four-year anniversary.

Us: Crikey. Just to confirm—you spent months researching a company; you did seven interviews, in each of which you had carefully prepared questions to help you understand whether this would work for you; and two weeks in you'd not only decided to leave but given yourself a timeline. Is that right?

Lisa: Yes, that's it. I knew fifteen days in that I wasn't there long term.

Us: And the main reason for that was your manager, and her style?

Lisa: Yes. And it wasn't just my manager—other leaders seemed to operate based on fear, too.

Us: When you were at Company B, were you introduced to their Core Values or Leadership Principles or anything like that?

Lisa: Yes! I was handed a laminated page of them at my orientation. I was thrilled!

Us: Why was that?

Lisa: I read them and thought, "These are great!" There was one I remember in particular—it was about disagreeing and then committing, about having the courage to speak up if you disagreed with what was being said, but then committing wholeheartedly to the ultimate decision when it was made. I thought that was really exciting, and would make for a great environment. But then I started work, and I realized—darn, these just aren't true. Worse than that, some people here use them for evil.

Us: For evil?

Lisa: Yes, they justify bad behavior by pointing to the Leadership Principles. So if they want to silence dissent, they tell people it's time to commit to the direction they want to go. Which is the opposite of what that idea is meant to be about.

Us: Ah, OK. So pretty quickly you decided to find a path back to Company A, right?

Lisa: Yes.

Us: And in the light of this experience with Company B, what was important to you as you looked for this next role?

Lisa: Three things—culture, leadership, and the work I'd be doing.

Us: What do you mean by culture?

Lisa: It's the tenets of how we behave. I think of it like a family creed—this is how we operate and treat one another in this family.

Us: What are some words you'd use to describe Company A's culture?

Lisa: Let me see. *Inclusive, collaborative, kind, generous, trusting, fair, supportive.* And I think the senior leaders are good people who lead ethically.

Us: Were those things uniform across Company A, in your experience?

Lisa: I think I was fortunate—they showed up in the teams I worked on for sure. But I know people who were less fortunate, who didn't see these things.

Us: How do you explain that?

Lisa: For me, it's a question of whether each team leader believes in the culture of the company—whether they get the culture or not. If they do, you're fortunate. If not, you're not.

· · ·

From the outside looking in, it's pretty hard to figure out what it might be like to work for a particular company. If you're job hunting, you might start by searching online as Lisa did—perhaps on Glassdoor or one of the other job boards where employees can rate their current company—or by talking to friends about where they've worked and what their experiences were. You might try to talk to a recruiter, although it's tricky to do that if you're not yet sure you're going to apply. You might try to figure it out by reading the coverage of a company in the press, but this can be frustrating, since articles tend to focus more on a company's products or its strategy, rather than on its culture per se. Wherever you look, you'll find yourself wondering if what you're discovering is really representative of the company, and is giving you a good sense of the inside story. In search of more objectivity and breadth, then, you might turn to *Fortune* magazine's annual ranking of the 100 Best Companies to Work For.

Fortune publishes its ranking every January, and this issue of the magazine is one of the most widely read of the year. The ranking is based on an anonymous survey of the employees at each company (known as the "Trust Index"), together with a submission that each company puts together describing how it invests in its people and what it has to offer them (called the "Culture Audit"). From all this, the editors at the magazine and the analysts at the Great Place to Work Institute (which conducts the research) put together a list that tells you which companies are the best to work for that year, together with descriptions of the various perks they offer and brief testimony from current employees. In 2018 the top six, in order, were Salesforce, Wegmans, Ultimate Software, Boston Consulting Group, Edward Jones, and Kimpton Hotels, selected for reasons ranging from the pragmatic (paying bonuses for employee referrals, offering Starbucks gift cards during busy times, on-site child day care) to the noble (giving millions of dollars' worth of reclaimed food to the hungry, building environmentally friendly offices, always trying to promote from within) to the quirky (Salesforce has an entire floor dedicated to *ohana*, the Hawaiian for *family*, while Kimpton offers all new hires a welcome care package complete with each person's favorite snacks).

If you are indeed looking for a job, you read *Fortune*'s list in search of insights about a given company. What will your colleagues be like? How will they treat you? What will a typical day be like? Will your work be interesting, challenging, and valued? Is this a company that really cares for its people? If you go through the long process of applying, and interviewing, and negotiating an offer, and ultimately landing a job there, will this be a company that puts as much into you and your career as you're going to put into it?

What, precisely, is this list measuring about these companies? Read the submissions, the press releases, and *Fortune*'s own descriptions of the winners, and the word you land on is *culture*. Salesforce has a "family culture," hence the Ohana floor. Wegmans has a culture based on its mission to "help people live healthier, better lives through food." Kimpton Hotels has an "inclusiveness culture." Each of these companies, it appears, has figured out what kind of culture it wants to build, and then has made it onto the list because it has been resolute and effective in its pursuit. Judging by these and other examples, this thing called culture really matters. It is potentially more important than what the company does—"Culture eats strategy for breakfast!"—how the company does it, how much the employees get paid, or even the company's current stock price.

Culture matters, according to the voluminous literature on the topic, because it has three powerful contributions to make. First, it tells you who you are at work. If you're at Patagonia, you'd rather be surfing. You work in beautiful Oxnard, California, and your onboarding consists of a day-long beach party where you are gifted the CEO's autobiography—*Let My People Go Surfing*—and where your first meeting takes place around a campfire. If you're at Goldman Sachs, then never mind the surfing—you'd rather be winning. You wear your bespoke suit every day because you're a winner. It means something to say that you work for Deloitte, or for Apple, or for Chick-fil-A—and this meaning says something about you, something that locates you and differentiates you, that defines your tribe.

Second, culture has come to be how we choose to explain success. When Tesla's stock was on the rise in the early part of 2017, it wasn't because people were finally getting the electric cars they'd paid deposits for a year earlier—they weren't. Rather, it was because Elon Musk had created a culture of cool, a place where you couldn't even see the cutting edge because it was so far behind you. When Toyota had to recall over six million vehicles, the direct cause was a problem with the shift-lever assembly, but the deeper explanation we arrived at was that it was a problem with their polite yet win-at-all-costs culture.

And third, culture is now a watchword for where we want our company to go: almost overnight, a big part of the job description of senior corporate leaders has become to create a specific sort of culture, a culture of "performance," perhaps, or a culture of "feedback," or a culture of "inclusion," or a culture of "innovation"; to shape the direction of the company they lead by infusing it with particular traits that govern how people behave. Beyond explaining the now, culture has become our handle on the next.[1]

As a team leader you are going to be told, repeatedly, that you must take stock of all this because you are responsible for embodying your company's culture, and for building a team that adheres to these cultural norms. You will be asked to select only applicants who fit the culture, to identify high-potentials by whether or not they embody the company culture, to run your meetings in a way that fits the culture, and, at company off-sites, to don the T-shirts and sing the songs.

All of which is fine, right up to the point where you start to wonder what, precisely, you are being held accountable for. Read the *Fortune* list again and you'll be struck by the fact that a very small percentage of what's written about your company is in your job description. Having an on-site day-care facility, giving all employees 20 percent of their time to pursue their own interests, offering large rewards for referring a new hire, and building solar panels on the roof are all admirable initiatives, yet none of them is within your control. They are commitments made by others—the executive committee or the board—and while you may think them worthy, and may indeed be proud that they are something your tribe contributes to the world, you can't do anything about them. They are off in some other place, far from the day-to-day projects and deadlines, the ongoing actions and interactions, that actually comprise your world of work.

When people ask you what it's "really like" to work at your company, you immediately know you're going to tell them not about the solar panels and the cafeteria, but about what it's really like. So you'll get real, and talk about how work is parceled out, whether many managers play favorites, how disputes get resolved, whether the real meeting happens only after the formal meeting is over, how people get promoted, how territorial the teams are, how large the power distance is between senior leaders and everyone else, whether good news or bad news travels fastest, how much recognition there is, and whether performance or politics is most prized. You'll get down to the two-foot level of how work actually gets done, and try to tease out what your company truly feels like to the people on the ground.

You won't know whether to call this "culture" or not, just as you won't necessarily know how to label each of these two-foot-level details, but in every fiber of your being you'll know that this ground-level stuff is what'll decide how hard people will work once they've joined, and how long they'll stay. This ground-level stuff is what they truly care about. Indeed, this ground-level stuff is what *you* truly care about.

In which case, your most pressing question, as a team leader, will be something like this: If I am to help my team give their best, for as long as possible, which of these details are most critical? Tell me the most important ones, and I'll do my level best to pay attention to those.

We've spent the last two decades attempting to answer this question for you. In the next few pages we'll outline what we've found, and then we'll focus the rest of this book on going deeper, and on giving you insights and prescriptions for how you can address the things that matter most.

And in so doing, the first lie we'll need to expose is precisely that *people care which company they work for.* It sounds so odd to label this a lie, since each of us does indeed feel some sort of connection to our company, but read on, and we think you'll see that while what each of us truly cares about may begin as "company," it quickly morphs into something else rather different.

• • •

All quantitative research requires qualitative digging, which is why, a little while ago, we spent a few hours with a team of people in Cisco's office in Krakow, Poland.* We were curious about their experience of work, and what their team was like. The team had about fifteen members overall, engaged in various jobs supporting Cisco's customers. We asked the group about the things they did frequently—daily or weekly or monthly or quarterly—that were important to them. Three of the team members answered by talking about lunch. We always bring our lunches to work, they said, instead of going to the cafeteria. And there's a spot on the patio outside where we eat together. We always eat at the same time as one another, no matter what is happening that day, and sometimes we talk about work, and other times about stuff outside work—this is what we do every day.

Later on, we saw where the fifteen-person team worked (our initial discussion had taken place in a conference room). They worked at a long row of workstations, each separated from its neighbors by vertical dividers. The three people who ate their packed lunches together pulled us to one side. Look! they said, pointing to an unremarkable spot on the floor, a few feet from the workstations. This is where we huddle! We asked what they meant. They said that when something happened

---

*One of the great joys of writing as a team of two is that it allows us to bring both of our perspectives and, critically, experiences and stories to the task, resulting in what we hope is a richer book. This presents, however, one small challenge when writing about an experience that one but not both of us had, and it's the challenge of which pronouns to use. Joint authors before us have taken various approaches to this, either by referring to themselves in the third person ("When Marcus interviewed such-and-such . . .") or by beginning every story with some sort of parenthetical clarification ("When one of us [Ashley] was in Poland . . ."), neither of which we feel makes up in clarity what it takes away in readability. So we've decided that whether an event described here was experienced by one of us alone or by both of us, we'll just say "we." We hope you will forgive us a little pronoun flexibility in the service of easier reading.

during the day that they needed to talk about, they would leave their workstations and form an impromptu huddle where they could figure out what to do.

Here we have a team of fifteen people, doing real work in the real world, and within it a sub-team of three people, also doing real work in the real world. And the three take time every day to eat together, and also—maybe because of the lunches, or maybe not because of them, or maybe just because—have a way of quickly breaking the routine configuration of their workspace to solve problems together.

What is the "culture" of this three-person team-within-a-team? Is it different from the "culture" of the bigger, fifteen-person team, and if so, how? Who knows? All we do know is that both the three-person miniteam and the fifteen-person team are extremely productive and highly engaged. Back at Cisco's headquarters in San Jose, California, the CEO, Chuck Robbins, is doing his best to build an enthusiastic, committed workforce, but he is thousands of miles and several organizational levels away from the day-to-day realities that these team members face, and he knows that there's a limit to what he can control from the center. All he can hope to do is to encourage these local teams—and every other of his thousands upon thousands of teams—to build the sort of work experience that gets the best from each and every team member.

What, then, should he be asking them to focus on? What are, in fact, the most important aspects of our experience of work?

The only way to rigorously answer this question is as follows: First, create two groups of people, one group from teams with high performance (high productivity, high innovation, high customer satisfaction, low voluntary turnover, low lost work days, whatever *performance* means in a given company or business unit), the second group from teams with low or average performance.

Next, start asking questions about what these teams are like on the inside. Ask many, *many* questions of the high performers, and then ask the same questions of the low performers. Search for those few questions where the people on the high-performing teams say that they strongly agree and the people on the mid- to lower-performing teams do not. The goal here is to try to find what is distinctive about the high-performing teams through the eyes of the people on those teams.

Over the last several years we've repeated this research hundreds of times in many different companies, always zeroing in on the questions that most clearly sort the best from the rest. We are not the first to undertake this kind of research, of course. Back in the late 1990s the Gallup Organization did pioneering work on engagement, eventually identifying twelve conditions as the drivers of it, and since then organizations such as the Corporate Executive Board, Korn Ferry, and Kenexa have added to our growing body of knowledge and our understanding of engagement at work, and of how we can measure it most reliably and with the most validity. Our work built on this existing research, as all sound research should—research findings are provisional, after all—and, in the end, we wound up identifying just a few aspects of the employee experience that exist disproportionately on the highest-performing teams. These eight aspects, and these eight precisely worded items,* validly predict sustained team performance:

1. I am really enthusiastic about the mission of my company.

2. At work, I clearly understand what is expected of me.

3. In my team, I am surrounded by people who share my values.

4. I have the chance to use my strengths every day at work.

---

*Strictly speaking, an item is a statement that a survey-taker responds to. As items are statements, not questions, they don't come with question marks. However, they are often referred to as questions, to ensure maximum confusion for those of us trying to figure out what's going on.

The eight engagement items discussed in this book are copyright ADP.

5. My teammates have my back.

6. I know I will be recognized for excellent work.

7. I have great confidence in my company's future.

8. In my work, I am always challenged to grow.

You might notice a few things about these items right away. First, the team members are not directly rating their team leader or their company on anything—they are rating only their own feelings and experiences. This is because, as we'll see in chapter 6, people are horribly unreliable raters of other people. When we ask someone to rate someone else on an abstract quality such as empathy or vision or strategic thinking, their responses tell us more about the person doing the rating than the person being rated. To get good data we have to ask people about their own experiences.

Second, you may also notice that the eight items fall into two broad groupings. The first is the odd-numbered items:

1. I am really enthusiastic about the mission of my company.

3. In my team, I am surrounded by people who share my values.

5. My teammates have my back.

7. I have great confidence in my company's future.

These deal with the elements of a person's experience created in their back-and-forth interactions with others on the team—the communal experience of work, if you will. What do we all *share*, as a team or as a company? We can think of these as the "Best of We" questions.

The second group comprises the even-numbered items:

2. At work, I clearly understand what is expected of me.

4. I have the chance to use my strengths every day at work.

6. I know I will be recognized for excellent work.

8. In my work, I am always challenged to grow.

These deal instead with the individual experience of work. What is unique about *me*? What is valuable about *me*? Do *I* feel challenged to grow? We can think of these as the "Best of Me" questions.

These two categories of experience—We experiences and Me experiences—are the things we need at work in order to thrive. They are specific; they are reliably measured; they are personal; they reveal a local individual experience intertwined with a local collective experience. They are everyday. And if we think about the team in Poland, while we might not know what its "culture" is, we do know that lunching together and huddling together will have some bearing on the team members' feeling that their teammates have their backs, that they share a sense of what excellence is, that they are called on to do their best work frequently, that they catch each other doing things right, and so on. What we see in the eight questions is a simple way of measuring experience-at-work, and one that you, the team leader, can do something about.

And what more than two decades of research into teams and their leaders has to tell us is this: what distinguishes the best team leaders from the rest is their ability to meet these two categories of needs for the people on their teams. What we, as team members, want from you, our team leader, is firstly that you make us feel part of something bigger, that you show us how what we are doing together is important and meaningful; and secondly, that you make us feel that you can see us, and connect to us, and care about us, and challenge us, in a way that recognizes who we are as individuals. We ask you to give us this sense of universality—all of us together—and at the same time to recognize our own uniqueness; to magnify what we all share, and to lift up what is special about each of us. When you come to excel as a leader of a team it will be because you've successfully integrated these two quite distinct human needs.

Over the course of this book, we'll explore precisely *how* the best leaders do this—what they pay attention to and how they interact with the people around them. At the same time, we'll explore the eight items in more detail, and we'll see how the lies we're told at work push back, hard, against each of these eight critical aspects.

· · ·

But what of our first lie, that *people care which company they work for*?

Well, we now know that these eight questions measure very precisely those aspects of our experience of work that matter the most—in other words, the aspects that drive performance, voluntary turnover, lost work days, accidents on the job, and customer satisfaction. So, if it is true that in large part people's experience at work is driven by the company they work for, then when we ask these eight questions to every person in every team at a particular company, we should get, generally, the same responses. There shouldn't be variation from team to team, because the day-to-day experience of working at this particular company should remain mostly consistent.*

But that's not the case—in fact, it's *never* the case. The statistical measure of variation is called range, and we've found that these scores always have a greater range *within a company* than *between companies*. Experience varies more *within a company* than *between companies*.

Here's what this looks like. This is how 5,983 teams at Cisco answered the second question, "At work, I clearly understand what is expected of me." (See figure 1-1.)

Now, this is a very basic question. If you've spent much time in business organizations, you'll know that they devote a lot of energy to talking about strategies and plans and priorities and themes and critical

---

*More precisely, we would see only as much variation within teams as we would within the company as a whole.

FIGURE 1-1

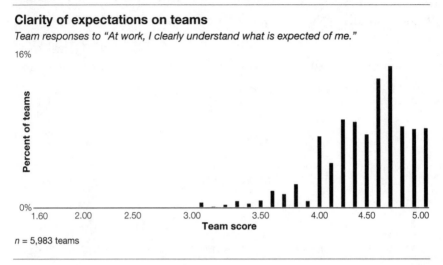

Clarity of expectations on teams

Team responses to "At work, I clearly understand what is expected of me."

n = 5,983 teams

initiatives and business imperatives, and Cisco is no different. Yet for all this effort, these nearly six thousand teams had a widely varying sense of what was expected of them. And we saw this variance across *all* teams at *every* company that we surveyed.

Here's how 1,002 teams at Mission Health answered the seventh question, "I have great confidence in my company's future." (See figure 1-2.)

If there's any item that should vary between companies rather than within them, it would surely be this one. After all, one company will presumably have only one future, and this future should seem the same regardless of which team you're on. Yet it doesn't feel like that. People's responses to this question vary significantly depending on which team they're on, within the same company: different team, different level of confidence in the future.

We see similar patterns on all eight of the questions—we see, in other words, that when we zero in on the critical aspects of our experience at work, they vary more team-to-team than they do company-to-company. Any ideas—like the idea of culture—that rest on the assumption that our experience of a company is uniform, no

FIGURE 1-2

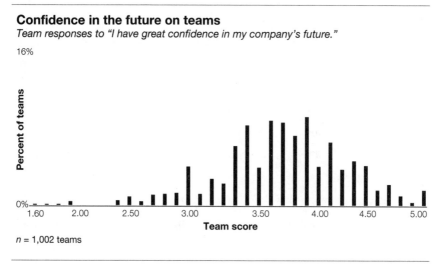

Confidence in the future on teams

Team responses to "I have great confidence in my company's future."

n = 1,002 teams

matter where we sit, don't hold up. Any ideas—again, like the idea of culture—that rest on the assumption that our experience will vary company to company are incomplete, because our experience will vary more within a company than between companies. And any ideas— again, like the idea of culture—that rest on the assumption that this broad, unchanging company-ness is what defines our experience of work are simply wrong.

Instead *local* experiences—how we interact with our immediate colleagues, our lunching-on-the-patio companions, and our huddling-in-the-corner partners—are significantly more important than company ones. At least, that's what all this research is telling us.

Moreover, if we care most which *company* we work for, it follows that there should be no connection between our experience on a given team and our choice to stay with a given company—because company trumps team. But whenever we run an analysis, we find that when a team's score is low on these items, members of that team are significantly more likely to leave the company. At Cisco, for example, we've seen that when someone's experience of their team moves from the top half, companywide, to the bottom half, their likelihood of leaving the company increases by 45 percent. When people choose not to work somewhere, the somewhere isn't a company, it's a team. If we put you in a good team at a bad company, you'll tend to hang around, but if we put you in a bad team at a good company, you won't be there for long. The team is the sun, the moon, and the stars of your experience at work. As Edmund Burke, the Anglo-Irish writer and philosopher put it as far back as 1790, "To love the little platoon we belong to in society is the first principle (the germ, as it were) of public affections."[2]

When we push on the data, and examine closely its patterns and variations, we arrive at this conclusion: while people might care which company they join, they don't care which company they work for. The truth is that, once there, *people care which team they're on*.

• • •

Recently the ADP Research Institute conducted a nineteen-country study on the nature of engagement at work—what drives it, and what it drives. We've included a summary of the findings in the appendix, but here are three highlights that you'll want to know. First, virtually all work is in fact teamwork. In companies with over 150 employees, 82 percent of people work on teams, and 72 percent work on more than one team. Even in small companies, of fewer than twenty people, this finding holds: 68 percent of those in small companies report working on a team, and 49 percent say they work on more than one team. This proved to be so in every single country in the study.

Second, we know that if you do happen to work on a team you are twice as likely to score high on the eight engagement items, and that this trend linking engagement to teams extends to multiple teams—in fact, the most engaged group of workers across the working world are those who work on *five* distinct teams.

Third, just like Lisa, those team members who said they trusted their team leader were *twelve* times more likely to be fully engaged at work.

The good news in all this for you, the team leader, is that what people care most about at work is within your control. You might not be able to weigh in on your company's parental-leave policy, or the quality of its cafeteria, but you can build a healthy team—you can set clear expectations for your people, or not; you can position each person to play to his or her strengths every day, or not; you can praise the team for excellent work, or not; you can help people grow their careers, or not. And you can, over time, build trust with your people, or not. Of course, given the "always-on" nature of your daily work, attending to each of these is challenging, but at least they are indeed part of your daily work.

The bad news for you is that your company, most likely, looks past this, so while you're doing your best to create these experiences for your people, your company may not be holding your fellow team leaders accountable for doing the same on their teams. Companies almost universally miss the importance of teams, as evidenced by the fact that most companies don't even know how many teams they have at any moment in time, and who is on them, let alone which are the best ones—we are functionally blind to teams. And our overemphasis on culture leads companies to remove responsibility from where it resides—with the team leaders—and instead to focus on generalities. You now know that your company does not have a uniform culture, that if there is something distinct about your company's culture then it is unmeasurable, that the total score of your company's employee survey is simply the clumping together of lots of highly varied team-level surveys, and that these clumps mask what really matters. You now know that when a CEO sets out to build a great company, all she can do—and it's a lot—is strive to build more and more teams like her company's best teams.

And you now know that often what's written about company cultures are stories masquerading as data—stories of one world, and then another, and then another, vivid, intriguing, charming, and occasionally a bit scary, but not real. Like Narnia, or like Middle-earth, if hobbits had jobs.

• • •

If the most important experience of work is the experience of team, what should we make of all the "culture of . . ." things with which we began? Are they all entirely irrelevant?

In his fascinating book *Sapiens*,[3] and again and in more depth in its sequel, *Homo Deus*,[4] the historian Yuval Noah Harari asks what it is that explains the success of humankind over all other species. Having examined and rejected the usual explanations—we're not alone, as a species, in using tools, or in having language, or in making plans, or in experiencing consciousness—he moves on to explore our notions of reality. Objective reality, as we know, is a reality that exists independently of our attitudes or feelings about it: if you stop believing in gravity, you'll still fall to the ground if you jump out of the window. Subjective reality, on the other hand, is defined precisely by your attitudes and feelings: if you have a toothache yet your dentist tells you she can't find anything the matter (there is no objective problem), your tooth still hurts.

But Harari goes on to argue that there is a third kind of reality, that this kind of reality is unique to humans, and that this kind of reality explains the dominance (for good or ill) of our species. There are some things that are real simply because we *all* agree they're real—things whose existence depends not on any objective reality, nor on any individual's subjective reality, but rather on our collective belief in them. By this logic, money, for example, exists *only* because all of us agree it does. Initially this might sound odd—surely money is just money, not some sort of mass belief system—but here's the rub: when we all cease to believe in these realities, they cease to be real. If you and everyone else stop believing, all of a sudden, that a particular piece of paper is worth $10, then it actually and rather immediately ceases to be worth $10. This is more or less what happened in India on the evening of November 8, 2016, when the government announced that the very next day certain bills would no longer be legal tender, and those bills turned instantly from *Things That Are Valuable Because We All Agree They Are* to *Things That Are Valueless Because Some Of Us Don't.*

Harari calls these extended, communal realities *intersubjective realities,* and tells us that they're the reason our achievements as a species are so different from those of our planet-mates. They enable us to coordinate our actions with those of people we may never meet, across distance and across time. Our belief in the intersubjective reality of nation, for example, enables us to cooperate with our fellow citizens to finance and build monuments, or to wage war; our belief in the intersubjective reality of democracy allows us to elect governments and to follow their laws. Our intersubjective realities are the distinguishing feature—the apex technology—of *Homo sapiens.*

What are our intersubjective realities in the world of work? One, obviously, is the idea of the company. We can't touch it; it exists only in the realm of laws (another intersubjective reality), and when we stop agreeing it exists, it ceases to exist. Obviously, the stock-market value of a public company is another example. As is that company's brand and brand value. And its bank balance. All of these are useful—essential, even—to our ability to organize lots of people to achieve complex and enduring goals. Without them, and the many other intersubjective realities in the world of work, we would have none of the things that "companies" have produced since we invented them. But that doesn't make them real, in the sense that gravity is real, or in the sense that a toothache is real. Or in the sense that the other people at work—your team—are real.

And just as the idea of the company is, in this particular sense, unreal, so is the idea of company "culture." It's a useful fiction. That doesn't mean we should dispense with it; it *does* mean, however, that we should be careful not to mistake it for something it isn't. Culture locates us in the world. It consists of stories we share with one another to breathe life into the empty vessel of "company." But—and here's the kicker—so powerful is our need for story, our need for communal sense making of the world, that we imagine that our company and its culture can explain our experience of work. And yet it can't. So strong is our identification with our tribe that it's hard for us to imagine that other people inside our company are having a completely different experience of "tribe" from ours. Yet they are—and these local team experiences have far more bearing on whether we stay in the tribe or leave it than do our tribal stories.

• • •

How can you make sense, then, of the things that are clearly different from one company to the next, things to which you're accustomed to attaching such importance? Patagonia *does* have a drastically different type of onboarding than Salesforce. Goldman Sachs *does* have a very different dress code from Apple. What are these things, and how are they different from the real-world experience of work?

The difference is this: these things are signifiers, designed to lure you in. You may not care which company you work for, but since you do care about which company you *join*, these signifiers are crafted to help a company attract a certain kind of person by highlighting what the company thinks this kind of person values. This is why these signifiers show up time and again in promotional materials, and why they are so prominent in various company rankings—because companies want it that way. These kinds of perks are plumage—peacock feathers for people. They sound cool because they're designed to get your attention, just like plumage is. So when you read about how a certain company gives each employee "twenty-percent" time to focus on personal projects or claims to always promote from within, just remember that these beautiful feathers are designed almost exclusively to attract you, and that this attraction, as most attractions tend to, will fade.

The biggest difference, of course, between cultural plumage and the real world is that the *impact* of plumage on how you and your team do your work every day is slight. That's not what it's for. It is a shared fiction, and it exists to attract a certain kind of person to join the company. And as with all shared fictions, the moment you all stop collectively believing in the plumage, it vanishes. Team experience, on the other hand (how you talk to one another and work with one another), has large and lasting impact on how you do your work, and it doesn't require all of you to agree to believe in it. It is what it is. And whether or not you all believe in it or can all describe it in the same way, it will nonetheless influence both how effectively your team works and for how long, and how many of your teammates will choose to stay.

• • •

When you study excellence and what leads to it—what creates it— there is a dog that doesn't bark.* Actually, a couple of them. Company doesn't bark. And cultural plumage doesn't bark. Instead, sitting there in plain sight is what was in plain sight in Poland. What the three people there shared, as a key part of their experience of work, was not about a place to eat, but rather—critically—about the people to eat with. While they might think of Cisco as a place that affords them a table to sit at or a corner of the office to huddle in, if we give them those

---

*GREGORY: "Is there any other point to which you would wish to draw my attention?"
HOLMES: "To the curious incident of the dog in the night-time."
GREGORY: "The dog did nothing in the night-time."
HOLMES: "That was the curious incident."
—Sir Arthur Conan Doyle, "The Adventure of Silver Blaze," in *The Memoirs of Sherlock Holmes* (London: George Newnes, 1894).

things yet take away their teammates, or change the sorts of interactions they have with those teammates, their experience vanishes. In a very real sense the spot they huddle on with a couple of teammates matters more to them than all the perks Cisco well-intendedly throws their way. What's in plain sight, when we study excellence at work, is the groups of people doing actual work together—what's in plain sight is teams.

This is why teams matter, and it's why they matter much more than cultural plumage matters.

Teams simplify: they help us see where to focus and what to do. Culture doesn't do this, funnily enough, because it's too abstract.

Teams make work real: they ground us in the day-to-day, both in terms of the content of our work and the colleagues with whom we do it. Culture doesn't.

And teams, paradoxically, make homes for individuals. Whereas culture's focus leans toward conformity to a common core of behaviors, teams focus on the opposite. Teams aren't about sameness—they aren't, at their best, about marching in lockstep. Instead they're about unlocking what is unique about each of us, in the service of something shared. A team, at its finest, insists on the unique contribution of each of its members, and is the best way we humans have ever come up with of harnessing those distinctive contributions together in the service of something that none of us could do alone.

In the last few years, there has been a lot of talking and writing about teams in corporate circles. Sadly, much of it has yet to grasp the main point. The general direction of the discussion so far has been that we should pay attention to teams because there are a lot of them at work. This is, of course, true—although one could make the case that this isn't news. Granted, given new communications and information technologies, teams can now be assembled spanning more geographies and time zones and organizational units than ever before, but the fact that there are now more teams and more different sorts of teams than ever before isn't the big thing. The big thing is that only on a team can we express our individuality at work and put it to highest use.

In a sense, that's what the rest of this book is about. To see it clearly, we have to let go of our ideas about cultural plumage, because only when we do so does the fact of team emerge—quietly, simply, powerfully— from its shadow. And as we do this we come to realize what is perhaps the biggest problem of all with the idea of culture: it doesn't actually help us understand what to do more of, less of, or differently. Whether culture is a real thing or not, whether it defines our tribe at work or not, whether it's a marker of what sort of company we're joining or not, it won't tell you, the team leader, what to do to make things better. For that, we must take you to where the experience lives: to your team, and networks of teams, and their leaders. That's what matters most.

· · ·

There are three things for you to do as a leader of a team. First, you should know the answers to the eight questions for your team, all the time. There are technologies available to help you do this, but the easiest place to start is to ask your team members, one person at a time. Whatever their answers are, you'll *always* be smarter because of them, and you'll *always* know you're paying attention to something that matters.

Second, read on to understand more clearly how to build a great team, and how the lies you'll encounter get in the way of that. Your role as team leader is the most important role in any company. And who your company chooses to make team leader is the most important decision it ever makes. You have by far the greatest influence on the distinctive local experience of your team. This is a weighty responsibility, but at least it's yours. We want to help you step into it.

And third, when you're next looking to join a company, don't bother asking if it has a great culture—no one can tell you that in any real way.

Instead, ask what it does to build great teams.

The best plan wins

George Clooney had a plan.

"I have a question," says Carl Reiner early on in the movie *Ocean's Eleven*, after Clooney has laid out his scheme for breaking into the impressively secured vault of a Las Vegas casino.

"Say we get into the cage, and through the security doors there, and down the elevator we can't move, and past the guards with the guns, and into the vault we can't open . . . say we do all that. We're just supposed to walk out of there with $150 million in cash on us, without getting stopped?"

There's a silence. The members of Ocean's handpicked team eye one another nervously, unsure what's coming next.

Clooney pauses, and then nods, and then: "Yeah."

And Carl says, "Oh." And then, "OK." And in an instant, we know that Clooney has a plan for that, too, and that Carl realizes there's a plan, and doesn't need to know what it is, just that there is one, and that it'd better be a good one, because, as everyone knows, *the best plan wins*.

The thrill for us, the viewer, is seeing whether the plan will work—will Matt Damon's pickpocket skills succeed in lifting the badge from the security guard? Will Casey Affleck and Scott Caan's goofy antics and handy-dandy birthday balloons block the casino cameras? Will Clooney charm Julia Roberts? (Yes to all. Duh.)

But ponder for a minute the thrill each team member would have felt. Even though they were coming together under challenging circumstances, they had the plan, whose raw material was a specific role that each of them should play. Each person's role was tightly circumscribed, time-bound, and sequential—Brad Pitt would place the call to Julia Roberts, but not until Clooney had slid the phone into her jacket pocket—so all could feel secure in the knowledge that if they learned how to perform their role well, and executed it well, then, like a mathematical algorithm, the sequence would play out perfectly, the plan would work, and the money would be theirs.

If you've recently been promoted to team leader, the first thing you'll be expected to do is create a plan. You'll be asked—before you even start, most likely—what your plan is for your team, or, more specifically, what your ninety-day plan is for your team. You'll have to sit down, think hard, survey your team members (many of whom you will have inherited), and then do your best George Clooney impression and make your plan.

And when you do this, you'll quickly realize one of the many differences between your team and Clooney's: his team works alone, while yours appears to be connected to a whole host of other teams, each with their own version of the plan. In fact, poke your head above the parapet of your team for a second and look out across all the other teams in the company, and you'll discover something of a planning frenzy. Every team is about to go, or is away on, or is just back from, or is just debriefing from, their off-site, during which they formulated, or perhaps reformulated, their current version of the plan.

It won't be immediately obvious to you, but after a few years you'll discern that there is a pattern to this planning, a predictable rhythm that repeats itself year after year: in September, in advance of the

November board meeting, the leaders of your company will go away on a senior leadership retreat. They may do a SWOT analysis (Strengths/Weaknesses/Opportunities/Threats—and it's just as fun as it sounds); they may bring in outside consultants to help them; and after much analysis and debate and proposal and counter-proposal, the white smoke will emerge from the chimney, and the leaders will emerge with The Strategic Plan. They will then present this plan to the board, and once it's approved, they will share it with their direct reports. This plan will then be sliced up into many other plans (departmental plans, divisional plans, geographic plans, and so on), each slice finer and more detailed than the preceding one, until you, too, are asked to take your team off-site and construct your version of the plan.

We do this because we believe that plans are important. If we could just get the plan right, we think, and weave every team's plan into the broader company plan, then we could be confident that our resources were allocated appropriately, that the correct sequence and timing were laid out, that each person's role was clearly defined, and that we had enough of the right people to fill each required role. Buoyed by this confidence, we'd know that we'd only have to galvanize our teams to give their all, and success would follow.

At the same time, there is a yearning quality to all this planning. We are attempting to shape our future, and our plans can feel like scaffolding stretching out into the months ahead, upon which we'll build our better world—their function is perhaps as much to reassure us as it is to make that world real. Plans give us certainty, or at least a bulwark against uncertainty. They help us believe that we will, indeed, walk out of the casino with the cash.

And yet, just as this cycle of big plans leading to medium plans leading to small plans is familiar to you, so—surely—is the nagging realization that things rarely, if ever, turn out the way you hope they will.

Sure, planning is exciting in the beginning, but the more you sit in all these planning meetings, the more a feeling of futility creeps in. While it all looks great on paper, tidy and perfect, you sense it's never really going to play out like this, and that as a result you'll soon be back in yet another planning meeting. You'll leave this one with the broad contours of your plan sketched out, and you'll agree on the next steps necessary to refine those contours into something specific and actionable, and then the meeting to make things actionable will get postponed a bit, and then, when it finally happens, it will drift off in another direction. And then, when your team finally gets around to nailing the details, some new idea or thought or realization will emerge that leads you to rethink what you started off with. George Clooney never had to deal with this.

But in the real world you'll have to. The defining characteristic of our reality today is its ephemerality—the speed of change. If *Ocean's Eleven* took place in the real world, then after Clooney had put his plan together, and picked his perfect team, and defined each person's role, and pressed play, they'd arrive in the vault, open the safe . . . and it would be empty, because Nevada would have changed its gambling regulations, and Andy Garcia's casino owner would have ditched the cash, replaced it with Bitcoin, and, in hopes of jumping a few spots on the *Fortune* list, turned the vault into a subterranean romper-room-cum-fitness-center to aid his employees' well-being. In the real world, the *Ocean's Eleven* team would burst into the vault to discover the 11:30 a.m. hot-yoga class.

• • •

General Stanley McChrystal had to grapple with this alarmingly changing world, and the stakes he faced were far higher than yours will be (we hope). In his book *Team of Teams* he reveals what it was like to try to come up with "the plan" as he assumed command of the Joint Special Operations Task Force.[1] This group had brought together the special-operations units of each branch of the US military—the Army's Delta

Force and 75th Ranger Regiment, Marine Force Recon, Navy SEALs, and Air Force Pararescue and Combat Control Teams—and its mission was to deploy these units in the ongoing struggle with al-Qaeda in Iraq in the aftermath of the 2003 invasion. Within a few months of assuming command, McChrystal and his staff had created an "awesome machine"—the planning, execution, and debriefing of targeted raids was now conducted at greatly increased speed. But still they were losing the war. They faced an enemy who was spontaneous, decentralized, and agile, made up of terrorist cells that could plan and execute attacks without recourse to a chain of command, and as much as McChrystal's planners tried to optimize their process, they were never quite fast enough to be ahead of events. Even if their traditional system—intelligence gathering, leading to analysis, leading to target identification, leading to raid planning, leading to action, leading to after-action review—could be made to run at the speed of light, it was never quite fast enough. McChrystal's forces were still too often caught unawares by the latest attack, were still too often turning up at a house in search of a target that had been there when the plan was created, only to find no one there.

Everywhere we look we see this speed of change. When you put your plan together in September, it's obsolete by November. And if you look at it in January, you might not even recognize the roles and action items you wrote out in the fall. Events and changes are happening faster than they ever have before, so dissecting a situation and turning it into a meticulously constructed plan is an exercise in engaging in a present that will soon be gone. The amounts of time and energy it takes to make a plan this thorough and detailed are the very things that doom it to obsolescence. The thing we call *planning* doesn't tell you where to go; it just helps you understand where you are. Or rather, were. Recently. We aren't planning for the future, we're planning for the near-term past.

And where are the people who are making the plan? So far behind the front lines of the company that they don't have enough real-world information upon which to make the plan in the first place. How can you make a plan to sell a particular sort of product to a particular sort of customer when you're not out selling every day? You can't, not really. You can make a theoretical sales "model" based on your conceptual understanding of an abstract situation, or on an averaged data set that summarizes trends. But if it's not grounded in the real-world details of each actual sales conversation—when do the prospects' eyes glaze over, when do the prospects lean forward, when do they start to finish your sentences—your plan will always be more assumptive than prescriptive.

In terms of General McChrystal's challenge, this is the difference between building a plan around generalizations (say, that "25 percent of the time we show up at the wrong house") and building one that grapples with very specific realities (such as, "How do we hit *this particular* target, when he might leave *this particular* house, at *this particular* time, tonight?"). Unfortunately, most plans—particularly those devised high up in the company—are built like the former, not the latter.

And even if you do weave together the most carefully filigreed plan, your people inevitably chafe at being told what to do in the context of something so static, so conceptual, and potentially so out of touch with the real world they face. Although Ocean's Eleven were initially happy to be given prescribed roles with crystal-clear expectations, imagine how they'd feel if they played their roles to perfection as defined in the plan, and yet still found no money in the vault. And then imagine if they had to keep doing this month after month, because that was the plan, and because that was what the senior leader had decided would work, even though they kept telling their team leader that the money was gone, that the yoga instructor was getting annoyed, and that they felt just plain daft in their masks and overalls in the hundred-degree heat.

Your people want and need to engage with the world that they're really in, and to interact with the world as it really is. By harnessing them to a prefabricated plan, you're not only constraining your people but, quite possibly, also revealing how out of touch with reality you are.

This is not to say that planning is utterly useless. Creating space to think through all of the information you have in your world, and trying to pull that into some sort of order or understanding, has some value. But when you do that, know that all you've done is understand the scale and nature of the challenges your team is facing. You'll have learned little about what to do to make things better. The solutions can be found in the tangible and changing realities of the world as it really is, whereas your plans are necessarily abstract understandings of the recent past. Plans scope the problem, not the solution.

So, though you are told that *the best plan wins*, the reality is quite different. Many plans, particularly those created in large organizations, are overly generalized, quickly obsolete, and frustrating to those asked to execute them. It's far better to coordinate your team's efforts in real time, relying heavily on the informed, detailed intelligence of each unique team member.

• • •

In late 1940, Hitler's armies had swept across Europe to the shores of France, and Britain's Royal Air Force was all that stood between them and the conquest of the British Isles. Although the RAF had been able to increase the number of fighter aircraft available over the course of the summer months, what it had was still not enough. The accepted model of the time for aerial defense was that, because it was impossible to know where the next attack would come, defenders—in this case the Spitfires and Hurricanes of the RAF—should fly continuous patrols in shifts, in the hope of encountering attackers. But the length of the English coastline, and the number of planes and pilots required to patrol its entirety without pause, made this approach prohibitive. So the only possible alternative was to guess where the attack might come, and too much of the time the guess was wrong—a "good" interception rate was considered one where the enemy was sighted on half the sorties flown. In the history of air warfare to this point, this had always been true—hence the dictum of the day: "The bomber always gets through."

What the RAF needed, if the country were to be saved, was a force multiplier—something that made their limited roster of planes and pilots vastly more effective. The force multiplier they came up with was a room.

If you were to stand in this room today, here's what you'd see. Spanning one entire wall would be a series of twenty-six white vertical boards, each with the number of a squadron at the top, and each with rows of four colored lights underneath. The lights represent each flight in each squadron. There are twelve planes in a squadron, divided into four flights of three planes each, and the lights show at a glance the status of that flight—whether it's ready for action, ordered into the air, engaged with the enemy, returning to base to refuel, and so forth—together with how long each flight has been airborne. These boards (the so-called tote boards) show which orders have been given to which planes, capturing the status of each of four flights for each of twenty-six squadrons—so, 104 pieces of information.

Below the tote boards, you'd see two rows of numbers, showing the number of planes and the number of pilots available for each squadron at the beginning of that day—so, two numbers for each squadron, another 52 pieces of information.

Farther below on the same wall, you'd see four displays showing the heights at which barrage balloons are deployed, together with the day's weather forecast—5 more pieces of information.

In the center of this wall, you'd see an unusual-looking clock, the face of which is divided into five-minute increments colored alternately red, yellow, and blue, and whose purpose relates to the large map table that covers most of the floor area of the room. This table shows a large-scale view of a portion of the coastline, the English Channel, and the coast of France. Around it, you'd see a number of women, each wearing headphones and each wielding a croupier's stick. And in the middle of the table, you'd see a number of wooden blocks with numbers affixed to them and other numbers added to the tops of them on sticks, roughly the size of toothpicks.

Each wooden block represents a group of aircraft—either attackers, defenders, or unidentified planes. If the aircraft are over France or the sea, their location is given by two radar systems, collectively called Chain Home, whose information is relayed from forty stations along the coast. If they are over land, their location is given by telephone reports from the 30,000 members of the Royal Observer Corps, deployed at 1,000 observation posts (because the radar system faces only out to sea). The planes' location, together with information from a third system identifying whether they are friend or foe, is passed to the women around the table—the plotters. The plotters then move the wooden block to the right location and affix to it a numerical identifier, together with indicators of the number of planes, their altitude, whether they're friend or foe, and, for enemy planes, which squadrons have been dispatched to intercept them—this last information being the numbers on the toothpicks. And all of these various numbers are color-coded, and the colors match the colors on the unusual-looking clock, so that everyone can see at a glance how up-to-date each piece of information is.

The map table, then, captures thousands of returns from the Chain Home radar system each minute, plus thousands more from the friend-or-foe system, plus, for every twenty-four hours, a million individual reports from the Royal Observer Corps, each relayed to the room within forty seconds.

And what the room does is bring together all of these data points in real time and then present them so that front-line team members—called controllers—can exercise their judgment and can send their forces to where they know the enemy is. The room (now called the Battle of Britain Bunker) and its design, together with the network of identical rooms across the country and the many information systems flowing into each of them, formed what came to be called the Dowding system, after Hugh Dowding, the RAF commander who created it.

It made all the difference. It was a force multiplier that increased average interception rates from the prewar level of between 30 percent and 50 percent to an average of 90 percent, and often 100 percent, which is to say it *doubled* the effectiveness of the defending force.[2] It wasn't, in any sense, a planning system, acting slowly on stale and summarized information. Instead, it acted fast on current, raw, and detailed information. The RAF's force multiplier was an *intelligence system*.

· · ·

When we understand the characteristics of an intelligence system, as distinct from a planning system—accurate, real-time data, distributed broadly and quickly, and presented in detail so that team members can see and react to patterns in deciding for themselves what to do—we begin to see them everywhere. The Battle of Britain Bunker was an early example of what, today, we'd call a war room, a name that has grown from its literal roots to encompass more metaphorical uses. Think of the famous war room at the heart of Bill Clinton's first campaign for the US Presidency, for example, or of the war rooms used in project or crisis management. Think of NASA's Mission Control Center in Houston, Texas, or of a live-TV production room. Or think of something like Cisco's Security Operations Centers, where engineers can monitor performance across a group of customers' networks, and immediately respond to problems.

What all of these things have in common is that they move information across an organization as fast as possible, and do so to empower immediate and responsive action. Their underlying assumption is that people are wise, and that if you can present them with accurate, real-time, reliable data about the real world in front of them, they'll invariably make smart decisions.

It's not true that the best plan wins. It is true that *the best intelligence wins*.

• • •

What can you do as a team leader to create such an intelligence system for your team?

First, *liberate as much information as you possibly can*. Think about all the sources of information you have, and make as many of them as possible available to your team, on demand. Planning systems constrain information to those who "need to know." Intelligence systems don't—they liberate as much information as possible, as fast as possible. So don't worry too much at first about whether your team will understand the data or be able to make use of it. If you think the information will help your people gain a better understanding of their real world in real time, share it. And encourage your team to do the same. Help them understand that sharing what they know about the world, frequently, is vital. Make sure your team is swimming in real-time information, all the time.

Second, *watch carefully to see which data your people find useful*. Don't worry too much about making all this data simple or easy to consume, or about packaging it for people, or weaving it together to form a coherent story. The biggest challenge with data today isn't making sense of it—most of us deal with complexity all the time, and are pretty good at figuring out what we need to know and where to find it. No, the biggest challenge with data today is making it accurate—sorting the signal from the noise. This is much harder, and much more valuable for our teams. So be extremely vigilant about accuracy; watch which information your people naturally gravitate toward; and then, over time, increase the volume, depth, and speed of precisely that sort of data.

Third, *trust your people to make sense of the data*. Planning systems take the interpretation of the data away from those on the front lines, and hand it off to a select few, who analyze it and decipher its patterns, and then construct and communicate the plan. Intelligence systems do precisely the opposite—because the "intelligence" in an intelligence system lies not in the select few, but instead in the emergent interpretive powers of all front-line team members. You are not the best sense maker. They are.

McChrystal, describing the system he ultimately created in Iraq, makes this same point: "In the old model, subordinates provided information and leaders disseminated commands. We reversed it: we had our leaders provide information so that subordinates, armed with context, understanding, and connectivity, could take the initiative and make decisions."[3] And what he created was perhaps the most extreme example yet of an intelligence system in action.

• • •

A pretty good way to ruin someone's day is to fill it with meetings. Meetings, for most of us, are a way of taking time that could be put to good use in doing real work, and instead using that time to hear presentations of varying relevance to our immediate challenges, or to discuss topics that might appear important in the grand scheme of things, but that hardly seem urgent on any given day. And while countless meeting "best practices" (have a written agenda, document follow-up items, and so on) at least ensure some degree of utility, the fact remains that most meetings contain one or more people thinking to themselves that they could be doing something useful, if only they weren't doing this.*

Which makes what General McChrystal came up with in Iraq all the more remarkable, and all the more counterintuitive. Because what he did was to create a meeting, and moreover a meeting that took place six days a week, for two hours a day. For two thousand people.

---

*Pointy-Haired Boss: We're having a meeting to discuss employee retention.
Dilbert: Tell them that employees quit because there are too many useless meetings.
Pointy-Haired Boss: We won't be getting into reasons at the first meeting.
© 2001 United Feature Syndicate, Inc.

The meeting was called the O&I—the Operations and Intelligence meeting. Every day, at 9:00 a.m. Washington time, 4:00 p.m. Iraq time, McChrystal's entire command—and, ultimately, anyone from any other agency with an interest in understanding what was happening— would join, via video from wherever they were in the world, what amounted to a two-hour information-sharing session. The time was filled with brief updates, each a minute long, from anyone who had something pertinent to share, followed by four minutes of Q&A from the leadership team, or from anyone else who wanted to know more. The O&I had existed before McChrystal, but in a very different form. It had been shorter, and more exclusive, limited to those who had a "need to know" any particular piece of information—it was part of a quintessential planning system.

McChrystal's O&I was a very different beast. It was open to anyone who wanted to learn or share information. It was democratic, in the sense that giving updates and asking questions could be done by anyone, not just senior officers. It was spontaneous, in that updates were not required to be polished or vetted, only brief. And it was frequent. His system embodied these few truths: that information grows stale fast, and must therefore be shared fast; that the best way to enable coordinated action on the ground is to coordinate not actions themselves, but rather the information the ground needs right now; that the best judges of what information is and isn't valuable are the end users of that information; and, critically, that the best people to make sense of information are the users of that information. And finally, that the best way to make sense of it was *together*.

When McChrystal arrived in Iraq, and did everything he could to accelerate the planning system he inherited, the number of raids his troops conducted each month increased from ten to eighteen. When he created his intelligence system, that number shot all the way up to *three hundred*.[4]

And while this is an example of an intelligence system at huge scale, if you study the best team leaders you'll discover that many of them share a similarly frequent sense-making ritual—not with two thousand people, but with two. It's called a check-in, and in simple terms it's a frequent, one-on-one conversation about near-term future work between a team leader and a team member.

How frequent? Every week. These leaders understand that goals set at the beginning of the year have become irrelevant by the third week of the year, and that a year is not a marathon, planned out in detail long in advance, but is instead a series of fifty-two little sprints, each informed by the changing state of the world. They realize that the key role of a team leader is to ensure that Sprint Number Thirty-Six is as focused and as energizing as was Sprint Number One.

So, each and every week these leaders have a brief check-in with each team member, during which they ask two simple questions:

What are your priorities this week?

How can I help?

They are not looking for a to-do list from the team member. They simply want to discuss the team member's priorities, obstacles, and solutions in real time, while the work itself is ongoing. Making sense of it together can happen only in the now. The generalizations that emerge once the passage of time has blurred the details are not the stuff of good sense making. So, doing a check-in once every six weeks or even once a month is useless, because you'll wind up talking in generalities.

Actually, the data reveals that checking in with your team members once a month is literally worse than useless. While team leaders who check in once a week see, on average, a 13 percent increase in team engagement, those who check in only once a month see a 5 percent *decrease* in engagement.[5] It's as if team members are saying to you, "I'd rather you not waste my time if all we're going to do is talk generalities.

Either get into the nitty-gritty of my work and how you can help right now, or leave me alone."

Each check-in, then, is a chance to offer a tip, or an idea that can help the team member overcome a real-world obstacle, or a suggestion for how to refine a particular skill. Check-ins can be short—ten to fifteen minutes—but that's plenty of time to do a little real-time learning and coaching. And, like all good coaching, this has to be rooted in the specifics of the particular situation the team member is facing, the psychology she is bringing to it, the strengths she possesses, and the strategies she might already have tried. Again, the only way to surface these sorts of microdetails is to make sure that the conversations are frequent.

This leads us to one of the most important insights shared by the best team leaders: *frequency trumps quality*. They realize that it's less important that each check-in is perfectly executed than that it happens, every week. In the intelligence business, frequency is king. The more frequently and predictably you check in with your people or meet with your team—the more you offer your real-time attention to the reality of their work—the more performance and engagement you will get. In this sense, checking in is akin to teeth-brushing: you brush your teeth every day, and while you hope that each brushing is high quality, what's most important is that it happens, every day. Twice-a-year super-high-quality teeth-brushing is as absurd as it sounds. So is twice-a-year super-high-quality intelligence. A team with low check-in frequency is a team with low intelligence.

And this realization in turn gives the lie to the complaint—heard so often from senior leaders and HR executives—that "our team leaders aren't skilled enough to coach their people!" The data reveals only that those team leaders who check in every week with each team member have higher levels of engagement and performance, and lower levels of voluntary turnover. It doesn't have anything to say about the quality of those check-ins. We know for sure that if a team leader checks in often with a team member, the team member gets something really positive out of it—even if the team leader is no Pat Summit.* And besides, if the team leader struggles initially with her check-in quality, at least she's able to practice it fifty-one more times with each team member every year. No matter what her starting point, or her level of natural coaching talent, she's going to get a little better.

Now, you, the team leader, might think, *Well, I would love to check in with my people every week, but I can't. I've simply got too many people!* If that's you, then yes—you have too many people. One of the longer-running debates in the world of people and organizations is the span-of-control debate, which grapples with exactly how many team members every team leader should manage. Some say between one and nine employees. Others say between one and twenty. Some nurses manage staffs of forty; some call-center managers lead seventy or more.

But by pinpointing the weekly check-in as the single most powerful ritual of the world's best team leaders, we can now know the exact span of control that's right for every single team leader: it's the number of people that *you*, and only you, can check in with every week. If you can check in with eight people, but you can't fit nine into your schedule, your span of control is eight. If you can find a way to check in with twenty people, then your span of control is twenty. And if you're one of those people who can legitimately manage a weekly check-in with only two people, your span of control is two. Span of control, in other words, isn't a theoretical, one-size-fits-all thing. It's a practical, function-of-team-leader's-capacity-to-give-attention thing. Your span of control *is* your span of attention.

---

*In case you don't know Pat Summit, she was the best coach of the last century. She was the coach of the University of Tennessee women's basketball team, and she had the most wins in college basketball history: 1,098. She won eight NCAA championships (a record at the time); was an Olympic medalist and coach, guiding the US women's basketball team to a gold medal in 1984; and in 2000 was named the Naismith Coach of the Century.

In the service of intelligence, then—in the service of making sense of real-time information together—the weekly check-in is the anchor ritual. You need to design your teams, and their size, to enable it. And if ever you become a leader of leaders, you'll need to ensure that your leaders know that this check-in is the *most important part* of leading. Checking in with each person on a team—listening, course-correcting, adjusting, coaching, pinpointing, advising, paying attention to the intersection of the person and the real-world work—is not what you do *in addition to* the work of leading. This *is* the work of leading. If you don't like this, if the idea of weekly check-ins bores or frustrates you or you think that once a week is just "too much," that's fine—but, for the love of Hugh Dowding, don't be a leader.

In the previous chapter we saw how critical it was for team members to come to trust their team leader. Frequent sense making together— whether in McChrystal's O&I meeting, or your weekly check-ins—can help with this since it leads not only to better decisions but also to the building of trust. Two of the eight engagement items directly address this issue of trust: "In my team, I am surrounded by people who share my values" and "My teammates have my back." When these items receive low scores on a team it's easy to assume that the problem is one of intent—that team members don't really care for one another or want to support one another. More often than not, however, low scores are a function not of bad intent but of poor information: team members don't know *how* to support one another, because they don't know what's going on in enough detail to offer assistance. If they don't know what one another is doing, how can each learn what the others truly value? Likewise, if they don't know what work each is engaged in, how can any one of them feel safe? You can't watch someone's back if you don't know where his or her back is.

The more frequent sense-making rituals you establish on your team, the more information you will liberate, the more intelligence you will generate, and the more trust you will engender. Trust can never emerge from secrecy. Frequency creates safety.

• • •

The lessons of Dowding and McChrystal are not just lessons about systems and information and processes; they are lessons about the role of a leader in a fast-moving world. And their shared insight, across the span of sixty years, is that it is far more powerful for a leader to free the most information and the most decision-making power than it is for that leader to craft the perfect plan.

Another of the eight aspects that distinguish the best teams, as we've seen, is the sense of every team member that, "At work, I clearly understand what is expected of me." Whether informed by Taylorism and Scientific Management in the early part of the twentieth century, by Management by Objectives in the latter part of it, by any number of management truisms in between, or simply by what seems intuitive, our assumption has most often been that the best way to create clarity of expectations is to tell people what to do. It turns out, however, that by the time you've managed to do this, your directions are wrong because the world has moved on. In this way, the systems we've built to tell people what to do at great scale—planning systems—fail.

The best, most effective way to create clarity of expectations is to figure out how to let your people figure it out for themselves. This isn't a question of removing complexity, but is rather one of locating it in the right place—not hidden from view as the input for a grand plan, but rather shared for all to see. To do this, give your people as much accurate data as you can, as often as you can—a real-time view of what's going on right now—and then a way to make sense of it, together. Trust the intelligence of your team.

The best companies cascade goals

Recently a friend told us about a goal of hers: She said she was going to run a marathon. More precisely, she told us she was going to run the Prague marathon in seven months' time, in May. And when we asked her why, off the top of her head she shared a few of her reasons: that May was far enough away to give her time to go from "the couch to the course"; that the only marathon she could find around that time was in Prague; that she'd never been to Prague; that the course in Prague was known to be a mostly flat course and that a marathon was hard enough without throwing in those darn hills.

But of course none of these was the real reason she was running the marathon in Prague, in May. The real reason was that she wanted to significantly improve her physical stamina, and running a marathon seemed like the best way—albeit a tad drastic—to achieve that end. All the other details—May, Prague, a flat course—were simply her way of making that end more tangible, and therefore more hers.

This, at their best, is what goals do for us. They enable us to take what we value most and, by adding detail and timelines, to "chunk" these values into a describable outcome, something vivid and tangible. Visualized in our mind's eye, our goal pulls us forward, up and off the couch, and onto the road early one frigid Saturday morning in January, late one drizzly evening in March. Our goal becomes our companion, nestled in one corner of our psyche, pulsating, nudging us onward, guiding our thoughts and actions, and giving us the energy to push through the tiredness, the injuries, and the self-doubt, until one day we round the corner in Wenceslas Square and, alongside other people with other goals, complete our marathon.

And if goals did this in the corporate world—if they helped us step toward what's most important to us—they would be supremely useful.

• • •

Goals are everywhere at work—it's hard to find many companies that do not engage in some sort of annual or semi-annual goal-setting regimen. At some point in the year, usually at the start of a fiscal year or after bonuses and raises have been paid, the organization's senior leaders set their goals for the upcoming six or twelve months, and then share them with their teams. Each team member looks at each of the leader's goals, and figures out what to do to advance that goal, and thus sets a sort of minigoal that reflects some part of the leader's goal. This continues down the chain, until you, and every other employee, has a set of goals that are miniversions of some larger goal further up in the organization.

In some organizations, goals are also grouped into categories, so that each person is asked to set, say, strategic goals, operational goals, people goals, and innovation goals. Once the goals have been created, each is then approved by the person's immediate leader, and then by the leader above that person, and so on, with each layer assessing whether each goal is sufficiently challenging, and whether it's properly aligned with the goals above, up and up and up the chain.

As the year unfolds, you may well be asked to record what percentage of your goals you've completed. This "percent complete" data is then aggregated into bigger and bigger groups so that the company can, at any point during the year, say things like, "65 percent of our teams have completed 46 percent of their goals. We need to speed up!"

And, at the end of the year, you're asked to write a brief self-assessment reflecting how you feel you've done on each goal, after which your team leader will review this assessment and add her own, in some cases also saying whether she thinks each goal was actually met, or not. After HR has nudged her a couple of times, she'll input all this information into the company performance management system, whereupon it'll serve as a permanent record of your performance for the year, and will guide your pay, promotion opportunities, and even continued employment.

If you're in sales, your sales quota will work in a similar way—an overall corporate sales goal is sliced into parts and distributed across the organization. The only difference being that your quota, or your team's quota, is usually just a single number handed down to you from above, defining you and your work throughout the year—which is why salespeople, in most companies, are referred to not as people but simply as "quota carriers."

And, in the era of the smartphone, once-a-year goal-setting has been deemed Not Enough, and so your phone will soon be dramatically upping the frequency of all this goal-setting, assessing, and tracking, if it hasn't done so already—all because we have come to believe that *the best companies cascade goals.*

• • •

The names we give these goals have changed over the years. We started with MBOs, or Management by Objectives, first popularized by Peter Drucker in his 1954 book *The Practice of Management.* Then came SMART goals, goals that are specific, measurable, actionable, realistic, and time-bound, followed shortly by KPIs (Key Performance Indicators) and BHAGs (big hairy audacious goals, in Jim Collins's memorable framing). The latest incarnation, OKRs (Objectives and Key Results), originated at Intel and is now used by much of Silicon Valley for defining and tracking goals and measuring them against your "key results."

Across all the different technologies and methodologies, massive amounts of time and money are invested in this goal-setting. To give you a sense of the scale of the investment, the consulting firm Deloitte estimated that it spent $450 million on goal-setting, tracking, and evaluating every year, while Accenture, its consulting cousin, with more than 500,000 employees, spent more than twice that. When companies like these shell out close to $1 billion on something every year, there must be some truly extraordinary benefits.

What are they?

Well, every company is different, of course, and each makes its own calculus, but the three most common reasons put forth for all this goal-setting are, first, that goals stimulate and coordinate performance by aligning everyone's work; second, that tracking goals' "percent complete" yields valuable data on the team's or company's progress throughout the year; and third, that goal attainment allows companies to evaluate team members' performance at the end of the year. So, companies invest in goals because goals are seen as a *stimulator*, a *tracker*, and an *evaluator*—and these three core functions of goals are why we spend so much time, energy, and money on them.

And this is precisely where the trouble begins.

In terms of goals as a stimulator of performance, one great fear of senior leaders is that the work of their people is misaligned, and that effort is being wasted in activities that drag the company hither and yon, like a rudderless boat in a choppy sea. The creation of a cascade of goals calms this fear, and gives leaders the confidence that everyone on the boat is pulling on the oars in the same direction.

Of course, none of this alignment is worth very much if the goals themselves don't result in greater activity—if the boat doesn't actually go anywhere. As it happens, no research exists showing that goals set for you from above stimulate you to greater productivity. In fact, the weight of evidence suggests that cascaded goals do the opposite: they limit performance. They slow your boat down.

Have you ever tried to hail a cab in New York City on a rainy day? It's not easy. You stand there on the corner of 52nd and 3rd waving frantically at any vehicle that's even vaguely yellow, and bemoaning the fact that every one of the (suddenly scarce) cabs is taken. If you're up on your economics, you might even surmise, as the water drips off your nose, that the rain has increased the number of taxi hailers (demand) while not changing the number of taxi drivers (supply), hence the problem. But actually that's not quite what's going on. Cab drivers have an informal daily goal, or quota, for the fares they want to earn before they allow themselves to stop working—for most cabbies that number is twice the cost of renting the cab for the day.[1] The moment the day's receipts add up to twice their rental fee, they head home and rest up for the next day of battle. Now, they have this goal every day, but on rainy days—because more people choose to take a cab—they hit that goal earlier in their shift, and the moment they do they vanish off home.

The same thing happens with sales quotas. Leaders set quotas because they want to stimulate the performance of their salespeople. But quotas don't actually work like that. The very best salespeople hit their quota months before the end of the year, whereupon they do the sales equivalent of vanishing off home—that is, they start to delay the closing of their deals so that they can "bank" them and ensure that they begin the next year with a head start. Sales goals actually degrade the performance of top salespeople—they function, as they do for New York City cab drivers, as a ceiling on performance, not a catalyst for more of it.

But what about salespeople who are struggling, or middle-of-the-road? Won't goals serve to stretch them upward toward their quota, in much the same way as our friend's marathon goal will help to stretch her upward toward greater endurance? Well, again, not exactly. In reality, what happens to middling or struggling salespeople is that their imposed quota increases the pressure on them. And this is not the self-imposed pressure that comes from attempting to achieve something we feel is important—the sort our marathon-training friend will feel on a Sunday morning when she forces herself to get up and go running. No, this pressure to achieve company-imposed goals is coercion, and coercion is a cousin to fear. In the worst cases, fear-fueled employees push and push and, falling short, resort to inappropriate and sometimes illegal tactics in order to meet their goals.

This is what happened at Wells Fargo with its cross-selling goals for each branch: if someone came in to open up a checking account, the Wells Fargo personal banker was also supposed to sell them a savings account, a credit card, a demand deposit account, and a loan. But having these goals didn't lead to more cross-selling, or at least, not just that. Instead, it led to the creation of more than 3.5 million fake accounts.

None of which is to say that sales quotas are useless. In fact, they can be an excellent forecasting device. Senior leaders can use them to estimate what the company's top line is going to be for any given period, and then announce this to the board and the investment community so that all interested parties can get a sense of the expected revenues, against which costs, investments, and ultimately cash flow can be assessed. The best executives are good guesstimators—they have a sense, born of long experience, of what the median quota should be, the "line of best fit" around which the variation of salespeople's performance will cluster. Some will outperform their quota by 10 percent, others will fall short by 10 percent, and thus at year's end the sales goals, when guessed well, will be hit.

But these sales goals don't beget more sales; they just anticipate what the sales will be. Sales goals are for performance *prediction*, not performance creation.

How about tracking performance—do goals allow companies to do that? Hardly. Even though so many companies ask employees to write down their yearly goals and track their progress using some sort of software; even though books like *The Progress Principle* by Teresa Amabile and Steven Kramer say that humans love to track their progress and that they derive joy from each achievement;[2] and even though, in the last few years, we have seen more goal tracking and not less; none of this tracking does what it is intended to, for the simple reason that your progress toward a goal is not linear.

Take our marathon-running friend. If, at the end of February, she calculates that her training regimen is 62 percent complete, does that mean that she has only 38 percent of her marathon goal left to go? Obviously not: she has 100 percent left because she hasn't yet started her actual marathon. And what happens when she does indeed run her race? When she has finished her first thirteen miles does that mean she is now thirteen out of twenty-six miles, or 50 percent of the way toward completing the race? Again, no. As every marathon runner discovers, the first half of the marathon is the comparatively easy part. It's the last half—in particular, the last six miles—that's brutal. Only when you pass the twenty-mile mark do you begin to feel the legs harden and the mind weaken; only then do you know whether you have the physical and mental strength to complete your goal. And what percentage of the whole does the refining fire of the last six miles represent—40 percent? 60 percent? 90 percent? It's impossible to put an accurate number on it because, in truth, the first twenty miles of a marathon are one thing, and the last six miles a very different thing.

So our friend can't be 62 percent done with her marathon preparation, nor she can be 50 percent done with her actual marathon. She can only either complete the goal or not complete it. All goals, at least in the real world, function in this same way. You are either done, or you are not done: goal attainment is binary. You might want to set some intermediate goals along the way, and tick these goals off as they are done (or not done). But you won't ever be able to assign a "percent complete" to your bigger goal as you tick off these mini-goals. And if you attempt to, or if your company asks you to, you will only be generating falsely precise data about the state of your progress.

Finally, what about evaluating employees? Can we evaluate a person based on how many goals he or she has achieved? Many companies do, for sure. But here's the snag: unless we can standardize the difficulty of each person's goals it's impossible to objectively judge the relative performance of each employee.

Let's say we have two employees we're evaluating, Victoria and Albert. Each is aiming to complete five goals, and at year's end Victoria has achieved three goals and Albert has achieved five. Does that mean Albert is a higher performer? Not necessarily. Maybe one of Victoria's five goals was "Govern an empire" and one of Albert's five goals was "Make a cup of tea." For us to use goal attainment to evaluate Victoria and Albert, we need to be able to perfectly calibrate each and every goal for difficulty—we need each manager, with perfect consistency, to be able to weigh the stretchiness or slackness of a given goal in exactly the same way as every other manager.*

---

*A condition known more properly as inter-rater reliability, and another finicky-but-importantly-true thing that, as we'll see later, explains in part why 360-degree assessments don't work and why performance ratings are such a problem.

And as it happens this sort of calibration is a practical impossibility, so we can't. Sorry, Albert.

• • •

Despite this evidence, however, it remains true that goals, and cascaded goals in particular, have an intuitive appeal to many leaders who find themselves in search of ways to ensure efficient and aligned execution in their organizations. And, at the same time, it also remains true that for those of us in the trenches, our experience of goals feels nonintuitive, mechanical, fake, even demeaning. Why is that?

Well, in the real world, this is what's going on. Firstly, and oddly, when you sit down to write your goals, you already have a pretty good idea of the work that you're about to do. After all, it's not as though you roll up to the office on a Monday morning desperately trying to figure out how you're going to fill the time. So what the goal-setting process is asking you to do is to write down work that you already know you're going to do. Your work goals aren't out ahead of you, pulling you along like our marathoner's goal; instead they're just behind you, being tugged along by your own preexisting understanding of the work you're going to do anyway.

The goal categories—strategic, operational, innovation, people, and so on—are odd simply because work doesn't come in categories. You don't plan your time by thinking, "Well, on Tuesday I'll do some operational, and hopefully make time for a bit of innovation on Thursday afternoon." Work usually comes in projects, with deadlines and deliverables, and so when you're asked to translate it back into category goals, you (and most every other employee) fudge it and force-fit your work to the categories, while hoping no one will mind too much.

And while it's not unreasonable to hope that the work you do matches up to what your team leader wants you to do, setting goals that are a subset of his goals, or reviewing your goals against his, is actually a pretty strange way of going about this. Your team leader already knows what you're doing, because in the real world you talk to him about it, all the time. If you're off working on origami and he'd rather you were working on quilting, he'll tell you. And when something changes, a few days later, and he needs you to shift your focus over to glass-blowing, again, he'll just tell you. Even if he doesn't tell you, and you continue to potter away at something that's all of a sudden out of whack, the very last thing he'd think of doing to communicate this to you is to go back into your goal form, change your goals, and hope you'll notice. Again, cascaded goals are tagging along behind the work, not out ahead of it: as used in the real world, goal setting is more a system of record keeping than a system of work making.

Then there's the fact that you don't go and look at your goals once you've set them. If they were supposed to be guiding your work, you'd think you might.

And what about the gritty point of it all, at year's end, when you're supposed to self-evaluate against your goals? While your boss may imagine that you're engaging in honest and earnest reflection on the year gone by, you're probably trying to find the elusive sweet spot between, on the one hand, saying that you hit all your goals out of the park, by which you'd risk seeming arrogant or deluded, and, on the other, acknowledging that some things didn't go as planned, by which you'd risk giving your boss—or some unseen higher-up—an excuse to decrease your bonus. Self-evaluation of goals isn't really about evaluating your work, in other words: it's a careful exercise in self-promotion and political positioning, in figuring out how much to reveal honestly and how much to couch carefully.

This is no comment on you, by the way. Carefully calibrating your self-evaluation to find this sweet spot is a practical response to a bizarre situation. The company has asked you to evaluate yourself against a list of abstract goals that were irrelevant a couple of weeks after you wrote them down. You're being asked to do something meaningless and pretend it's meaningful. It's enough to make you a little crazy.

And your team leader's in on the crazy. When the end of the year comes around and she has to sit down with a stack of goal forms and write—under each goal you typed in months and months ago—one or two little sentences describing how you've done against each one, what must be going through her mind? More than likely it isn't related to you or how she thinks you've done, but is more about how quickly she can get through the stack and cross "goal review" off her to-do list. Like you, she's got a nagging feeling that she's wasting her time—because what's in front of her now is a random subset of things you thought you might be doing a while ago, shoehorned into whatever categories you thought you could get away with at the time, written so as to look maximally impressive for anyone reading the form, and now garnished with your delicately positioned self-evaluation. She knows that the work changed an equally long time ago and has very little to do with what's on the form, and that she's already told you how well you did on the work that actually happened, by talking to you about it as the year went along. To her this form filling is the worst kind of administrivia-masquerading-as-management, so she writes the little sentences and hopes that no one will complain if they're shorter than last year's.

In the real world, there is work—stuff that you have to get done. In theory world, there are goals.

Work is ahead of you; goals are behind you—they're your rear-view mirror.

Work is specific and detailed; goals are abstract.

Work changes fast; goals change slowly, or not at all.

Work makes you feel like you have agency; goals make you feel like a cog in a machine.

Work makes you feel trusted; goals make you feel *dis*trusted.

Work is work; goals aren't.

But it doesn't have to be this way. Goals can be a force for good.

• • •

Look again at our soon-to-be-marathoner friend: she has taken something she deems valuable (fitness) and turned it into a tangible achievement (the marathon). She has made it real. This, ultimately, is what goals are for: to help you manifest your values. They are your best mechanism for taking what's inside of you and bringing it out where you and others can see it, and where you and they can benefit from it. Your goals define the dent you want to make in the world.

And this in turn means that the only criterion for what makes a good goal is that the person working toward it must set it for him- or herself, *voluntarily*. The only way a goal has any use at all is if it comes out of you as an expression of what you deem valuable. It doesn't have to be SMART, or big, hairy, and audacious. It doesn't need to contain key performance indicators or be built from objectives and key results. If a goal is going to be useful, if it is going to help you contribute more, then the *only* criterion is that you must set it for yourself, voluntarily. Any goal imposed upon you from above is an un-goal.

This doesn't mean, though, that there is nothing we should cascade in our organizations. Since goals, done properly, are only and always an expression of what a person finds most meaningful, then to create alignment in our company we should do everything we can to ensure that everyone in the company understands what matters most. And so the truth:

The best companies don't cascade goals; *the best companies cascade meaning.*

• • •

The research into the best teams gives us the first clue to this. When you have a measurement instrument like the eight questions we shared in chapter 1, one of the things you can do is something called factor analysis. This, in essence, tells you how many different sorts of things your questions are measuring—how clumpy they are. In all the years of researching teams, company by company by company, we had only ever found one factor in our eight questions—one clump of experience that all eight questions were illuminating for us—and we called this clump "engagement."

But when we ran the numbers at Cisco, something unexpected happened. First, two of the eight questions behaved differently from the other six in one slice of the analysis. We weren't sure what this meant, as it didn't show up anywhere else. But later on, we ran our factor analysis, and then, all at once, there it was: a second factor appeared.

It was made up of these two questions:

1. I am really enthusiastic about the mission of my company.

7. I have great confidence in my company's future.

So we began thinking of these as the "company" factor, and the remaining six questions as the "team" factor—and these two factors *together* as "engagement."

To be clear, the "company" things—excitement about the mission and confidence in the future—still vary from a good team to a bad team, and still explain team performance. But at the same time, it appears that they may not originate from within the team, as the other six things—safety and trust, a sense of excellence, challenging work, and so on—clearly do, but instead originate from outside the team and then become amplified, or not, within the team. Put another way, while a team left to its own devices can take care of many of its own needs, it apparently can't create a sense of the broader mission and confidence in the future from out of thin air. So, in addition to giving our teams and their members a real-time understanding of what is happening in the world, we need to give them a sense of which hill we're trying to take. Instead of cascading goals, instead of cascading instructions for actions, we should cascade meaning and purpose.

The best leaders realize that their people are wise, that they do not need to be coerced into alignment through yearly goal setting. These leaders strive instead to bring to life for their people the meaning and purpose of their work, the missions and contributions and methods that truly matter. These leaders know that in a team infused with such meaning, each person will be smart enough and driven enough to set goals voluntarily that manifest that meaning. It is shared meaning that creates alignment, and this alignment is *emergent*, not coerced. Whereas cascaded goals are a control mechanism, cascaded meaning is a release mechanism. It brings to life the context within which everyone works, but it leaves the locus of control—for choosing, deciding, prioritizing, goal setting—where it truly resides, and where understanding of the world and the ability to do something about it intersect: with the team member.

Our prevailing assumption is that we need goals because our deficit at work is a deficit of aligned action. We're mistaken. What we face instead is a deficit of meaning, of a clear and detailed understanding of the purpose of our work, and of the values we should honor in deciding how to get it done. Our people don't need to be told what to do; they want to be told why.

• • •

To see what this looks like in practice, take a closer look at Mark Zuckerberg and Sheryl Sandberg of Facebook, and Truett Cathy of Chick-fil-A. Though separated in age, religious affiliation, geography, and company product, they all demonstrate a similar fixation with cascading meaning. Now, given the challenges that both Facebook and Chick-fil-A have faced lately, whether because of their use of their customers' data, in Facebook's case, or because of their position on gay rights, in Chick-fil-A's, you might ask why we chose these people as examples. Our reasoning is this: people are imperfect, and so if we are going to learn from real people, then, by definition, we are going to have to learn from imperfect people. It is up to us all to sort what is useful and valuable about these people and their companies, from what is not.

Ten years ago, in a post intended to clarify his company's mission, Zuckerberg wrote that Facebook's purpose was to make the world more connected. As we were writing this chapter, he added what he sees as meaningful nuance to this mission, saying:

> . . . we're making a major change to how we build Facebook. I'm changing the goal I give our product teams from focusing on helping you find relevant content to helping you have more meaningful social interactions.[3]

You may not see the distinction, but he does, and so today—just as he's done every six months for the last ten years—he's intent on announcing another distinction to the world and, more importantly, to all of the people who work for him. This is what Zuckerberg does. He takes his values so seriously that with each new insight of his, he tweaks and course corrects and tweaks and learns and tweaks again, and then with great weight and import he announces the tweak to the world.

To some people, these small shifts of focus and their accompanying announcements might seem portentous, exhibiting no more than the narcissism of minor differences, but to he and Sandberg they are part of a relentless effort to cascade to their teams what they truly value, with the implicit message that if you don't value what they value then you may well be on the wrong team. And indeed the constant iteration and "improvement" of this message is, in and of itself, part of that message, because Zuckerberg's and Sandberg's meaning in the world is not just to help people get more connected but also to do so in a way that confesses to being a work in progress. They've both made it very clear—Sandberg in her book *Lean In*, and Zuckerberg in his numerous blogs and congressional testimony—that they don't necessarily know all the answers. They know what they want to build at Facebook, *and* they know they don't always know how to get it, and neither do you, and neither does any of us. What they've told us is that each of them, and everyone else at Facebook, are constantly making it up as they go along, constantly experimenting.

If you join Facebook on Thursday, you're at onboarding boot camp on Friday, writing and honing code over the weekend, and potentially having that code shipped on Monday. Things move fast. Facebook's address, 1 Hacker Way, reinforces this ethos, and if the symbolism of that didn't register with you, there's always the massive "The Hacker Company" sign, bought from a strip mall in Florida, that now hangs proudly over the company's town square.

These types of things—the signage, the street address—are different from the cultural plumage we encountered in our first chapter, designed to lure you in. Rather, they exist to help us understand what we are working toward—what our work is for, and what it means. Indeed, Facebook's entire campus seems to have been constructed to bring Zuckerberg and Sandberg's meaning to life. Though the exteriors of many of the buildings are Frank Gehry masterworks of fluid beauty and sustainable energy, the interiors scream "temporary." It feels like the entire company just moved in yesterday, and might move out tomorrow: concrete floors, exposed AC ducts, a pile of keyboards sitting in one corner, handmade posters tacked up on the walls.

When we were there a couple of years ago, we noticed that each conference-room door was made of glass and had a logo etched onto it—and that this same logo stretched off into the distance, repeating on door after door, for the length of a football field. Which might not be particularly unusual if the logo—there in Facebook's offices where Facebook's code gets written by Facebook's employees to go into Facebook's applications—was actually Facebook's logo. But it wasn't: it was Sun Microsystems' logo.

"What's with the logos?" we asked Facebook's head of facilities.

"Oh that," he said. "Well that's because this used to be the Sun Microsystems building."

"Could you perhaps afford to buy new doors," we offered, "with the Facebook logo on them?"

"We could," he replied. "But Mark and Sheryl made the decision to keep the logo on the doors because it reminds everyone that unless you make quick decisions, move fast, and figure out better solutions, you might go the way of Sun Microsystems."

Look on the walls, and you'll see another Facebook oddity: posters. Physical, printed posters. Outside, on the conference-room walls, behind the reception desk; posters next to posters next to yet more posters. Each one is an announcement of something someone is passionate about, some hobby, event, or activity—underwater skateboarding, Time's Up, Black Lives Matter, or the local tiddlywinks group. Why would something as old-economy as a poster proliferate at a high-tech digital-media company? It's all part of Facebook's stated mission to facilitate and reinforce real human connection. If you want people to connect with other people then you have to be curious about what each person is interested in and passionate about, and then find ways to surface and celebrate these passions. Just as we draw on our cave's wall, so we put up our posters. And in this way we learn about one another.

With all of these deliberate actions Zuckerberg and Sandberg have cascaded their meaning to their team of teams, and again, while we can quibble with the results, or worry that speed and connection at

Facebook have been emphasized to the detriment of security and accuracy, we can still learn from the way in which speed and connection have, indeed, been emphasized.

If you love genuine human connection, Zuckerberg and Sandberg tell their people, you'll find meaning at Facebook.

If you love the idea that the future is a work in progress, you'll find meaning at Facebook.

If you love speed over beauty, you'll find meaning at Facebook.

But, if you want beauty—carefully considered, precise, perfect beauty—then Facebook is not for you. If you want to live in a world where things are either not yet begun or already perfected, but never in between, don't work here. Instead, go just a couple miles down the road and work for Apple. There, it does not look like they moved in yesterday and are about to move out tomorrow. There, it looks like an alien spaceship—perfectly circular, complete, whole, and utterly finished—has landed in downtown Cupertino, and welcomes in only those who are attracted to its beautiful closed system. If that's what gets you going, if that's where you find meaning, work there. Because Facebook will leave you cold.

• • •

Chick-fil-A is the most profitable and fastest-growing quick-service restaurant company in the world, which is perhaps surprising. Facebook's growth is surely tied to the power of network effects. Google's success can be traced to the monopolistic powers of its search algorithm. Amazon relied on its first-mover status and disdain of margins to secure its leadership position. But what's Chick-fil-A got? It's got a chicken sandwich, some waffle fries, and a shake, which, though all distinctly yummy, wouldn't on their face seem differentiated enough to explain the company's outlandish and continued success.

What Chick-fil-A had was Truett Cathy, its founder, a man who was just as relentless, as precise, and as deliberate at bringing his meaning to life as Facebook's leaders have been.

Unlike Facebook, where the work never seems to stop, Chick-fil-A isn't open on Sundays, despite the boost in sales and profit that the extra day would bring. Why? Because Cathy was a devout Christian who followed the Bible's injunction to reserve Sunday as a day of rest.

The closed-on-Sunday policy is perhaps the most obvious example of the way that Cathy cascaded meaning to his teams. A less well-known one is Chick-fil-A's franchise agreement. Your typical franchisee-franchisor agreement is a mechanism designed to leverage capital through the multiplier of brand—the franchisor brings the brand, the franchisee the capital. The franchisor selects the franchisee based on how large and how stable a hunk of capital the franchisee can bring to the agreement, and the franchisee assesses the franchisor based on how powerful and attractive the brand is. The goal of the franchisor is to secure lots of capital; the goal of the franchisee to secure as many locations as possible. So, for example, Arcos Dorados Holdings Inc., McDonald's largest franchisee, has over $4.5 billion in sales from over two thousand locations.

The Chick-fil-A franchise agreement does not work this way. As a Chick-fil-A franchisee you cannot own two thousand locations, no matter how much capital you have. Instead, you are allowed to own one.* You can throw as much money at Chick-fil-A as you like, and it won't be swayed into giving you any more locations: the franchise agreement, unchanged since Cathy devised it in the mid-1950s, forbids it. At its founding, Cathy decided that the mission of his company was less to sell chicken than it was to build leaders in local communities. Some of us might scoff at this, but Cathy stayed true to it, and devised his franchise agreement accordingly. He reasoned that if he

*In exceptional circumstances, Chick-fil-A will allow you a second freestanding location, if your first is in a mall. But 95% of their operators have only one.

was to grow local leaders, he would have to ensure that each person he brought on as a franchisee had a good reason to stay close to their local community. The best way to do that, he thought, was to keep these leaders in their stores, and the best way to ensure that, in turn, was to allow them only one. If you have only one, he figured, then you will be in this store all the time, staying close to your guests and close to your team members, knowing intimately the concerns of each—what the community is interested in and what it's worried about. And over time you will respond to these needs and take action, and therefore, over time you will grow as a community leader.

Guided by the purity of his vision, he crafted this extraordinary franchise agreement and then selected his franchisees (or operators, as they are known in the company), not on the size of their capital but on their commitment to their community. And in case you're thinking to yourself that while this makes for a nice story (the sort of founding myth we're all used to hearing), it can't possibly be true in the second decade of the twenty-first century, then you should know that to this day, you need zero capital to become an operator, and yet such is the care with which Chick-fil-A selects these future community leaders that it is harder to become one than it is to get into Harvard.

Over the years, Chick-fil-A has doubtless scared away countless billions of dollars of capital that could have been pressed into service to grow its brand, but what it has gained instead are tens of thousands of people who have embraced Cathy's meaning. These local leaders are the heroes of the organization. Every year, the company gathers them all together at an event called Seminar, where one of the highlights is a magazine-worthy spread of photos and stories and testimonials, all in celebration of the unique contribution that each operator has made in his or her community. At each Seminar the very best operators are brought up on stage, one-by-one, to have their story told.

• • •

None of this is to say that Mark Zuckerberg, Sheryl Sandberg, or Truett Cathy are exemplars of perfection—they aren't, and we don't imagine any of them would have claimed to be. But if you want to create alignment in your team, or your company, then you can learn from the way in which each of them deliberately, relentlessly, precisely, and pervasively cascaded meaning.

To be specific, here are the three levers they used to such great effect.

The first is *expressed values*: what you write on the walls. We don't mean that you should literally write out your "values." Many leaders and many companies set about doing this and wind up with a list of generic values such as *integrity*, *innovation*, or, God forbid, *teamwork*—which are about as meaningful as Muzak—and then wonder why the whole exercise doesn't seem to have made much difference. Instead, apply some creativity to how you want to bring your meaning to life for your people. Don't *tell* them what you value, *show* them. What do you actually want them to see and to bump into at work? Facebook's Sun Microsystems logos, its love of posters, and the "Hacker Company" signage are all vivid examples of this.

What are your expressed values? What have you written on your walls? What do your people encounter when they walk in through the door. What do they see when they turn to the left? And what do those things tell them about who you are?

A second way to cascade meaning is through *rituals*. Facebook has their famous bimonthly hack-a-thon; Chick-fil-A stops work on Sundays. Sam Walton, founder of Walmart and Sam's Club, had a ritual he practiced every single Friday until he was physically unable to do it anymore: he would pick a store, move the merchandise around on a particular end-cap display, and come back on Saturday to see what had sold.

It was his own version of QMI, or quick market intelligence, and what it signaled, to his employees, was his deep belief that no one, not even the boss, knows the brain of the customer better than the customer.

You already have rituals, whether they are conscious or unconscious, and these rituals—the things you do repeatedly—communicate to your people what is meaningful to you. If we followed you around for a week, we'd see them. Let's say you have a meeting: What time do you show up? Are you five minutes early, or five minutes late? What are you wearing? Do you catch up with your team members about their personal lives or do you launch right into business? Who talks first? Do you allow your team members to speak, or do you cut them off? Does the meeting go long? Do you hold people back to finish things up?

These are all aspects of your rituals, and we, your team, see them, make sense of them, and draw our conclusions—whether you want us to or not. The question, then, isn't whether you have rituals or not. The question is whether or not you are deliberate about what your rituals communicate.

To see the power of a ritual to vividly communicate a leader's meaning, juxtapose Facebook's rituals with Steve Jobs's. At the end of every week, either Zuckerberg or Sandberg goes to Facebook's largest cafeteria and holds an all-hands meeting during which any employee can ask any question that he or she wants to, and the two top leaders commit to answering each question as best they can. The purpose of these meetings is contained not so much in the actual substance of the answers as it is in the reinforcement that Facebook values transparency and openness so much that they will dedicate a significant chunk of top leaders' time to it each week.

Jobs, by contrast, valued aesthetic beauty far higher than openness, and so his all-hands meetings, which he held every three months or so, and which the rest of the world mistook for product launches, looked very different. At each "launch" he would describe in precise detail the beautiful design of each product, or the intricate ecosystem of hardware and software, or the exquisite integration of content and code, and while we, the consumers, were oohing and ahing at the new products, the real audience—Apple employees—were watching and taking note. They could see their leader extolling the virtues of aesthetics, of beauty for its own sake, of the joy in refined creation, and they would lean into that shared meaning.

Or they would lean out and go work for Facebook. Either way, the product launch had served its true purpose: to cascade Jobs's meaning across his teams.

The third lever is *stories*. Chick-fil-A makes an art of its storytelling through the operator profiles during Seminar. The company dedicates time to going out to each operator's store, taking photos, and learning about his or her family and community, precisely so it can share these stories with the rest of the company.

Many of the best leaders are storytellers, not in the sense of writing a novel or a screenplay, but because they cascade meaning through vignettes, anecdotes, or stories told at meetings, on email chains, or on phone calls. They are always telling these little stories, because the stories that they choose to tell convey what they value. Stories make sense of the world: they are meaning, made human. That's why religions tell stories about their messiah and the creation of the earth, and include parables within those stories that help us learn what is meaningful. And that's why you can tell a lot about what matters to a team by the stories that the team members tell themselves.

For example, on a much larger scale, if you've spent any sort of time in Great Britain you'll know that there are three battles that the Brits can't stop talking about: the Charge of the Light Brigade in the Crimean War, and the Battle of Britain and the evacuation from Dunkirk in the Second World War. There's nothing odd, of course, about a country repeating the tales of its battles long after they've been fought. What is odd, however, is that Britain didn't win any of these battles. The Charge of the Light Brigade was a disaster, and the Battle of Britain and the Dunkirk evacuation were more about avoiding defeat than securing victory. Why, then, do we keep talking about them?

Because they define what we Brits think is most meaningful about us: that we never give up, and we never give in. We value determination and grit *more* than we value winning, so we tell story upon story of keep-going-ness that usually ends up on just the wrong side of victory.* In so doing we create shared meaning.

You tell stories, whether you know it or not, and you're telling them all the time, in every conversation and at every meeting. What stories are you telling, and what do they say about what you find meaningful?

• • •

As a leader, you are trying to unlock the judgment, the choices, the insight, and the creativity of your people. But, as we've seen in the last two chapters, the way we go about this doesn't make much sense. We cloister information in our planning systems, and we cascade directives in our goal-setting systems. Instead, we should unlock information through intelligence systems, and cascade meaning through our expressed values, rituals, and stories. We should let our people know what's going on in the world, and which hill we're trying to take, and then we should trust them to figure out how to make a contribution. They will invariably

---

*Here's another one: Our most famous explorer is not Ernest Shackleton, who successfully rescued his team after they became stranded in the ice on an expedition to Antarctica. Neither is it James Cook, who was the first European to discover Australia. No, it's Robert Falcon Scott, who lost the race to the South Pole to Roald Amundsen and was therefore the *second* person to reach it, and who died of hypothermia and starvation on the way back, persisting to the very end. He's the one we talk about most.

make better and more authentic decisions than those derived from any planning system that cascades goals from on high.

For Ethan Floquet—or, more accurately, for his mother—his cascaded goals became an ever increasing burden with each passing year.[4] Ethan has autism, and every year since his early childhood his mother has been asked to write an individualized education plan, or IEP, setting out her and her husband's goals for Ethan for the upcoming year—their aspirations for their son—to aid and guide his educators and therapists. But as time went by, their goals diminished. It became clear that Ethan would never live independently, or hold down a job without help, or marry. His goals became smaller and smaller; the annual meeting to discuss his development became more and more somber; and each year's IEP became shorter than the preceding year's. It ultimately shrank to a single sentence, at a time when Ethan had found a farm program that seemed to offer some promise ("We hope that Ethan can remain with this program for the year"), before vanishing altogether the following year. Ethan's mother had been too busy, and the task of once again revisiting all his shortcomings—for the eighteenth year in a row—too painful.

But that year, unbeknownst to his mother, Ethan had written his own goals. He had written them, of course, in ignorance of his cascaded goals, and had instead focused on something else. Here they are, in full:

> After I graduate from high school I plan to work at Prospect Meadow Farm until I retire and live at home with my family as long as I can. I'd like to keep taking classes at Berkshire Hills Music Academy. For fun, I want to play Special Olympics basketball, go to our cabin in Vermont and the shore in New Jersey, mow lawns, and collect business cards. My goals for the future are to take the PVTA bus into town to make purchases, and someday learn how to drive a zero-turn lawn mower.

Goals set by others imprison us. In creating his own, Ethan had found freedom.

LIE #4

The best people are well-rounded

Watch Lionel Messi dribble. Go on YouTube, type in "Best Messi Dribbles," click on any of the clips that come up—there will be hundreds to choose from; any one will do—and you will see a small man with magical feet, running at what seems like double time past one defender after another until he gets into the penalty area and shoots. If you are a soccer fan, you will have seen him do this countless times already, but if you aren't, it's worth taking a moment to watch this man. All of us who are interested in excellence can benefit from studying preternatural ability in action: we can wonder at what caused it, analyze the technique of it, and dissect the steps involved, or we can simply revel in the fluid mastery of it and try to imagine where in our lives we, too, can experience flow such as this.

Lionel Messi is from the port city of Rosario in Argentina. He was always a speedy kid. In videos his mom took of his first soccer games, you see him sprint past one opponent after another, as though the outsize ball is pulling him along on a string. Such a prodigy was he that, from across the Atlantic, scouts from F.C. Barcelona came calling, and at the tender age of thirteen Messi was spirited away from home to La Masia, "The Farmhouse," Barcelona's legendary youth academy. There, his little body refused to grow, so they gave him growth hormones and waited for the size of his frame to catch up with the size of his talent. It never did: he topped out at five feet seven, and stayed as skinny as a kid playing on the streets of Buenos Aires' *villa miseria*. But somehow this didn't seem to matter. His gift was so extraordinary— the ball looking as if it were magnetically attached to his boots, no matter his speed or his jackrabbit changes in direction—that it rendered irrelevant his lack of size and stature. He joined Barcelona's first team at the age of seventeen and since then has proven himself the best soccer player in the world, and in many people's eyes, the greatest of all time. Watch him now, and watch carefully, because we may never see his like again.

Although any of the YouTube videos could serve as a highlight reel, the one that best illuminates his gifts shows a goal that Messi scored against Athletic Bilbao in the final of the 2015 Copa del Rey.[1] It's worth playing it out in detail because, while so much of what he does in just a few seconds is astonishing (not least the cannon of a shot he unleashes at the end of the run), this clip reveals something about him that is at once truly bizarre and the very foundation of his genius.

He receives a pass on the halfway line, and for a moment stands perfectly still with the ball at his feet, one defender in front of him and the rest of the opposing players staking out their positions between him and the goal. Then, as though seized by a sudden thought, he darts to his left, jukes back to his right, leaves the nearest defender flat-footed, and takes off down the sideline. Three other opponents converge on him, trying to squeeze him into the corner and away from the goal. He slows for a second, dips his shoulder right, accelerates left, touches the ball past the legs of one defender, and then at once is free of all three of them and bursting toward the penalty area. Two more

Bilbao players sprint over to cover him, but somehow he ghosts past this new threat, his legs on fast-forward, the ball now rolling out to his left, perfectly positioned for a strike on goal. He shoots. He scores. The Barcelona players celebrate with him as only soccer players can, and as he walks back toward the halfway line for the restart, even the Bilbao supporters clap in admiration. The greatest ever.

Watch this clip over and over and you find many things to marvel at: his zero-to-top-speed quickness, his innate sense of the pitch and of the most dangerous angle to take toward goal, his counterintuitive decision to shoot for the near post. But by far the most remarkable discovery awaiting you is that, as he races from the halfway line through seven defenders and into the penalty area, he uses only one foot. Count the touches from the start of his run to his actual shot on goal and you realize that of the nineteen times he kicks the ball, only two of them are with his right foot. Everything else he does during the dribble, including the shot at the end of it, is done with his left.

Click on other clips, watch other dribbles in the magnificent Messi oeuvre, and you discover that this is always the case. His ratio of strong-foot to weak-foot usage stays constant at around 10 to 1. For the sake of comparison, the right-footed Cristiano Ronaldo's ratio is around 4.5 to 1. Messi is not just a left-footed player, in other words. He is a player who does virtually everything that needs to be done with a ball with only his left foot. Passing, dribbling, shooting, tackling—all of it.

Messi's left-footedness, then, is truly extreme. And, of course, everyone on the opposing team is acutely aware of this, yet even with the foreknowledge that he is going to play with his left foot time after time after time, they are still bamboozled as he swerves around them. Messi has taken his natural left-footedness and cultivated it to such an extent—developed it to work with such speed and precision—that instead of being a limitation, it bestows on him a consistent, dramatic, and unfair advantage.

We get the sense, watching him, that acquiring this advantage was no rational calculation on his part. For sure, he must have practiced ten thousand hours and more, but what he conveys as he swerves and skips toward goal is not diligence and discipline, but joy: pure, unconscious, unstoppable joy in his craft. To see him run with the ball at his feet is to see the fullest and best and most authentic expression of this man. It delights us, and lifts us up, as it always does when we see someone shine as only he or she can shine. And just like the opposing supporters, we look in wonder at this little man, clap our hands, and smile.

· · ·

Messi plies his trade on the world's largest sporting stages, but you may have experienced similar admiration for colleagues at work. One of them puts together a presentation and delivers it with wit and clarity, and you smile. Another handles a grumpy customer with just the right mix of empathy and practicality, and you marvel at how easy she made it look. Another defuses a complex political situation, and you look at him in awe and wonder how on earth he did it. As humans we are wired to find joy in seeing someone else's talents in action. We resonate with the naturalness, the fluidity, and the honesty of a thing done brilliantly well, and it attracts us and draws us in.

You will have recognized the Messi joy when it is your *own* performance that you're experiencing, too—that is, when you are expressing your own strengths. This sensation is not, at root, created by how good you are at something. Rather, it's created by how that activity makes you feel. A *strength*, properly defined, is not "something you are good at." You will have many activities or skills that, by dint of your intelligence, your sense of responsibility, or your disciplined practice, you are quite good at, and that nonetheless bore you, or leave you cold, or even drain you. "Something you are good at" is not a strength; it is an ability. And, yes, you will be able to demonstrate high ability—albeit briefly—at quite a few things that bring you no joy whatsoever.

A *strength*, on the other hand, is an "activity that makes you feel strong." This sort of activity possesses for you certain definable qualities. Before you do it, you find yourself actively looking forward to doing it. While you are doing it, time seems to speed up, one moment blurring into the next. And after you've done it, while you may be tired and not quite ready to suit up and tackle it again, you nonetheless feel filled up, proud. It is this combination of three distinct feelings—positive anticipation beforehand, flow during, and fulfillment afterward—that makes a certain activity a strength. And it is this combination of feelings that produces in you the yearning to do the activity again and again, to practice it over and over, to thrill to the chance to do it just one more time. A strength is far more *appetite* than ability, and indeed it is the appetite ingredient that feeds the desire to keep working on it and that, in the end, produces the skill improvement necessary for excellent performance.

Of course, it's possible there are a few activities in which you seem to have boatloads of appetite and very little natural ability. Florence Foster Jenkins was, according to one historian, "the world's worst opera singer. No one before or since has liberated herself quite so completely from the shackles of musical notation."[2] The songwriter Cole Porter used to have to bang his cane repeatedly against his leg in order to stop himself from laughing out loud at the unremitting awfulness of her voice. And yet she loved to sing, and even managed to buy her way onto the stage at Carnegie Hall.

Look closer at Lady Florence, however, or at anyone who appears to love an activity in which his or her performance is woeful, and you discover that often what such a person loves isn't the activity itself but instead the trappings of the activity. In Lady Florence's case it was most probably the attention given to a public performer: she had been a successful pianist in childhood, even performing at the White House, until an injury curtailed her piano playing and she had to find another way to get onstage. Other times, you see someone become addicted to brief moments of greatness in a sea of otherwise mediocre performances, and what keeps pulling that person back to the activity is the endless quest to re-create those flashes of brilliance. Anyone who has ever hit a perfect seven iron on the golf course, and then spent years toiling to recapture that one moment, will know what we mean. In any case, it appears that as a rule we humans are congenitally incapable of deeply loving an activity in which we are awful.

Instead, we are drawn to activities in which we find joy. We can't always explain why, but some activities seem to contain ingredients that breathe life into us, that lift us up out of ourselves to reveal something finer, more resilient, and more creative. Each of us is different, of course, so each of us finds this joy in different activities, yet each of us knows this feeling. And when our work does indeed bring us this joyful ingredient, when we do indeed feel love, even, for what we do, then we are truly magnificent. Stevie Wonder, who clearly knows a thing or two about cultivating and contributing one's strengths to the world, said it best: "You will never feel proud of your work if you find no joy within it. Your best work is always joyful work."[3]

This is what work does to Stevie Wonder when he composes and sings—he finds joy. This is what work does to Lionel Messi when he dances round defenders and finds the net from impossible angles—he finds delight. This is what we see when we see anyone who is really good at their work—we see someone who has found love in what they do. And this is what your company hopes your work will do for you. When your leaders say they want you to be creative and innovative and collaborative and resilient and intuitive and productive, what they are really saying is, "We want you to fill your working hours with activities that bring you joy, with tasks that delight you."

Oddly—and sadly—this set of observations is often dismissed in business circles, perhaps because business is meant to be about rigor and objectivity and competitive advantage, next to which the idea of looking for joy in work, as a precursor to excellence in work, seems rather soft. Fixing shortcomings, no matter how hard that might be, seems like the hard-boiled business of business; finding delight is the province of poets.

Yet the data does not lie. Of the eight conditions that are the signature of the highest-performing teams, there is one in particular that stands out—in study after study, irrespective of industry and irrespective of nationality—as the single most powerful predictor of a team's productivity. It is each team member's sense that "I have the chance to use my strengths every day at work." No matter what kind of work your team is doing and no matter which part of the world you're working in, your team will always be most productive when more team members feel delight and joy in what they do every day. Now, when we remove the words "every day" from the question, reasoning that perhaps the quotidian frequency is too high and that perhaps we should ask only whether people get a chance to feel a "good fit" between their strengths and their job, the item ceases to work—that is, the link between those who strongly agree to it and the performance of the team vanishes. The "every-day-ness" of the feeling that your work plays to your strengths is a vital condition of high performance. Somehow, on the best teams, the team leader is able not only to identify the strengths of each person but also to tweak roles and responsibilities so that team members, individually, feel that their work calls upon them to exercise their strengths on a daily basis. When a team leader does this, everything else—recognition, sense of mission, clarity of expectations—works better. But when a team leader doesn't, nothing else that he or she tries, whether in the form of money or title or cheerleading or cajoling, can make up for it.

Ongoing work-strengths fit is the *master lever* for high-performance teams: pull it, and everything else is elevated; fail to pull it, and everything else is diminished.

Nothing thus far should be particularly surprising. We've all seen people like Lionel Messi demonstrate their brilliance, and been uplifted by the sight. We've watched colleagues excel, and we've felt happy wonder in their success. We've experienced the joy of being at one with an activity, and the pride of knowing everything we've been able to contribute through our unique combination of strengths. Even the data shouldn't be particularly shocking—of course the best teams are built around the optimal fit between strengths and roles. For any of us with much experience of the world, there is (or at least there should be) no earth-shattering revelation here.

Which makes it all the more surprising (or frustrating, or depressing) that companies are not, in fact, built to help us pinpoint and then contribute our unique strengths. In their systems and processes and technologies, in their rituals and language and philosophies, they evidence exactly the opposite design: to measure us against a standardized model, and then badger us to become as similar to this model as possible. They are built, that is, around the lie that *the best people are well-rounded*.

• • •

At some point in your career, if you haven't already done so, you will bump into a thing called a competency model. A competency is a quality you are supposed to possess in order to excel in your job. They look like this: strategic thinking, goal orientation, political savvy, business acumen, customer focus, and so on. The idea behind them is that excellent performance in a job can be defined in terms of the right grouping of competencies. Thus the company's top leaders will be asked to examine a long list of these competencies—there are literally thousands to choose from—and then pick the ones that everyone agrees each incumbent in each job should possess. One widely used model, for example, identifies five categories of competencies (core, leadership/management/business/interpersonal, job functional, job technical, and technical-task specific) and then a further list of competencies within each of these, so that "core," in this case, includes 22 leadership competencies, 18 management competencies, 45 business competencies, and 33 individual competencies, for a total of 118.[4] Entry-level jobs are assigned fewer or simpler competencies, and the further up the hierarchy a job is, the more numerous and the more complex the competencies assigned to it tend to become. Having defined competencies for each role, the leaders will also usually define a desired proficiency level for each competency on a scale of 1 to 5, so that they can say, for instance, that such-and-such a job requires strategic thinking at a proficiency level of 3, whereas it needs customer focus at a proficiency level of 5.

This entire construct—the chosen competencies and their required proficiency levels, for each seniority level, for each job, across some or all of an organization—is called a competency model. In a typical model, a given job might be defined to require a few dozen competencies at varying proficiency levels.

So far, this might seem unobjectionable, if a little unwieldy: a group of leaders getting together to define what they feel the ideal employee should look like. It might not be our first choice for how they should spend their time, but at least no one has been harmed in the making of this model. It's what happens next, however, that leads us into choppier waters, because once created, the competencies show up everywhere. Your manager and your peers will rate you on them, and your overall performance rating will be derived in large part from how much of each of them you possess. During annual talent reviews, the competencies will be the language used to describe your performance and potential: if the consensus is that you possess them all, you will be considered for promotion, or paid more, or selected for plum assignments; whereas if you do not possess them, or display gaps in a few of them, you will be told to take the relevant training programs, and work on proving to your company that you have plugged your gaps. These competencies will become the lens through which your company sees you, understands you, and values you.

All of the major Human Capital Management tools—the enterprise software systems that companies use to keep information about you, pay you, allocate benefits to you, promote you, develop you, and deploy you—are built around competency models, and how closely you and your colleagues match up to the models. There is even, in one of these platforms, a robot that takes over the mundane chore of providing written feedback for team members: The team leader first selects which competency to evaluate, from the required list for the team member; then picks from a list of behaviors that someone is supposed to exhibit if they are either failing at, meeting, or exceeding this competency; then watches as the system generates a sample sentence to convey this feedback; then is given the opportunity to adjust this sentence to sound more or less positive, using buttons that adjust the feedback in one direction or the other; and then clicks a final button to add the finished sentence to someone's feedback form—all without typing a single word. The robot produces such eye-glazing prose as, "Barbara . . . puts thought into her budget requests and reviews her costs throughout the year to identify appropriate adjustments," these insights being produced with a few speedy clicks, and in complete ignorance of (and apparent indifference to) whether Barbara actually does any of those things.[5]

What concerns us here, however, is not so much the soul-crushingly automated implementation of competency models, but rather the theory of work that they embody and that underlies so much of what we do in organizations today. The theory goes something like this: we live in a world of machines, code, and processes, and when these break, we have to identify the faulty component or line of code or process step and fix it—to take dysfunction and repair it. The first part of this competency theory of work, then, extends this thinking to performance. Once we've located you on our proficiency scales, we tell you that your lowest scores—those where you are most "broken"—are your "development areas," and that the best path to greater performance will come from unrelenting focus on these areas.

The second part of our theory takes this line of thinking to its logical conclusion: we reason that if improvement in performance comes from remedying shortcomings, then high performance—excellence—must be the result of having removed shortcomings across the board, from having a high score on every scale. Excellence, in other words, is a synonym for all-round high ability: well-rounded people are better.

This is the lie that underpins the tyranny of competencies, and it is persistent and pervasive. But to see the truth, we need only to understand two particular facts.

First, *competencies are impossible to measure.* Take "strategic thinking" as an example. Is this a state, something that is variable and subject to flux? Or is it a trait, something that is inherent and relatively stable over time? In the field of psychometrics we measure these two phenomena quite differently.

When we are measuring states, we either devise surveys that ask a person about his or her state of mind, or we create tests with right and wrong answers to determine whether a person has acquired the necessary knowledge. A person's voting preference is a *state*, as expressed in a survey. We presume it can change, such that when we ask a person about it at Time 1, and then give her new information, we expect her preference might well be different at Time 2. Mood is a *state*. Although it does appear that each of us has a unique happiness set point, we assume that a person's mood can change around that point, such that when we ask about it at Time 1, and then a change in situation or circumstance occurs, we may well observe a difference in the person's mood by Time 2. Similarly, skills and knowledge are *states*. If we test you on a certain skill or knowledge base at Time 1, and then give you more training in these areas, it's likely that you will get more of the answers right at Time 2.

These are all *states*, and we expect them as such to change over time.

Traits, on the other hand, are inherent in a person. Extroversion is a trait, for example, as is empathy, and competitiveness, and need for structure. Each of us possesses certain unique predispositions and recurring patterns of thought, feeling, and behavior, and the overwhelming evidence is that, while each of us can learn over time to be more intelligent and effective at contributing through these patterns, the patterns themselves persist throughout our lives.

Traits cannot be measured with a survey or a skills test. Instead, they have to be measured using a reliable and validated personality assessment. The two most prevalent kinds of personality assessments are *self-assessments* (involving a number of carefully worded statements measured on a strongly agree–to–strongly disagree scale) and *situational judgment tests* (involving a number of situations with a list of possible response options from which the test taker selects the one that fits her best).*

Before you set about measuring something you have to decide which of these—states or traits—you are trying to measure, so that you can properly select your measurement method.

Here's the point. Seen in this light, what is a competency such as "strategic thinking"? Is it a state or a trait? We need to know, if we want to measure it—and the entire purported purpose of competencies is to measure something. If we think a competency is the former, a state, then we should measure it either with a survey asking about the person's state of mind or with an actual test that has correct and incorrect answers. We should never ask your manager or your peers to rate you on it, because they can't possibly know how much of this abstract quality you possess, any more than they can accurately divine

---

*If you are familiar with Marcus's work, StrengthsFinder is an example of a self-assessment and StandOut is an example of a situational judgment test.

your voting preferences or the score you would get on a test. And if we think a competency is the latter, an inherent trait, then we should use a personality assessment to measure it, and we should never tell you to take a "strategic thinking" class so that you can improve in it, because if it's a trait, then, by definition, it probably won't change much.

But the truth about competencies such as strategic thinking, political savvy, or any of the others is that they are a haphazard mix-up of states and traits. We don't know whether goal orientation, say, derives from the way you are wired, or from what you have learned to do, or from what you have been told to do. We don't know whether customer focus is a different piece of your wiring, or a different skill you have learned, or the same skill used differently, or something else entirely. A scientific approach to performance would start with what is measurable, and only then study how those things contributed to performance. But competencies are built in the other direction. They start with a listing of every quality we can think of that we feel is important to performance, and only then ask how each one might be measured. By this point it is too late to disentangle the states from the traits, so we fall back on rating one another on the resultant abstractions (which measures, sadly, neither state *nor* trait) and hoping that are all improvable in some way.*

And because competencies are unmeasurable, it is impossible to prove or disprove the assertion that *everyone who excels in a particular job possesses a particular set of competencies*. It is equally impossible to show that *people who acquired the competencies they lacked outperformed those who did not*—that, in other words, well-rounded people are better. These two statements together are the foundation for most of what companies do to develop the talents of their people, yet each of them is unfalsifiable—you will find no academic papers in any peer-reviewed journal proving the necessity of possessing certain competencies, and

---

*We'll talk more about the perils of rating other people in chapter 6.

no proof that acquiring the ones you lack nets you any increase in performance. Both of these assertions, despite the good intentions that created them, are conjured from thin air—and we can never know if they are correct.

• • •

But hang on, you may say: Isn't the art of business the art of making decisions with incomplete data? Isn't that what businesspeople get paid for—taking risks in the face of uncertainty? Isn't all this psychometric stuff a bit precious? Even if we can't prove, measurably, that acquiring a list of competencies helps a person to excel, what's wrong with trying nonetheless? Surely a good team leader should encourage each of her people to pinpoint capability gaps, to strive to plug these gaps and thereby become more well-rounded. Surely both the team and the individual would benefit from getting each person to conform ever more closely to the well-rounded ideal. Indeed, surely that's what growth *is*—the process of gaining ability where we have little.

Again, no. Which brings us to the second fact: the research into high performance in any profession or endeavor reveals that *excellence is idiosyncratic*. The well-rounded high performer is a creature of theory world. In the real world each high performer is unique and distinct, and excels precisely because that person has understood his or her uniqueness and cultivated it intelligently.

We see this most easily in the world of professional sports. If we were to design the theoretical model of a high-performing attacker on a soccer team, we would not create a Lionel Messi, with his diminutive stature and ineffectual right foot. Instead we might devise a player who looks more like Cristiano Ronaldo—a taller, more physically imposing player who is equally at ease with his left foot, his right foot, and his head (though even here we would likely erase from our theoretical design Ronaldo's ego, individualism, and occasional petulance). In the world of tennis we would obviously include in our design the fluidity and grace of Roger Federer, but we'd also probably want to add a hunk of Rafael Nadal's muscle, dollops of Novak Djokovic's cocksureness, and just a hint of Andy Murray's soft hands at the net. In our theoretical world, in other words, we would pick and mix the qualities we thought preferable. But obviously, in the real world no one gets to do this, whether they're a soccer player, a tennis player, or a team leader. In the real world each of us learns to make the most of what we have. Growth, it turns out, is actually a question not of figuring out how to gain ability where we lack it but of figuring out how to increase impact where we already have ability. And because our abilities are diverse, when you look at a great performance you see not diversity minimized but rather diversity magnified; not sameness but uniqueness.

We find the same idiosyncrasy among the best musical performers. We expect Adele to belt out soaring, maudlin ballads, but were we to ask Lorde or Halsey or Britney Spears or, God forbid, Miley Cyrus to sing or sound the same as Adele, we'd all be as alarmed as the Carnegie audience at a Florence Foster Jenkins concert. Now, we might assert that every role has some minimum requirements without which a person cannot succeed, no matter how extraordinary his or her other gifts (the customary name for these things, or rather for the lack of them, is career derailers). Even here, though, we would need to be careful in specifying our minimum requirements. After all, if we include "fluency in musical notation" in our list of musical skills, we'd knock out some big names. Frank Sinatra, for instance, couldn't read a note. Neither can Elton John. And if we include "having two hands" in our list of required traits for a pianist, we'd be forced to exclude Paul Wittgenstein, a classical pianist who lost his right arm in the First World War, who subsequently commissioned piano concertos for the left hand from the leading composers of his day, and without whom we would not have masterpieces by Benjamin Britten, Paul Hindemith, Sergei Prokofiev, Richard Strauss, and Maurice Ravel.

But these are all extreme examples, and might seem remote from the real world of work. What happens when we measure the strengths and skills of a regular job? Do we find idiosyncrasy or well-roundedness?

. . .

In the early 1980s, a man set out to predict performance. His name was Don Clifton. He was trained as a mathematician and a psychologist, and he set out to identify, quantitatively, the factors that could be identified in a job candidate—specifically, the factors that would predict success in the role the candidate sought.

Clifton was leading a team of researchers at a company called Selection Research, Incorporated (SRI), which in the 1990s acquired and took on the name of the Gallup Organization. One of the early studies SRI did sought to predict the success of pub managers for a large brewery chain, as it had long been recognized that a big part of the difference between a so-so pub and a great pub depended, in some hard-to-pin-down way, on the characteristics of the manager. Clifton and his team began, as they always did, by asking questions—lots of questions—of the brewery chain's best and average pub managers, as measured by their business results. "What is the best way to manage someone?" "How closely should an employee be supervised?" And so on. They asked these questions of the average managers and of the great managers, and looked for differences in their answers. Questions that didn't yield a difference were thrown out, and when all was said and done they had a set of 108 questions that seemed to identify the secrets of pub-manager performance. Now they did a blind test, using their questions on a different selection of managers, without knowing how well these managers were doing, and they demonstrated that their list of questions could reliably and consistently sort the best from the rest.

The questions measured various qualities—from a pub manager's sense of mission, to his or her instinctive contingency planning, to his or her ability to develop others—and the researchers were curious to see if one of these, or a small group of these, was the master key, the one thing or combination of things that, time and time again, unlocked great performance. But as they looked at the scores of the best managers, they found something subtly and wonderfully different. The high scores of the best managers moved around—one manager would do well on questions about creating a particular ambience in the pub, say, while another would excel on questions about inventory and budgeting. There was no pattern at all. Or, rather, there was just one big pattern—the only way to predict a manager's performance was to look at his or her *total* score. They had found a list of ways in which managers could excel, and they could define excellence on each of these dimensions. Yet it seemed to make no difference which of these a candidate excelled at, *as long as he or she excelled somewhere.*

This was not an anomaly for the role of pub manager. Every single occupation the Gallup Organization studied—salesperson, teacher, doctor, housekeeper—displayed this same pattern: those who excelled did *not* share all the same abilities, but instead displayed unique combinations of different abilities, strongly. Excellence in the real world, in every profession, is idiosyncratic.

In the theoretical world that exists inside most of our large organizations—a world preoccupied with the need for order and tidiness—the perfect incumbent of every role possesses all the competencies that can be dreamed up and defined. In the real world, however, these long lists of intricately defined competencies don't exist, and if they did, they wouldn't matter. If, as someone once said,* the British fox hunt is the unspeakable in pursuit of the inedible, then the

---

*Yes, it was Oscar Wilde.

competency model is the unmeasurable in pursuit of the irrelevant. In the real world, each of us, imperfect as we are, strives to make the most of the unique mix of traits and skills with which we've been blessed. Those of us who do this best—who find what we love about what we do, and cultivate this love with intelligence and discipline—are the ones who contribute most. The best people are not well-rounded, finding fulfillment in their uniform ability. Quite the opposite, in fact—*the best people are spiky*, and in their lovingly honed spikiness they find their biggest contribution, their fastest growth, and, ultimately, their greatest joy.

• • •

On some level, we have all long known this. From our earliest memories of school to our most recent experiences of work, the thought that *if only I could set this annoying thing aside and focus on what I really want to, then I could make a much bigger difference* is all too familiar. But then why do these competency models and their associated 360-degree assessments, feedback tools, and development plans exist? What could have prompted otherwise sensible people to have spent so much time and energy and money building models whose efficacy is intrinsically unprovable, that require enormous amounts of time and energy to create, and that fly in the face of our own experiences in the world?

The simplest answer is that, though we are deeply aware that each of us is unique, and that no amount of training or badgering will remove that uniqueness, it is still quite overwhelming for a busy team leader to allow himself to come face-to-face with the fact that each of his team members thinks differently, is motivated by different things, responds to relationship cues differently, and gets a kick out of different sorts of praise. Who has the time for all these subtle shadings of diversity? Better to just define a model, and then manage to the model (hence the automated feedback writer we encountered earlier).

For a company, it's all about control. The strong instinct of most corporate leaders, faced with the teeming diversity not just of gender, race, and age but of thought, drive, and relationship inside their organizations, is to look for some way to exert control—to rein it all in, to impose conformity on the chaos, and thence to be able to understand what's going on, and to shape what will happen next. And so companies have spent, and continue to spend, large quantities of time and money trying to work around each person's uniqueness—and this is where these models bubble up from. The models promise rigor—a clear set of characteristics against which *everyone* can be measured, a sort of "apples-to-apples" comparison (even though in the real world it is always "apples-to-oranges"). The models promise analytical insights— a way to understand the *entire* workforce. (It's no accident the systems are known as performance management systems, as oxymoronic as that sounds.) The models promise fact, evidence, truth. What is the job of an executive if not to know what's going on, in great specificity, and to be able to tweak the dials of the vast enterprise before him so that progress may be made? The creeping suspicion, on the part of more and more leaders, that the models offer none of the things they promise, is an inconvenience to be minimized.

And to be clear, it isn't just the competency models that are dubious but the ideas behind them. There is the idea that improvement comes from repairing our deficits. There is the idea that failure is essential to growth. And there is the idea that our strengths are something to be afraid of.

As we've seen, what's most striking when we look at excellent performance is not the absence of deficit but, rather, the presence of a few signature strengths, honed over time and put to ever greater use. But still the idea of fixing deficits appeals to us—it gives us the hope that we might corral, and thus tame, our imperfections, and it allows us to make amends for our shortcomings by toiling to fix them. And the fact that this toil is usually far from joyful is part of the allure.

"Pain + Reflection = Progress" is the mantra at Bridgewater, the hedge fund run by Ray Dalio, and in some way we thrill to the hard clarity of this prescription. The pain of working on our deficits seems like a worthy pain, a way to pay our penance and make our restitution with the world, and we are drawn to its salutary austerity.

And the idea that failure is important is attractive, in turn, because failure helps us understand our deficits—it helps us find more of them. If a technology company today is *not* talking about failing fast, there is presumed to be something wrong with it. "There is no way to 'get better' other than to first do it, however poorly you do," says Charlie Kim, CEO of Next Jump, and this makes perfect sense. But then the false syllogism: "So get started; go out and fail! We have become good at getting better because we are so good at failing." Beyond the obvious point—that if all a company did was to become brilliant at failing in more and more ways, faster and faster, it would be, well, a failure— the truth is that large success is the aggregation of small successes, and that therefore improvement consists of finding out, in each trial, what works, seizing hold of it, and figuring out how to make more of it. Failure by itself doesn't teach us anything about success, just as our deficits by themselves don't teach us anything about our strengths. And the moment we begin to get better is the moment when something actually works, not when it doesn't.*

And then there is the idea that our strengths are to be feared—that we should avoid overusing them because that will somehow pull us away from our proper focus on failure and shortcomings, and instead pull us toward laziness and complacency. Of course, if we were able

---

*As we're writing this, Facebook is facing numerous government inquiries into the use of its data to influence elections, Uber has curtailed its self-driving-car testing because one of its cars hit and killed a cyclist, and Yahoo has long since ceased to exist in any meaningful sense. It is unlikely that anyone is celebrating these and other failures, and the "fail fast" speed with which they've been achieved.

to watch a great athlete training, or a great writer writing, or a great coder coding, we would see that honing a strength is hard work—it is by no means easy to find that incremental margin of performance when you are already operating at a high level—and that a strength is not where we are most "finished" but in fact where we are most productively challenged. Yet we are told to resist the temptation to "just" play to our strengths, and instead to work constantly on our weaknesses. In common parlance, we are told to avoid "running around our backhand."[6] This betrays, perhaps, a misunderstanding of what a strength actually is. It is not, for each of us, where performance is *easiest*—it is where performance is most *impactful* and *increasing*. We would never tell Lionel Messi to try to play with his right foot. We would instead watch as he works, tirelessly, to make his left ever more powerful. And the only reason that "running around your backhand" has become an idiom for avoiding a weakness is that this is *exactly* what we see great tennis players do, time and time again, whether it's Juan Martín del Potro, Rafael Nadal, or countless others. The phrase describes the act of avoiding a weakness in order to play to a strength, and the lesson from the best is that this leads *toward* high performance, not *away* from it.

Yet these are the ideas that competency models, 360-degree assessments, talent reviews, feedback tools, and much more are built on—that what is most important for us is to understand our deficits, embrace failure, and be wary of our strengths. To be clear, we are not, here, making an absolutist argument: we are not saying that there is nothing to be gained from trying to improve our shortcomings, or that we shouldn't try new things for fear of failure. We are, however, arguing for priority, for focusing first, and predominantly, on our strengths and our successes, because that is where the greatest advantage is to be had. And the great shame in all of this is that the very systems that we might hope would be aimed at discovering and unleashing each person's unique talents have, in fact, the effect of inhibiting those talents, and denying what makes each one of us unique. They don't, in the end, help performance. They hinder it.

• • •

What, then, should we do in the face of all of this? How do the best team leaders in the real world go about building great teams? Here are three strategies we've seen used by the best team leaders.

The first strategy is this: *Get into the outcomes business.* A team leader at one of the early Silicon Valley startups faced an unusual situation. He had assigned a new hire to work with one of his experienced engineers, and now the experienced engineer was complaining. The new hire was arrogant and prickly, he said, but worse than this, he had awful body odor—the team leader should fire him. But the team leader saw something in his unusual employee, and worked out a different solution. He figured that the two could work together as long as they weren't in the office at the same time, and instead passed work back and forth. And so, in the early days of Atari, Steve Jobs worked nights.[7]

Others may have confused you into thinking you are in the control business, and competency models will have left you languishing in the method business. But you're in neither of these. As a team leader, you are in the outcomes business. You are being paid to create certain outcomes for your company, as efficiently, as predictably, and as sustainably as possible, and to do this with enough creativity and intuition and excitement to engage the sort of talent that you and your company will need tomorrow. The lesson we learn from Hugh Dowding's bunker, Stanley McChrystal's daily O&I call, Facebook's conference-room logos, and Chick-fil-A's franchising agreement is that leaders *can't* be in the control business and *must* be in the intelligence, meaning, and empowerment business—the outcomes business.

Lionel Messi's manager needs the team to score goals. And Messi's bizarrely magical left-footedness is only intriguing because it results in Messi, or one of his teammates, putting the ball in the back of the net. Everything his manager does to coach him makes sense only if they both keep focused on the outcome of scoring goals, and thereby helping the team win. It's not the idiosyncrasy that ultimately matters. It's the goals that matter, and the idiosyncrasy is only useful because it is *always* the best way to get more goals.

Tennis is the same. If we were coaching Andy Murray, we would never try to define for him some model of universal tennis excellence and tell him to try to play like that. Instead we'd say something like, "Hey, Andy, we know what winning looks like, and feels like, so what strengths do you have that can give you an unfair advantage over everyone else, and thereby help you win? You will never have Roger's backhand, or Rafa's spin, but you do have speed, and touch, and a weird, relentless, hangdog determination. How can we make those dominate for you?" Billie Jean King once said that the best tennis players have to practice their winning combinations, the one-two-three sequences that end the point in their favor. So we might continue by asking Andy how his strengths can be combined, and then encourage him to spend time honing those combinations, so that in pressure situations he can call upon them with unthinking confidence. We would, in other words, try to help him figure out how his particular strengths, alone or in combination, could move him toward the outcomes he's after.

The outcome of teaching is helping a student learn. There is no universal recipe for that, any more than there is a universal recipe for writing a beautiful song. The outcome of managing a pub is not creating a great atmosphere, or designing a fun quiz night, or having the best-priced, best-tasting beer. These are methods, and none of them matter in and of themselves. Instead the outcome is having a pub full of happy punters. The very best district managers spend their pub visits paying attention to what each pub manager looks forward to, when he is in "flow," and which activities in the pub he naturally gravitates to. They then build their coaching strategies around these signs of his strengths, helping each manager combine them in the service of the desired outcome.

You can do the same. Define the outcomes you want from your team and its members, and then look for each person's strength signs to figure out how each person can reach those outcomes most efficiently, most amazingly, most creatively, and most joyfully. The moment you realize you're in the outcomes business is the moment you turn each person's uniqueness from a bug into a feature.

And what you will be doing, when you step back and look, is fitting the role to the person—which leads us to the second strategy: *Define the adjustable seat.*

In the years following the end of the Second World War, the United States Air Force was creating more and more innovative and expensive planes—jet-powered, fast, and fiendishly hard to control—which pilots were then proceeding to crash at an alarming rate. After various inconclusive inquiries, Air Force engineers began to wonder if the cockpit design was the problem—if, for some pilots, the controls were too hard to reach and operate—and if the standardized cockpit dimensions, created in 1926 from studying hundreds of pilots and calculating their average size, were in need of revision. The engineers decided to recalculate the average, and to this end set out in 1950 to measure the various physical attributes of 4,063 pilots. One of the team charged with doing the measuring was a young lieutenant named Gilbert S. Daniels.

Now, as Daniels thought about the problem the USAF faced, he realized that this wasn't only a problem of knowing the average per se, but also one of fit, between any individual pilot and a cockpit designed for the average pilot. So as the study proceeded, he began to think about another question. In addition to his assigned task of calculating the average, he asked himself how many of the pilots in the sample were actually average-sized—or close to average-sized, at any rate. (Daniels defined *average* as within the middle 30 percent of the range of measures on any given dimension.) If a good number of pilots were near average-sized, he reasoned, then the new cockpit dimensions stood a chance of solving the problem.

The researchers had measured ten dimensions for each pilot, so now Daniels set himself the task of going through the data, pilot by pilot by pilot, and counting how many of the 4,063 pilots were in the middle 30 percent on all of the ten dimensions.

The answer, when it came, was this: *none*. There were no average-sized pilots—none whatsoever. Even if you looked at just three of the ten dimensions, fewer than 5 percent of the pilots were average-sized on all three. Even in a population of humans deliberately *selected* against a set of criteria (if you were too tall or too short, for instance, you weren't qualified to become a USAF pilot in the first place), there was no one-size-fits-all, not even close.[8]

Just as Don Clifton discovered that the only predictor of performance was total score across a number of relevant variables—that there was no right *pattern* of abilities, only a right *sum* of abilities—Gilbert Daniels discovered that there were no average humans in a population of 4,063, and that the average is a mathematical concept, not something that exists in the physical world.[9] While the outcomes of high performance are visible and clear, the ingredients of high performance vary from person to person. There is no one-size-fits-all when it comes to human beings; and there is no one-size-fits-all when it comes to great performance.

What can you do, then, with all this unfettered diversity? You do what Daniels advised the US Air Force to do: design an adjustable seat. Fit the machine to the pilot, not the other way around. You can do the same with your team—it entails adjusting the outcomes you're asking individual team members to deliver to better match their idiosyncratic talents.

The first strategy suggests that we clarify the outcomes we're after, and then help each team member find his or her path to these outcomes. This raises the question of what to do if the outcomes aren't right for a particular person. In response, the second strategy suggests that we fit the work to the person, and not the other way around, so as to maximize person-outcome fit. But this in turn raises a further question: if we are always fitting work to people, how do we address the full spectrum of work we have to get done? If we were to design an "adjustable seat" for each person, we may still end up with many necessary tasks left undone.

Hence the third strategy: *Use team technology.* To help you address everything that needs to be addressed, the real world has devised a supremely effective technology for integrating people's wonderfully imperfect capabilities in the service of a given objective. It's called a team, and the essential magic of a team is that it makes weirdness useful.

You are weird. You don't seem weird to you because you are with you all the time. But you are weird, to everyone else, and they are weird to you: gloriously, beautifully weird. It's weird that others don't get a kick out of the same things that we do. It's weird that some people love doing things we find excruciating. And when we see someone do something better than we ever imagined possible, it can be confounding, perplexing, astonishing—and also, of course, a source of relief. Thank goodness that woman there loves to confront people. Thank goodness that man there loves thorny political situations. Thank goodness that woman there is so impatient for action. If the people around us were not wired to be weird, then we'd have to spend all of our time scrambling to find someone who actually stood out. Instead, we can partner them up, and wire their weirdness together into a team.

Diversity isn't an impediment to building a great team—rather, it's the fundamental ingredient without which a great team cannot exist. If we were all the same, there would doubtless be things that all of us could not do, and that therefore the team could not do. We need to partner with people whose strengths—whose weirdness, whose spikiness—is different from ours if we are to achieve results that demand more abilities than any of us has alone. And this means, in turn, that the more different we are from one another, the more we need one another. The more different we are, the more we rely on understanding and appreciating the strengths of others, and on building a shared understanding of purpose, and an atmosphere of safety and trust, so that those strengths can be most usefully put to work. Well-roundedness is a misguided and futile objective when it comes to individual people; but when it comes to teams, it's an absolute necessity. The more diverse the team members, the more weird, spiky, and idiosyncratic they are, the more well-rounded the team.

Competencies, and all the other normative and deficit-focused tools we have, don't push in this direction—of expressing and harnessing diversity. They do just the opposite, as we've seen. But we don't need to throw them out completely. The process of creating them—involving a group of leaders, usually, debating what they value most—is not one that should result in any sort of measurement tool or one-size-fits-all standard. It is, however, exactly the sort of process that should create a statement of collective values, priorities, purpose, and ambition. Customer focus, innovation, growth orientation, agility—these are not abilities to be measured, they are values to be shared. So we should remove from our competency models the levels of ability, the individual evaluations, the feedback, and all the other things that they have become encumbered with, and we should instead simplify them, clarify them, recognize them (and name them) for what they are, and stick them on a wall for all to see. When we carry our competencies across the measurement bridge, we enter a fake and dangerous world—as a tool of assessment, order and control, they are worse than useless. But as public signifiers for what we deem most important, they are another way we can cascade meaning in our organizations, and thereby help our leaders and teams understand what's most important.

People need feedback

It is a truth universally acknowledged that a millennial in possession of a job must be in want of feedback.

Actually, not just millennials. It goes without question that feedback for each and every one of us at work is a good thing, and that more feedback is an even better thing. As a result, today we are blessed with upward feedback, downward feedback, peer feedback, 360-degree feedback, performance feedback, developmental feedback, constructive feedback, solicited, unsolicited, and anonymous feedback, and with all of these flavors and variants has emerged a cottage industry of classes to teach us both how to give this feedback and how to receive it with grace and equanimity. We seem certain that modern employees need, and indeed cannot but benefit from, a real-time, straight-up assessment of their performance, and an appraisal of where they stand in relation to their peers. Indeed, of all the things we "know for sure," in Twain's words, this is the one we know for surest.

If there is any complaint in all this, at least on the evidence of recent innovations in HR technology, it's that this feedback doesn't happen nearly *enough*, so coming soon to a phone near you is an array of tools designed to enable you and your company to generate feedback at any time, on any person, about any and all aspects of his or her performance.

You, as the team leader, will be told that one of the most important and tricky parts of your job is to convey this feedback to your people, no matter how negative the reviews might be. Your job is to accelerate team performance, and it'll be your responsibility to hold a mirror up to the performance of your people so they can see themselves as they really are, and see their performance as it truly is. This, you'll be told, is the secret to both success and respect as a team leader—so much so, in fact, that this sort of direct, clear, unvarnished feedback has its own special name at work: it's called *candid* feedback.

And this in turn means that you need to maintain a certain distance, lest you lose your objectivity and compromise your candor. Although you may sometimes wonder if people would give more and grow more if you showed that you genuinely cared about them, the refrain you'll hear is that if you get too close to your team members you'll never be able to give them the candid feedback they need.

To aid your development as a leader, others will recommend to you the many books on how to have tough conversations, and will suggest you read from the growing pile of articles describing just how much Gen Y and millennials crave constant corrective feedback. With titles such as "Why Millennials Actually Want More Feedback at Work" (*Fortune*), "Managers: Millennials Want Feedback, but Won't Ask for It" (Gallup), "Feedback Is the Unlikely Key to Millennial Career Happiness" (*Forbes*), and "Why Millennials Need Constant Feedback at Work" (*Business Insider*), these articles will make plain to you that millennials thrive on the stuff.

You'll be taught phrases such as, "Is now a good time for me to give you some feedback?" And, "Would you care for some feedback?" And the slightly more assertive, "I have some feedback for you. Are you sitting down?" Having learned how to give feedback, you'll also learn how to receive it through techniques such as *mirroring* ("Did I hear you say that I need to work on my 'organizational savvy and politics'?") and *active listening* ("Can you clarify what you mean by 'hopelessly naive' and give me a couple of recent examples?").

And of course, should you reject the feedback you receive from someone else because it feels odd, or confusing, or just plain wrong, you'll be helped to understand that this feeling is just a natural reaction to threat, and that to grow as a person and as a leader you will need to "let go of your ego," to "embrace your failures," and to always maintain a "growth mindset." If you can reframe all this feedback as valuable input to help you grow, then—you'll be told—you'll soon find yourself addicted to it. As the author and speaker Simon Sinek said recently in his spot as guest editor for Virgin's workplace blog, "So here's a way you can fulfill your potential in the workplace: negative feedback . . . Negative feedback is where it's at . . . After every project or anything that I do, I always ask somebody, 'What sucks? What can I do better? Where is there room for improvement?' I'm now to the point where I crave it. That's what you want. You want to get to the point where you crave negative feedback."[1]

· · ·

Seeing such enthusiasm for feedback, we might start to wonder what an entire company would look and feel like if everyone was giving everyone else reviews at every turn—if feedback were pervasive and continuous. If so we need look no further than Bridgewater Associates, the world's largest hedge fund. In addition to being extraordinarily gifted at securing returns for his investors—Bridgewater has made $45 billion in net gains since its founding in 1975, more than any other hedge fund—Ray Dalio, Bridgewater's chairman, co-CEO, and co-CIO, has decided to build his company around a commitment to "radical transparency." His belief—explained in his book *Principles*, in which he lays out 210 prescriptions for work and life—is that the way to be successful is to see and engage with the world as it truly is, no matter how positive or negative these realities are.[2] No hierarchy or office politics should prevent anyone, no matter their level in the company, from challenging an assumption or interrogating a course of action. The real world is right there, Dalio says: it is what it is. We must face it with all of our intelligence unfettered, and we can't allow our politeness or our fear of repercussion to prevent us from seeing what is there to be seen, and thereby changing it for the better.

Of course, people are part of this real world, and they too must be seen for who they really are, without filter, without delay. So at Bridgewater, not only is every meeting videotaped, archived, and made available for every person in the company to view in the company's "Transparency Library" (Dalio's commitment to radical transparency is total and without irony) but also each employee is issued an iPad loaded with a variety of apps for rating his or her fellow employees on sixty attributes, such as "willingness to touch the nerve," "conceptual thinking," and "reliability." Employees are expected to rate their peers after calls, meetings, and daily interactions, and all the resultant ratings are analyzed (by the team that created IBM's Watson, no less), permanently stored, and then displayed on a card that each employee carries with him or her at all times. Bridgewater calls this your "baseball card," and its intent is to hold you accountable for knowing "who you really are," and to give everyone else a radically transparent view of what you truly bring to Bridgewater—one of the metrics it displays is your "believability score."[3]

This is obviously an extreme example—back in 2016, Dalio and his COO got into such a heated spat that each demanded the other be rated on "integrity" by the entire firm—and it is difficult to prove what effect, positive or negative, this transparency has had on performance. (Despite the millions of data points collected, Bridgewater still has no reliable measure of each person's performance, as we'll see in chapter 6.) The company as a whole has produced outstanding results across decades and has grown from Mr. Dalio's two-bedroom apartment to occupying a gleaming office building in Greenwich, Connecticut, with 1,500 full-time employees. At the same time, however, the Glassdoor reviews of Bridgewater are mixed, and its first-eighteen-month turnover levels stand at 30 percent, three times higher than the industry average. People leave teams, not companies, as we've seen. That said, it does seem that Bridgewater has more than its fair share of teams that people want to leave.

But while Ray Dalio and Bridgewater may be outliers, they are at the same time clearly part of the established consensus that *people need feedback*, and that the best companies and the most effective team leaders must figure out how to give it to them.

$$\bullet \quad \bullet \quad \bullet$$

In part, this consensus is a perfectly reasonable reaction to the absurd infrequency of traditional performance reviews. Because companies report their financial results annually, we have all become used to altering people's compensation annually, and since many companies came to espouse "pay for performance," it was inevitable that goals would be set annually, and performance reviews conducted annually, and therefore feedback given annually. This cadence, though it worked for the financial folks, made little sense for either team leaders or members. Leaders felt burdened by the need to put everything into one set of goals at the beginning of the year and one set of laborious reviews at the end, while team members simply felt ignored. No one was served by this annual infrequency, yet there wasn't much to be done about it—if we hated filling out one long set of forms at the beginning and the end of the year, nothing would be gained by upping the frequency of the form filling.

And then technology came to the rescue, as it were. With the creation of app-enabled smartphones, the subsequent near ubiquity of these phones, and then their integration with corporate IT infrastructure, companies gained the ability to give every employee the power to launch a survey to anyone in the employee census file, and collect, aggregate, and report the results. Today we can get feedback from anyone, on anyone, at any time, quickly and easily.

But while this might explain why we are now *able* to give constant feedback, it doesn't help us understand why we would so desperately *want* to. To understand that we need to turn to two well-documented oddities of human nature.

Let's say that one of your colleagues is late for an important meeting. As you sit in mild annoyance waiting for him to arrive, you create a little story in your mind that explains his tardiness as a result of his disorganization and lack of prioritization, and his lack of concern for all the people he's keeping waiting. This sort of interpretation of others' actions is so commonplace that it would be unremarkable, except for the fact that it contains a kernel of reasoning that's demonstrably flawed, and that nevertheless has a huge impact on how we design our organizations. What we're doing, in creating our little story, is coming up with an explanation—an attribution, if you like—for our colleagues' actions, and those explanations, when they concern the people around us, overwhelmingly ascribe others' behavior to their innate abilities and personality, not to the external circumstances they find themselves in. In this case, your colleague is late because of his innate disorganization, for example, not because a senior leader grabbed him in the hallway to ask a pressing question. This tendency of ours to skew our explanations of others' behavior (particularly negative behavior) toward stories about *who they are* is called the Fundamental Attribution Error. Show us someone doing something that annoys us, or inconveniences us, and we're instantly certain that it's because there's something wrong with that person.

And the Fundamental Attribution Error has a cousin. While our stories of others center on *who they are*, we are much more generous to ourselves in our interpretation of our own actions. When it comes to our self-attributions, we skew the other way, and overascribe our behavior to the external situation around us, to *what's happening to us*. If we're doing something that annoys someone else, then that person is annoyed only because he or she doesn't understand the situation that's forcing us to act that way. This tendency is called the Actor-Observer Bias, and it's one of a number of human-reasoning biases that fall into a category called self-serving biases, because they serve to explain away our own actions in a way that props up our self-esteem.

These biases lead us to believe that your performance (whether good or bad) is due to *who you are*—your drive, or style, or effort, say—which in turn leads us to the conclusion that if we want to get you to improve your performance we must give you feedback on who you are, so that you can increase your drive, refine your style, or redouble your efforts. To fix a performance problem we instinctively turn to giving you personal feedback, rather than looking at the external situation you were facing and addressing that.

And by the way, if you think about it, much of the world of work is designed this way—it's designed for Those Other People, who need to be told what to do (hence planning instead of intelligence), whose work needs aligning (hence goals over meaning and purpose), and whose weaknesses put us all at risk (hence the deficit thinking we saw in the last chapter, instead of the focus on distinctive abilities). One of the inconvenient truths about humans is that we have poor theories of others, and these theories lead us, among other things, to design our working world to remedy or to insulate against failings that we see in others but don't see in ourselves.*

Add to this the wonky logic that since success is achieved only through *hard work*, and since giving negative feedback, receiving negative feedback, and fixing mistakes are all *hard work*, therefore negative feedback causes success,† and you can begin to see why our faith in feedback, and specifically negative feedback, is so firmly rooted—why we "know for sure" that feedback is helpful and that our colleagues need it.

But this just ain't so.

• • •

Let's go back to where we began, with millennials. The various books and articles argue that millennials crave feedback in part because they are addicted to social media, and to the dopamine hit of one more Facebook "like," or one more Instagram "love." We are asked to interpret this behavior as the result of millennials' need to always know how they are perceived by others and where they stand. And, according to

*The American philosopher John Rawls proposed, in 1971, a thought experiment to counter these theories of ours, an experiment he called The Veil of Ignorance. Essentially, he suggested that the best way to design the world was to imagine that when we were done designing it, we'd be randomly assigned some role in this new world, and that we should design in ignorance of what that role would be—whether we would be rich or poor, male or female, academic or athletic, and so on. He proposed, in other words, that we should design a world for ourselves, for any imaginable permutation of ourselves, rather than for others. And this is likely a very good way to design a workplace, too—not for those idiots, but for this one.

†This false syllogism is wonderfully memorialized in the British TV comedy *Yes, Prime Minister*, in the form of "We must do something. This is something. Therefore we must do this." Its equivalent: "All cats have four legs. My dog has four legs. Therefore, my dog is a cat." Logicians refer to this as the fallacy of the undistributed middle. For the rest of us, it's known as politicians' logic.

this reading, you're in big trouble as a manager if you aren't constantly attending to how they're doing and telling them how to do it better.

But if we look more closely—if we look at which features have become more popular on the various social-media platforms, and at the details of how users choose to interact with these platforms—a different picture begins to emerge.

Consider, for example, the very different approaches taken by Facebook and Snapchat to providing for user feedback. A couple of years ago Facebook had been researching additional response emojis beyond the classic "like." After much experimentation (and constant reassurances to its users that the company wasn't going to launch a "dislike" button), Facebook announced the addition of six new emojis so that users could offer more-nuanced feedback to other users' posts: the six finalists were "love," "haha," "yay," "wow," "sad," and "angry." Yet soon after the launch, Facebook discovered that, despite the company's careful research and testing, hardly anyone bothered with the new options.

Snapchat, meanwhile, was growing, and then growing some more. Snapchat didn't have six possible responses to a post—it didn't even have one, in fact, because there was no Snapchat "like" button, and there isn't to this day. Its appeal was precisely that on this new platform no one would rate you. The user just posts a story, or sends a friend a snap message; the friend responds or doesn't; and then— poof!—in twenty-four hours the story or snap is gone, permanently. If you talk to heavy users of Snapchat—and there are now over 200 million of them—you'll discover that what's attractive about Snapchat to millennials is precisely that they can go there, post there, and share there, all without feeling the pressure of feedback. They see the size of their audience. They keep their snap streaks alive with their friends. But they never have to worry about feedback at all: there is no judgment, let alone any permanent record of judgment. Instead there is just the connection to a friend or an audience.

For all of Snapchat's early users this was a relief. Snapchat became one of the precious few places in their lives where they were free to be themselves and connect with each other without filters. The very absence of permanent feedback allowed them to be more casual, more at ease, and more real, and this safe, attentive place attracted them in the millions. It is extraordinarily difficult to start a social-media platform and have it grow organically—users are busy and have established behavior patterns, and the power of the network effect to prevent those behaviors from changing is strong. Ning, Path, and latterly Myspace were all launched (in the case of Myspace, relaunched) with great fanfare, and all faltered because they didn't tap into the essence of human nature purely and powerfully enough. Snapchat's chances of success were arguably slim, and yet, because it found an important missing ingredient in young people's lives (a safe place filled with an admiring audience), it was able to find a path to exponential user growth. And then Facebook and Instagram, to their credit, got curious, listened and learned, and did whatever they could to make themselves more like Snapchat.

If the Snapchat example is any guide, it would seem that at root, social media is more about publishing—about positive self-presentation. It matters less to us whether this "self" is truly us, or whether, as many have observed, our online selves are aspirational projections, than it matters to us that others see us, and like us. We aren't looking for feedback. We're looking for an audience, and all of us—not just millennials—seem drawn to places that provide us with a way to meet our audience and gain its approval. What we want from social media is not really feedback. It's attention, and the lesson from the last decade is that social media is an attention economy—some users seeking it, some supplying it—not a feedback economy.

And ironically, while the design of today's social-media platforms reflects the fact that millennials are attracted most to environments without feedback, today's companies point to these very same social-media platforms as their primary evidence for why millennials crave feedback.

The Snapchat growth story is only the most recent addition to a large body of evidence about the human need for uncritical attention. In the late nineteenth century the philosopher Friedrich Nietzsche called us "the beast with red cheeks"—the lover of attention—and in the following decades the nascent field of social science proceeded to offer up one case study after another of just how right he was. The psychologist Harry Harlow, in a famous series of experiments in the 1950s, deprived baby monkeys of their mothers, gave them the choice of a wire "mother" holding a milk bottle or a soft towel "mother" with no milk bottle, and showed that primates, given this choice, will always crave warmth and attention and safety over food—the baby monkeys consistently and heart-wrenchingly picked the towel over the milk. More recently, epidemiologists, psychometricians, and statisticians have shown that by far the best predictor of heart disease, depression, and suicide is loneliness—if you deprive us of the attention of others, we wither.

In the workplace, the most well-known example of this phenomenon is the research undertaken in the 1920s and 1930s at the Hawthorne Works, a Western Electric facility just outside Chicago. The management, unsurprisingly, wanted to increase the productivity of the workers, and began a series of experiments to explore the relationship between working conditions and worker output. The researchers first made the factory brighter by turning the lights up, and sure enough, in the following days worker output jumped significantly. But then, in the interests of experimental rigor, they decided to turn the lights back down to see what would happen. Strangely, output increased once again. There followed more experiments—making the work stations cleaner, keeping the factory tidier, providing more food during breaks, varying the length of the breaks, keeping the total break time the same but dividing it into smaller or larger chunks—and in each case, when a condition was changed, output went up, yet when it was changed back to where it had been in the first place, output went up *again*. And then, more confounding still, when each experiment was concluded, output sank all the way back to its original level.

It took a while to figure out what was going on, but the consensus that ultimately emerged from the Hawthorne experiments has had a profound effect on the science of work. The conclusion was not that workers craved a brighter workplace or a tidier one, or, for that matter, a darker one or a messier one. Instead, what the workers were responding to was attention. Each of these interventions demonstrated to the workers that management was interested in them and their experience, and they liked that. And thus liking their work a little more, they worked a little better, and a little faster, and by the end of the day produced a lot more.

The truth, then, is that *people need attention*—and when you give it to us in a safe and nonjudgmental environment, we will come and stay and play and work.

. . .

But it's a bit more complicated than that, as it turns out, because feedback—even negative feedback—is still attention. And it's possible to quantify the impact of negative attention, if you will, versus positive attention, versus no attention at all, and thereby better understand what sort of attention we most want at work. In their ongoing study of engagement in the workplace, researchers at the Gallup Organization asked a representative sample of American workers whether their managers paid most attention to their strengths, to their weaknesses, or to neither, and they then asked a series of follow-up questions to measure how engaged each of these employees was. They then calculated the ratio of highly engaged employees to highly *dis*engaged employees for each type of attention.[4]

Their first finding told them, in effect, how to design the World's Worst Manager. To create pervasive disengagement, ignore your people. If you pay them no attention whatsoever—no positive feedback; no negative feedback; nothing—your team's engagement will plummet, so much so that for every one engaged team member you will have twenty disengaged team members.

The researchers' second finding might, on its face, look like a pretty encouraging outcome. They found that negative feedback is forty times more effective, as a team leadership approach, than ignoring people. For those employees whose leaders' attention was focused on fixing their shortcomings, the ratio of engaged to disengaged was two to one. But if we remember that "engagement" in this case is a precisely defined set of experiences that have been shown to *lead to* team performance; and if we recall that most of us have been taught that negative feedback is the best, and that most of us experience mainly negative feedback in our professional lives; and if we consider what the researchers found when they looked at positive attention, then this ratio of two to one becomes much more worrying. Because the third finding was this: for those employees given mainly positive attention— that is, attention to what they did best, and what was working most powerfully for them—the ratio of engaged to disengaged rose to sixty to one.

Positive attention, in other words, is *thirty times* more powerful than negative attention in creating high performance on a team. (It's also, if you're keeping score, *twelve hundred times* more powerful than ignoring people, but we haven't yet come across a management theory that advocates ignoring people.) So while we may occasionally have to help people get better at something that's holding them back, if paying attention to what people *can't* do is our default setting as team leaders, and if all our efforts are directed at giving and receiving negative feedback more often and more efficiently, then we're leaving enormous potential on the table. People don't need feedback. They need attention, and moreover, attention to what they do the best. And they become more engaged and therefore more productive when we give it to them.

• • •

So far, so good. We like positive attention, and it helps us do better work. But what about learning? If all we get is attention to our strengths, how will we ever develop? As Simon Sinek asked, what about those areas where he needs improvement? A team leader must surely want her team members to grow and get better, and won't this necessitate that she spend most of her time pinpointing flaws and fixing them?

Again, our informal theories of work—our "know for sure" theories —let us down. We seem to accept, on its face, the idea that "strengths" go at one end of the scale and "areas for improvement" or "areas of opportunity" go at the other, that areas of high performance are where we are most complete and areas of low performance are where we should, and can, grow.

But as we saw in the last chapter, the single most powerful predictor of both team performance and team engagement is the sense that "I have the chance to use my strengths every day at work." Now, we tend to think of "performance" and "development" as two separate things, as though development or growth is something that exists outside of the present-day work. But development means nothing more than doing our work a little better each day, so increasing performance and creating growth are the same thing. A focus on strengths increases performance. Therefore, a focus on strengths is what creates growth.

The best team leaders seem to know this. They reject the idea that the most important focus of their time is people's shortcomings, realizing instead that, in the real world, each person's strengths are in fact her areas of greatest opportunity for learning and growth; and that consequently, time and attention devoted to contributing to these strengths intelligently will yield exponential return now and in the future. Some of these leaders know this instinctively—or perhaps they've figured it out from their experience with real humans on their teams—but for the rest of us there is a wealth of biological data to reinforce the truth that positive attention accelerates development. At the microscopic level learning appears to be a function of neurogenesis: the growth of new neurons. And, as many recent studies have shown, the brain—though it goes through its most frenzied periods of synapse growth and synapse pruning during childhood and adolescence—never loses its ability to create more neurons and more synaptic connections between those neurons. This is referred to as "neural plasticity," and it's often pointed to as a sign that, since the brain can keep mutating through life, we should keep telling people what's wrong with them so that they can fix themselves, so that they can learn to do it right.

And of course, we *can* all learn to do it right, or at least, right-er. We *can* all learn to be slightly better at skills that we apply ourselves to with disciplined practice. However, what the brain science also reveals is that while the brain does continue to grow throughout life, each brain grows differently. Because of your genetic inheritance and the oddities of your early childhood environment, your brain's wiring is utterly unique—no one has ever had a brain wired just like yours, and given the brain's complexity, no one ever will. Some parts of your brain have tight thickets of synaptic connections, while other parts are far less dense. And when we examine your brain's growth—when we count the new neurons and their connections—it turns out that you grow far more neurons and synaptic connections where you already have the most preexisting neurons and synaptic connections. Perhaps this is caused by nature's harshly efficient use-it-or-lose-it design, or perhaps, with so much preexisting biological infrastructure supporting your densest synaptic regions, it is simply easier to forge new connections where you already have lots. Either way, we now know that, though every brain grows, each grows most where it's already strongest. The arrow of brain development points toward specialization. As the neuroscientist Joseph LeDoux memorably described it, "Brain growth is like new buds on an existing branch, rather than new branches."[5]

So the weight of the neurological evidence supports the notion that your strengths *are* your development areas—that these are, biologically speaking, one and the same. Neurological science can also tell us what happens in response to a deliberate focus on strengths instead of weaknesses. Consider, for example, an experiment during which scientists split students into two groups. To one group they gave positive coaching, asking about the students' dreams and how the students would go about achieving them, while with the other they probed about homework, and what the students thought they needed to do differently to be better. While these conversations were happening the scientists hooked each student up to a functional magnetic resonance imaging (fMRI) machine, so as to see which parts of the brain were most activated in response to these different sorts of attention.

Here's what they found. In the brains of the students who received negative feedback the sympathetic nervous system lit up. This is the "fight or flight" system, the system that mutes the other parts of the brain and thus allows us to focus only on the information most necessary to survive. When this part of the nervous system is triggered, your heart rate goes up, endorphins flood your body, your cortisol levels rise, and you tense for action. This is your brain on negative feedback: it responds as if to a threat, and it narrows its activity. The strong negative emotions produced by criticism "inhibits access to existing neural circuits and invokes cognitive, emotional, and perceptual impairment," psychology and business professor Richard Boyatzis said in summarizing the researchers findings.[6]

Negative feedback doesn't enable learning. It systematically inhibits it and is, neurologically speaking, how to create *impairment*.

In the students who received attention focused on their dreams and how they might go about achieving them, however, the sympathetic nervous system was not activated. Instead it was the parasympathetic nervous system that lit up. This is sometimes referred to as the "rest and digest" system. To quote the researchers again: "[T]he Parasympathetic Nervous System . . . stimulates adult neurogenesis (i.e., growth of new neurons) . . . , a sense of well being, better immune system functioning, and cognitive, emotional, and perceptual openness."[7]

In other words, positive, future-focused attention gives your brain access to more regions of itself and thus sets you up for greater learning. We're often told that the key to learning is to get out of our comfort zones, but this finding gives the lie to that particular chestnut—take us out of our comfort zones and our brains stop paying attention to anything other than surviving the experience. It's clear that we learn most *in* our comfort zone, because that's our strengths zone, where our neural pathways are most concentrated. It's where we're most open to possibility, and it's where we are most creative and insightful.

If you want your people to learn more, pay attention to what's working for them right now, and then build on that.

• • •

The question is, how? How can you stimulate learning and growth within your team, steer clear of the negative feedback that sets your people back, and still ensure that your team is running smoothly and efficiently?

There's one thing you can start to do immediately: get into the conscious habit of looking for what's going well for each of your team members. The pull to look at the negative is a very strong one—the Berkeley psychologist Rick Hanson sums up the research memorably when he says, "the brain is like Velcro for negative experiences, but

Teflon for positive ones"—which is why making this a *conscious* habit is so important.[8] It might not come naturally or easily for you, but with such a payoff in terms of performance, engagement, and growth, it'll be worth practicing it.

In the world of computing, there's an event called a high-priority interrupt. It tells the computer's processor that something requires its immediate attention, and so it needs to "interrupt" normal process- ing and jump the particular something to the head of the processing queue. In the real world of team leaders you'll have quite a few things that function in the same way—that grab your attention and force you to act. The majority of these high-priority interrupts are going to be problems, and that's normal. You don't want to administer medicine to a patient if it's the wrong medicine. You don't want to present some- thing to your executive if you've just received information that half of what you're presenting is now obsolete. Any system or process that breaks down will demand that you, the team leader, address it. This is a high-priority interrupt doing what it should do: stopping everything to seize your attention.

And the same high-priority interrupts will occur when one of your people messes up. You'll see something someone does wrong—a poorly handled call, a missed meeting, a project gone awry—and the same instinct will kick in: stop everything to tell that person what he did wrong, and what he needs to do to fix it.

The difficulty for you here is that people aren't processes, nor are they machines—what works for processes and machines doesn't work for men and women. Processes and machines are finite and static, and unless we change something about them, they either stay the same or gradually wear out. People, by contrast, are in a constant state of learning and growing, and, as we just saw, they grow the most under positive attention and the least under negative feedback. Paradoxically, then, the more your high-priority interrupts involve catching your people doing things wrong (so you can fix them), the less productive each person will become in the short term, and the less growth you'll see from your team members in the long run. Finding itself in negative-criticism territory, the human brain stiffens, tenses, and—in meaningful ways—resists improvement.[9] Machines and processes don't do that. You can fix a machine, you can fix a process, but you can't fix a person in the same way—people aren't toasters.

So, when it comes to your people, what should be your high-priority interrupt? If what you want is improvement, then it should be whenever someone on your team does something that really works. The goal is to consciously spend your days alert for those times when someone on your team does something so easily and effectively that it rocks you, just a little, and then to find a way of telling that person what you just saw.

This sounds as easy as "catch people doing things right," but as we'll see, there's a little more to it than that. Tom Landry, who coached the Dallas Cowboys for twenty-nine consecutive years, was one leader who figured this out. Early in his coaching career, with the Cowboys struggling at the bottom of the league and a bunch of misfits on his roster, he introduced a radical new method of coaching. While the other teams were reviewing missed tackles and dropped balls, Landry instead focused his players' attention on their wins, however minor. He combed through footage of previous games and created, for each player, a highlight reel of where that player had done something easily, naturally, and effectively. He reasoned that while the number of wrong ways to do something was infinite, the number of right ways, for any particular player, was not. It was finite, and knowable, and the best way to define and know the right way was to look at those plays where the player had done it right. So he set about capturing these distinctive moments of excellence and offering them up to each player. From now on, he said, "we only replay your winning plays."

Now, on one level, he was doing this to make his players feel better about themselves, because like all good team leaders, he knew the power of praise. The relevant survey item here is "I know I will be recognized for excellent work." And as we've seen, the data shows that people on the highest-performing teams strongly agree with this item far more than people on lower-performing teams.*

But Landry wasn't nearly as interested in praise as he was in learning. His instincts told him that each person would learn best how to improve his performance if he could see, in slow motion, what his own personal versions of excellence looked like. Really great performance often happens in a state of flow, such that we're barely conscious of what we're doing—Michael Jordan used to watch himself in post-game highlights and shake his head, saying, "Wow, I did that?" By replaying his players' winning plays Landry was taking them outside themselves and allowing them to see the contours and the rhythm of what "working" truly looked like for each one. In so doing, he hoped not only that they would feel more confident but also that they'd be in a better position to repeat and build on their unique strengths in action. David Cooperrider, professor of Social Entrepreneurship at Case Western Reserve University and creator of the theory of Appreciative Inquiry, has pointed out that organizational growth will always follow the focus of your attention.[10] Tom Landry, twenty years earlier, was applying the same principle to his Cowboys.

You can do this, too. Nowadays, *recognition* has become a synonym for *praise,* but in doing so has moved some way from its origins. It comes to us from the Latin word *cognoscere,* meaning *to know,* which in turn stems from the Greek word *gnosis,* meaning *knowledge* or *learning.* Thus, to *re*-cognize a person, in essence, means to come to know him anew. Recognition, in its deepest sense, is to spot something valuable

---

*And in case you're wondering which drives which—whether the performance leads to praise or vice versa—the data reveals that though high performance at Time 1 does indeed relate to a higher score on the recognition item at Time 2, the correlation coefficients are four times bigger when pointed the other way: praise leads to performance more than praise reflects performance.

in a person and then to ask her about it, in an ongoing effort to learn who she is when she is at her best.

The trick to doing this is not just to tell the person how well she's performed, or how good she is. While simple praise is by no means a bad thing, it captures a moment in the past rather than creating the possibility of more such moments in the future. Instead, what you'll want to do is tell the person what *you* experienced when that moment of excellence caught your attention—your instantaneous reaction to what worked. For a team member, nothing is more believable, and thus more powerful, than your sharing what you saw from her and how it made you feel. Or what it made you think. Or what it caused you to realize. Or how and where you will now rely on her. These are *your* reactions, and when you share them with specificity and with detail, you aren't judging her or rating her or fixing her. You are simply reflecting to her the unique "dent" she just made in the world, as seen through one person's eyes—yours. And precisely because it isn't a judgment or a rating, but is instead a simple reaction, it is authoritative and beyond question. It's also humble: when someone says to you "I want to know where I stand" she doesn't actually mean this, and you, frankly, are in no position to tell her—you are not the ultimate and definitive source of truth for where she stands. Instead, what she means is "I want to know where I stand *with you*." And happily, here your truth is unimpeachable.

With each replaying of these small moments of excellence, relayed through the lens of your own experience, you'll ease her into the rest-and-digest state of mind, her brain will become more receptive to new information and will make connections to other inputs found in other regions of her brain, and she will learn and grow and get better. It is, in short, the best recognition she could ever receive. You are learning about her, and relaying that learning to her, and, as on the best teams, she knows that tomorrow you will be doing so again. On such rituals is great performance built.

• • •

The nature of your attention is key. If a team member screws something up, of course you have to deal with it. But remember that when you do, you're merely remediating—and that remediating what's wrong, so a mistake won't happen again, moves you no closer to creating excellent performance. If a nurse gives someone the wrong medication, ignoring that mistake could be lethal. So you can, of course, say to him, "Don't ever do that again!" And you can, of course, design a process to ensure that the medicine is always triple-checked before being administered to a patient. But as you do this, know that if the nurse now consistently gives the correct medication to his patients, this does not mean he's now giving excellent care leading to a faster and more complete recovery. Correcting the nurse's mistake won't lead to this, any more than correcting someone's grammar will lead to her writing a beautiful poem, or telling someone the correct punchline to a joke will make this person funny. Excellence is not the opposite of failure: we can never create excellent performances by only fixing poor ones. Mistake fixing is just a tool to prevent failure.

To conjure excellence from your team requires a different focus for your attention. If you see somebody doing something that really works, stopping them and replaying it to them isn't only a high-priority interrupt, it is arguably your highest-priority interrupt. Get into this habit and you'll be far more likely to lead a high-performing team.

And what of balance? Landry said he would replay *only* each player's winning plays. Should we go to that extreme, or should we highlight the occasional winning play but focus mainly on mistake fixing? How many positive replays, in other words, should we have for every mistake-fix? What is the best ratio of 'Yes, that!' to 'Stop that!'? Research in other areas of social science sheds some light on this. Look at professor John Gottman's work on happy marriages, or professor Barbara Fredrickson's work on happiness and creativity, and the positive-to-negative ratio you'll arrive at is somewhere between three to one and five to one—three to five moments of appreciative attention for every one piece of negative feedback.[11] While there is no need to obsess over the mathematical precision of the ratios,[12] the science suggests that if you aim for this level of deliberate imbalance you and your team will be well served.

. . .

All that being said, however, there will inevitably come a day when, despite your best intentions and careful highlight flagging, one of your people will implore you to give him negative feedback or corrective action. Tell me what I'm doing wrong, he'll say. Or he'll say that he finds himself stuck in the middle of a difficult situation, or is struggling with his job and is turning to you for advice on how to move forward. What do you do?

To begin with, try to resist the powerful temptation to jump in with your very best advice.*

First, as we saw earlier in the chapter, your brain is wired uniquely, such that the world you see and the sense you make of it, the things in it that draw you in, or repel you, or drain you, or light you up, and the insights these things spark in your mind—all these are utterly different from everyone else's, and become even more different as you grow. As a result, the advice given to you by a leader who is not you will not necessarily work for you. The best team leaders know this: They realize that, for example, if you are struggling with public speaking, they cannot just advise you to organize your flow, practice your stories, and nail your ending, because what you mean by *flow* and *story* and *nail the ending* are going to be utterly different from what they mean by those very same words. They understand that the path you will take to your best performance will be unpredictably different from theirs.

---

*And the irony that we are here advising you not to give advice has not escaped us.

You'll need to remember this the next time you give someone a piece of perfectly crafted advice and then see him do something quite different from what you'd prescribed. Don't get mad at him: it wasn't that he wasn't listening, or had nodded his assent and then passive-aggressively gone and done the exact opposite. He'd heard you, and more than likely, he wanted to do what you wanted him to do. It's just that he couldn't make sense of your sense. All he had was his own sense, so he acted out of that, as best he could.

Seen in this light, much of what we call "advice" is perhaps better understood as *The Recitation Of A Set Of Tactics That Work For Me And Only Me*. Ray Dalio's principles are not universal, as interesting as we might find them to be. They are simply and only 210 tactics that work for Ray, or at most for people who share very many characteristics with Ray. In this sense, advice is akin to blood. Prior to the twentieth century doctors attempting blood transfusions found to their deep frustration that while in some cases they worked beautifully, in others the patient's body seemed to be allergic to the donor's blood and rejected it completely. It was only when the Austrian scientist Karl Landsteiner identified the existence of different blood types, and discovered that some blood types were physiologically incompatible with others, that doctors realized the importance of knowing the type of the donor and the patient before attempting a transfusion.

The same applies to "performance transfusions." To succeed, they depend on how individuals make sense of what they're hearing—how they metabolize it, and hook it into their own patterns of thought and behavior. Performance-transfusing advice, in other words, starts with the performer, not with the advice.

The second thing that great team leaders know, and that brain scientists have shown, is that an "insight" is brain food. These scientists aren't yet sure whether this is because insights come with a nice shot of dopamine or some other neurochemical transmitter, but what they do know is that the brain is built such that a new insight—"a feeling of knowing generated from within," to use their phrasing—feels good. Perhaps you have felt this. Perhaps you have noticed it in others when you've tried repeatedly to teach and advise but seen performance leap only when your team member has combined this advice with her own raw material to create a flash of new understanding. This insight then becomes her sense maker, her lens through which to view the challenge in front of her, her guide as she navigates her way forward. This insight is learning, and while it can be nudged from without, it is only ever generated from within.

We take such pains with our advice. We are so proud of its kindly intent, its perspective, its generosity, and its sequence: the way we begin with a simple setup and then walk our confused advice seeker step-by-step through our carefully constructed logic, until we bring her gaze all the way to the solution standing before her, clear as day. We offer this painting up to her, beautiful and complete.

But the most helpful advice is not a painting. It is instead a box of paints and a set of brushes. Here, the best team leaders seem to say, take these paints, these brushes, and see what you can do with them. What do you see, from your vantage point? What picture can you paint?

This, in the end, is why they are so intent on replaying for you what's working for you. By helping you to see what "working" looks like for you, they're offering you an image that you can use as raw material for your painting, and since it was your behavior that created the image in the first place, you've already felt it from within. Now it's their job to show it to you from without, so that you can recognize it, and re-create it, and refine it.

When a team member comes to you asking for advice, then, don't rush to your easel and start furiously painting away. Instead try this approach—the box-of-paints approach, if you will, containing some hues of *present*, some shades of *past*, and a few bright dabs of *future*.

Start with the *present*. If your team member approaches you with a problem, he is in it *now*. He is feeling weak, broken, or challenged, and you have to address that. But rather than dealing with it head-on, ask your colleague to tell you three things that are working for him *right now*. These "things that are working" might be related to the situation, or they might be completely separate from it. They might be significant or trivial. It doesn't matter. Just ask for three "things that are working." In doing that, you're priming his mind with oxytocin—what we sometimes call the "love drug," but which here is better thought of as the "creativity" drug. By getting him to think about some specific things that are going right, you are deliberately altering his brain chemistry so that he can be open to new solutions, and new ways of thinking or acting.

(By the way, you can be totally up-front with him about what you are doing—the evidence suggests that the more active a participant he is in this, the more effective the technique.[13])

Next, go to the *past*. Ask him, "When you had a problem like this in the past, what did you do that worked?" Much of our lives are lived through patterns, so it's highly likely that he has encountered this problem before and found himself similarly stuck. But on one of these occasions he will almost certainly have found some way forward, some action or insight or connection that worked for him and enabled him to move out of the mess. Get him thinking about that, and seeing it in his mind's eye: what he actually felt and did, and what happened next.

Finally, turn to the *future*. Ask your team member, "What do you already know you need to do? What do you already know works in this situation?" In a sense you're operating under the assumption that he's already made his decision—you're just helping him find it. At this point, by all means offer up one or two of your own paintings, to see if they might clarify his own. But above all keep asking him to describe what he already sees, and what he already knows works for him.

The emphasis here should not be on why questions ("Why didn't that work?" or "Why do you think you should do that?"), because these take both of you backward and upward into a fuzzy retrospective world of conjecture and concepts. Instead, rely on your what questions ("What do you actually want to have happen?" or "What are a couple of actions you could take right now?"). These sorts of questions yield concrete answers, in which your colleague finds his actual self doing actual things in the near future. Each answer he comes up with is a brushstroke to his painting, making his images ever more vivid, more compelling, and more real.

And if he starts big, as some do, with huge swaths of color that overwhelm the entire canvas—"What I need to do is quit my job, buy a dinghy, and sail round the Cape of Good Hope"—then put a couple of smaller brushes in his hand and direct his gaze to one corner of the canvas: Here's a figure, you might suggest. Can you repaint it, in a different color perhaps, or with one small shift in the perspective? Perhaps he will be able to come up with a few things he knows he can tackle right now, rather than up and quitting his job. And then, guided by the small but increasingly vivid image in his own mind, he will, little by little, create a new painting.

People can reliably rate other people

How much do you think you can know about a person simply by watching him? If you work with him every single day, do you think you can figure out what drives him? Could you spot enough clues to reveal to you whether he's competitive, or altruistic, or has a burning need to cross things off his list every day? How about his style of thinking? Are you perceptive enough to see his patterns and pinpoint that he is a big-picture, what-if thinker, or a logical, deductive reasoner, or that he values facts over concepts? And could you parse how he relates to others, and discern, for instance, that he's far more empathetic than he appears, and that deep down he really cares about his teammates?

Perhaps you can. Perhaps you are one of those people who instinctively picks up on the threads of others' behaviors and then weaves these into a detailed picture of who a person is and how he moves through the world. Certainly, the best team leaders seem able to do this. They pay close attention to the spontaneous actions and reactions of their team members, and figure out that one person likes receiving praise in private, while another values it only when it's given in front of the entire team; that one responds to clear directives, while another shuts down if you even appear to be telling her what to do. They know that each member of their team is unique, and they spend a huge amount of time trying to attend to and channel this uniqueness into something productive.

How about rating your team, though? Do you think you could accurately give your team members scores on each of their characteristics? If you surmise that one of your team is a strategic thinker, could you with confidence choose a number to signify how good at it she actually is? Could you do the same for her influencing skills, or her business knowledge, or even her overall performance? And if you were asked how much of these things she had in relation to everyone else on the team, do you think you could weigh each person precisely enough to put a number to each person's *relative* abilities? This might sound a bit trickier—you'd have to keep your definition of influencing skills stable, even while judging each unique person against that definition. But if we gave you a scale of one to five, with detailed descriptions of the behaviors associated with each number on the scale, do you think you could use that scale fairly, and arrive at a true rating?

And even if you are confident in your own ability to do this, what do you think about all the other team leaders around you? Do you think they would use the scale in the same way, with the same level of objectivity and discernment as you? Or would you worry that they might be more lenient graders, and so wind up with higher marks for everyone, or that they might define "influencing skills" differently from you? Do you think it's possible to teach all of these team leaders how to do this in exactly the same way?

It's a lot to keep straight—so many different people rating so many other different people on so many different characteristics, producing torrents of data. But keep it all straight we must, because this data represents people, and once collected, it comes to define how people are seen at work.

familiar with is the nine box. This is a graph showing *performance* along the x-axis and *potential* up the y-axis, with each axis divided into thirds—low, medium, and high—to create nine possible regions. Each team leader is asked to think about each person on his or her team and then place them, in advance of the talent review, into one of the nine boxes—to rate them, that is, on both their performance and their potential. This system is designed to allow a team leader to highlight that a particular person might have bags of potential, and yet not have translated that potential into actual performance, whereas another team member might contribute top-notch performance, and yet have very little potential upside—he's maxed out in his current position. With this data displayed in the talent review, the leadership team can define different courses of action for each person: the former will be given more training and more time, for example, while the latter might just be offered a healthy bonus.

Many companies also give people performance ratings on a scale of 1–5, either in parallel with or as an alternative to the nine-box process. Again, each team leader is asked to propose a rating for each person on his or her team. Then, before or as part of the talent review, there is a meeting called a "consensus" or "calibration" meeting, which goes something like this: your team leader talks about you and defends why she ended up giving you a 4 rating, and then her colleagues weigh in on why they gave their people 5s, or 4s, or 3s, whereupon debates ensue about what really constitutes a 4, whether a 4 on one team is the same as a 4 on another team, whether you truly deserve a 4 this year, and if you do, whether the organization has enough 4s left over to allow you to have one.

If the organization has run out of 4s—which happens often since many team leaders are reluctant to give a person a 3 or, perish the thought, a 2—then your team leader may have to give you a 3 and tell you that, though you truly deserved a 4, it wasn't your turn this year, and that she will look out for you next year. This is called "forcing

• • •

At least once a year, a number of your more senior colleagues will gather together in a room to discuss you. They will talk about your performance, your potential, and your career aspirations, and decide on such consequential issues as how much bonus you should get, whether you should be selected for a special training program, and when or if you should be promoted. This meeting, as you might know, is called a talent review, and virtually every organization conducts some version of it. The organization's interest is in looking one by one at its people—its talent—and then deciding how to invest differentially in those individuals. The people who display the highest performance and potential—the stars, if you like—will normally get the most money and opportunity, while those further down the scale will get less, and those struggling at the lower end of the scale will more than likely be moved into a euphemistically described Performance Improvement Plan (PIP) and thereby eased out.

These talent reviews are the mechanism that organizations use to manage their people. They want to keep the best people happy and challenged, and simultaneously weed out those who aren't contributing. Since, in most organizations, the largest costs are people's wages and benefits, these meetings are taken very seriously, and the most pressing question—a central preoccupation of all senior leaders in all large organizations—is, "How can we make sure that we are seeing our people for who they really are?" This is a wake-up-in-the-middle-of-the-night sort of question for senior leaders, because they worry that their team leaders might not, in fact, understand the sort of person the organization needs nearly as clearly as the senior leaders do, and further that the team leaders might not be objective raters of their own people.

To combat this worry, companies have set up all sorts of systems designed to add rigor to this review process. The one you may be most the curve," which is the name given to the rather painful process of reconciling the organization's need to have only a certain percentage of employees show up as super-high performers with the team leaders' tendency to give high ratings to everyone so as to avoid having unpleasant performance conversations. Forced curves are no one's idea of fun, but they are felt to be a necessary constraint on team leaders, and a way of ensuring that rewards are appropriately "differentiated," so that high performers get much more than low performers.

Perhaps wanting to add more precision to the words *performance* and *potential*, many organizations have created lists of competencies that team members are supposed to possess, and against which they are rated at the end of the year. In chapter 4 we questioned whether these models were true reflections of what performance looks like in the real world. (Does anyone really have all of the competencies? Can we really prove that those who acquire the ones they lack outperform those who don't?) Nevertheless, many organizations still rate each person against such standard checklists. To aid in this, each competency is defined in terms of behaviors, and then the behaviors are tied to a particular point on the rating scale. So, for example, on a competency called organizational savvy and politics, if you see that the person "Provides examples of savvy approaches to successfully solving organizational problems," then you'd rate her a three. If you see that she "Recognizes and effectively addresses politically challenging situations," you would rate her a four. Using your behaviorally anchored competency ratings as your building blocks, you would then be asked to construct an overall rating of her performance and potential, and this is how she'd be represented during the talent review.

Historically, the talent review has happened only once or twice a year, but as we saw with Bridgewater Associates, with the arrival of smartphones it's now technologically possible for an organization to launch short performance-ratings surveys throughout the year. Each person can be rated by their peers, direct reports, and bosses, and then the scores can be aggregated either at mid-year or at year's end to produce a final performance rating. A number of startup, venture-capital–backed companies are leading the charge in bringing constant ratings into the workplace, and have gained such traction that the more established Human-Capital-Management software providers are scrambling to create their own always-on rating tools, and large institutions such as PricewaterhouseCoopers and General Electric are building their own versions.

This race to real-time ratings appears as inevitable as it is frenzied, and all of it is in service of the organization's interest, which is to answer the question, "When it comes to our people, what do we *really* have here?"

Your interest in all this is related, but different. You won't be too worried about competencies, and calibration sessions, and behavioral anchors, all of which probably sound a bit esoteric. Instead, you'll be acutely aware of a few real-world practicalities that boil down to the fact that your pay, your promotion possibilities, and possibly even your continued employment are being decided in a meeting to which you are conspicuously not invited. The people who *are* in the room—some of whom you know, and some of whom know you, and others of whom you've never met—are talking about you, and people like you, and they are rating you, deciding which box you go in, and thereby deciding what you will get after a year of hard work, and also where your career will go next. You may not realize this during your first couple of years in the workforce, but once you do, it will preoccupy you. You'll think to yourself: I really want these people to think well of me. I really, really want these people not to think ill of me. But most of all, I want the truth of me in the room where the decisions are made. This is your interest.

You will come to wonder about these rating scales, these peer surveys, and these always-on 360-degree apps, and you will hope that there is enough science in them, enough rigor and process, that you—ideally, the best of you—will be portrayed accurately. After that, let the chips fall where they may. At least, then, you will have been given a fair hearing on your true merits as a person, and as a team member.

. . .

It is going to bother you greatly to learn, then, that in the real world, none of this works. None of the mechanisms and meetings—not the models, not the consensus sessions, not the exhaustive competencies, not the carefully calibrated rating scales—*none* of them will ensure that the truth of you emerges in the room, because *all* of them are based on the belief that *people can reliably rate other people*. And they can't.

This, in all its frustrating simplicity, is our sixth lie.

It's frustrating because it would be so much more convenient if, with enough training and a well-designed tool, a person could become a reliable rater of another person's skills and performance. Think of all the data on you we could gather, aggregate, and then act on! We could precisely peg your performance and your potential. We could accurately assess your competencies. We could look at all of these and more through the eyes of your bosses, peers, and subordinates. And then we could feed all this into an algorithm, and out would come promotion lists, succession plans, development plans, nominations for the high-potential program, and more.

But none of this is possible, despite the fact that many human-capital software systems claim to do exactly what's described above. Over the last forty years, we have tested and retested people's ability to rate others, and the inescapable conclusion—reported in research papers such as "The Control of Bias in Ratings: A Theory of Rating" and "Trait, Rater and Level Effects in 360-Degree Performance Ratings" and "Rater Source Effects Are Alive and Well After All"—is that human beings cannot reliably rate other human beings, on anything at all.[1]

We could confirm this by watching the ice-skating scoring at any recent Winter Olympics—how can the Chinese and the Canadian judges disagree so dramatically on the scoring of that triple toe loop?—but instead, let's take a look at the most revealing real-world study of our rating prowess, or lack thereof. It was conducted by two professors, Steven Scullen and Michael Mount, and one industrial/organizational psychologist, Maynard Goff. They collected ratings on 4,392 team leaders, from two direct reports, two peers, and two bosses. These team leaders were rated on a combination of leadership competencies, such as "manages execution" or "fosters teamwork" or "analyzes issues," with a short list of questions measuring each competency, for a total of just under half a million ratings from over twenty-five thousand raters.[2]

The researchers then asked a straightforward question: What best explained why the raters rated the way they did? Could ratings best be explained by relative positioning in the organizational hierarchy, in which case all your direct reports would give you similar ratings, which were measurably different from those given by your peers, which in turn were different from those given by your bosses? Or was the strongest effect a rater's sense of your overall performance—if someone thought highly of you overall, did this affect every single question he or she rated you on? Or was the most powerful factor driving your score on each of the six questions per competency how the person rated you on the other five questions for that competency? If he or she felt you had lots of political savvy, in other words, did this increase scores not only on one of the questions related to political savvy but on all of them? These three possible explanations—rater perspective, overall performance, and competency performance, as the researchers termed them—represented three increasingly close measures of the thing the ratings were trying to measure (your performance on a given skill), with the last of the three being closest to the mark.

Obviously, each rater had her own reasoning for each rating, but by slicing and dicing the data the researchers hoped to see what best explained the overall patterns, and what they found was that most of the variation in people's scores—54 percent of it—could be explained by a single factor: the unique personality of the rater. From the data it was apparent that each rater—regardless of whether he or she was a boss, a peer, or a direct report—displayed his or her own particular rating pattern. Some were very lenient raters, skewing far to the right of the rating scale, while others were tough graders, skewing left. Some had natural range, using the entire scale from one to five, while others seemed to be more comfortable arranging their ratings in a tight cluster. Each person, whether he or she realized it or not, had an idiosyncratic pattern of ratings, so this powerful effect came to be called the Idiosyncratic Rater Effect.

Here's what's going on. When Lucy rates Charlie on the various subquestions in the competency called strategic thinking, there is a distinct pattern to her ratings, which her organization believes reflects her judgment about how much strategic thinking Charlie has. For this to be true, however, when Lucy then turns her attention to a different team member, Snoopy, and rates him on the same competency, the pattern of her ratings should change, because she is now looking at a different person with, presumably, different levels of strategic thinking. What the Scullen, Mount, and Goff research reveals is that Lucy's pattern of ratings does *not* change when she rates two different people. Instead her ratings stay just about the same—her ratings pattern travels with her, regardless of who she's rating, so her ratings reveal more about *her* than they do about her team members. We think that rating tools are windows that allow us to see out to other people, but they're really just mirrors, with each of us endlessly bouncing us back at ourselves.

And this effect is not, by the way, associated with unconscious bias on the part of the rater for or against people of a particular gender, race, or age. These biases do exist, of course, and we should do everything we can to teach people how to see past them or remove them—but the discovery from this research is that the Idiosyncratic Rater Effect applies *regardless* of the gender, race, or age of both the rater and the person being rated. The idiosyncrasy of the rating pattern stems from the uniqueness of the rater, and doesn't appear to have much of anything to do with the person being rated. In fact, it's pretty much as though that person isn't there at all.[3]

The measurement community was understandably frustrated by the size of the Idiosyncratic Rater Effect, so it expended considerable effort trying to minimize it or remove it. The increasingly detailed descriptions of what constitutes a five versus a four, and the behavioral anchors attached to each point on the competency scales, are all part of that effort. Unfortunately, we now know that these increasingly detailed scales and anchors actually *magnify* the effect: the more complex the rating scale, the more powerful the influence of our idiosyncratic rating patterns.[4] It's almost as if we get overwhelmed by the complexity of the rating scale and revert to the "safety" of our natural rating pattern.

When we rate other people on a list of questions about their abilities, the Idiosyncratic Rater Effect explains *more than half* of why we choose the ratings we do. The three largest studies of people rating other people in the way that we do at work have reached strikingly similar conclusions: about 60 percent of the variability in ratings can be chalked up to the raters' differing responses to a rating scale.

Since you're most concerned that the truth of you be in the room, this should worry you enormously. The rating given to you tells us, in the main, about the *rating patterns of your team leader*, and yet, in the room, we act as though it tells us about the *performance patterns in you*.

And even if we could in fact correct for our rating idiosyncrasies, we'd still have another hurdle in front of us. The people you work with simply don't interact with you enough to be able to pinpoint the extent to which you possess, say, influencing skills, or political savvy, or strategic thinking, or frankly any abstract attribute. People at work are preoccupied (with work, mainly), and paying attention to you closely and continuously enough to be able to rate you on any of these abstractions is a practical impossibility. They simply don't see you enough. Their data on you is insufficient—hence the name for this second hurdle: *data insufficiency*. If Olympic ice-skating judges can't agree on the quality of each triple toe loop, when the only thing they are doing is sitting watching triple toe loops one after the other, then what hope does a busy peer, direct report, or boss have of accurately rating your "business acumen"?

Even if we changed the world of work, and created a job category of roving raters whose sole responsibility was to wander the hallways and meeting rooms, to watch each person act and react in real time, and then to rate each person on a list of qualities, we still wouldn't get good data, in part because our definitions are poor. A triple toe loop is defined as a take-off from a backward outside (skate) edge assisted by the toe of the other foot, followed by three rotations, followed by a landing on the same backward outside edge—and this is the only definition of it. Look up *business acumen*, on the other hand, and you'll find something like this:

> Business acumen is keenness and speed in understanding
> and deciding on a business situation . . . people with business
> acumen . . . are able to obtain essential information about a
> situation, focus on the key objectives, recognise the relevant
> options available for a solution, [and] select an appropriate
> course of action.[5]

And this is just one of many definitions you'll encounter. Furthermore, there is a world of difference between the specificity of "take-off from a backward outer edge" and the vagueness of "essential information," "key objectives," and "appropriate course of action." Essential to whom? Key objectives as determined by whom? Appropriate course of action as determined how? Of course, each of us reading the definitions thinks, "Well, I could easily define those for myself"—but that's the point. When we rate people on abstractions, there is even more scope for our ratings to reflect our own idiosyncrasies. And because one person's understanding of *business acumen* is meaningfully different from another's, even when two highly trained and focused raters rate the same person on the same quality, they find it extraordinarily difficult to arrive at the same rating for the same quality.

• • •

To all this talk of the *Idiosyncratic Rater Effect* and *data insufficiency*, however, some will tell you to calm your fears. The truth of you will indeed emerge in the room, they'll say, because even though one person might be an unreliable and idiosyncratic rater, many people won't be. If each person can just manage to get you "roughly right," and if we aggregate the "roughlys," then we'll wind up seeing you pretty clearly. This is the logic upon which 360-degree surveys are based: one person may be off base, but if ten people are telling you that you lack business acumen, then it's a safe bet that you do indeed lack business acumen.

Unfortunately, despite its ubiquity, this line of thinking is wrong. It contains two fallacies. The first of these concerns the wisdom of crowds. This was an idea popularized by James Surowiecki in his book of the same name, in which he described example after example of a well-informed majority being wiser than a sole genius.[6] He began the book with the story of Charles Darwin's half-cousin, Sir Francis Galton, who, while attending the West of England Fat Stock and Poultry Exhibition in 1906, came upon a competition to guess the weight of an ox. For sixpence, anyone who was interested could buy a ticket and write his guess on it, and the person whose guess was closest to the ox's actual weight would win a prize. Galton was fascinated by data, so he stuck around after the winner had been announced and asked if he could borrow the eight hundred tickets on which the guesses had been written. He divided the sum of the guesses by the number of them to find the average. The ox's actual weight was 1,198 pounds, and lo and behold, the average of all the guesses was 1,197 pounds. The crowd was wise.[7]

And this is entirely true—well-informed crowds are wise, and very often wiser than a small, privileged, expert elite. But the critical qualifier in that sentence is *well-informed*. The mechanism that creates wisdom in crowds is that lots of members of the crowd have real-world experience of the question being asked—in this case, most of them were from the surrounding farmlands and knew, roughly, the weight of oxen (and even if they didn't, they had a shared understanding of what "weight" was). Take all those "roughlys" and average them, and you do indeed get pretty close to the ox's actual weight.

But what happens if the crowd is ill-informed? What happens if instead of the ox's weight the crowd had been asked to guess the number of atoms in the ox's body? Or how "friendly" the ox was? The crowd, lacking any real-world frame of reference for the thing being guessed at, wouldn't be wise at all. This is what happens when lots of people who encounter you infrequently, and who each have different definitions of *business acumen*, are asked to rate you on it. We get the 360-degree-survey equivalent of West Country folk guessing the number of atoms in an ox.*

---

*In case you're curious, we did the math, and the answer appears to be something like 54,340,365,926,000,000,000,000,000,000, give or take. You might want to assemble your own crowd of West Country punters to check this.

The counterargument to this would be that in this analogy, business acumen is more like the weight of the ox than the number of atoms in the ox—we know what business acumen is, so we can indeed roughly rate one another on it. What we discover in the data, however, is that each person seems to have his own idiosyncratic definition of *business acumen*, and that the more we try to standardize the definition with behavioral descriptions such as those we saw earlier, the greater the idiosyncratic rater effect becomes.* The same applies to other characteristics such as influencing, decision making, or even performance. Each of these is an abstract vessel into which we pour our own unique meaning: we are not well-informed, and we are, as raters, about as effective as farmers would be estimating numbers of atoms. This is the first crowd-based fallacy—that all of us are (always) smarter than one of us.

The second fallacy is this: that although one person's rating of you might be bad data, if we combine it with six other people's equally bad ratings data, we will magically turn it into good data—that somehow the errors will be averaged out. But this is not how data works. Errors average out only if they are random. If they are systematic—if they stem, for example, from a faulty measurement instrument, as they do when we rate one another—then adding them up produces more error, not less. Noise plus noise plus noise never equals signal; it only ever equals lots of noise. In fact, the truth about data is that noise plus signal plus signal plus signal still equals noise, because the tiniest amount of bad data contaminates all the good data.

We found an intriguing example of this in the story of Ariel 6, the last in a series of scientific research satellites designed and built by

---

*One reason for this is that, to return to our earlier example, a toe loop jump existed before it was called a toe loop, so the precision of its definition is inherent in its name. Business acumen didn't exist as a thing until we named it, and as a result it's just an abstraction defined by other abstractions, and will always stubbornly resist any more precise definition.

the United Kingdom and launched by the United States in the 1960s and 1970s. It carried three instruments, a cosmic ray detector and two X-ray detectors. The X-ray detectors were aligned with the spin axis of the satellite, so to point them at a specific star, the entire satellite had to be pointed at a particular region of the sky. To achieve this attitude control, the designers came up with an ingenious way of using the Earth's magnetic field both to measure where the detectors were pointed and to change the actual orientation of the satellite. And in order to measure the magnetic field, the satellite was equipped with instruments called magnetometers. There were two of them, not only to provide redundancy but also to enable the two independent measurements to be combined and averaged so as to reduce any random errors.

In the summer of 1979, the satellite was carefully packed up, shipped from the United Kingdom to Wallops Flight Facility on the Eastern Shore of Virginia, mounted atop a Scout rocket, and launched into space. It immediately encountered problems: The satellite was not spinning about its designated axis and was slightly off-kilter. There were problems recharging the batteries. And for some reason the X-ray detectors were detecting fewer X-rays than scientists had expected they would. The scientists needed to run a test to figure out what had gone wrong, so they pointed the satellite at the strongest X-ray source in the sky, the Crab Nebula.

By comparing what they expected to see with what they were actually seeing, they made two discoveries. First, the surfaces of the mirrors of one of the X-ray detectors had become contaminated—as a result, in future missions X-ray mirrors were protected until it was safe to expose them to space. And second, it became obvious that the satellite wasn't pointing exactly where it should be—it was off by a few degrees. There was a fault, it turned out, with one of the magnetometers, so there was a systematic error in the averaged measurements. And with that bad data mixed with the good data from the other magnetometer, the satellite didn't know where it was—it couldn't be pointed accurately at the right star.

In the world of ratings, the idea that we can always cover for the possibility that any individual data source is bad by getting lots of data from lots of sources and averaging it is wrong and harmful. Adding bad data to good, or the other way around, doesn't improve the quality of the data or make up for its inherent shortcomings.

For Ariel 6, the solution was to ignore the readings from the faulty magnetometer and rely on those from the good one. But when it comes to the talent-review meetings aiming to identify our best people, we don't have this option. *All* our readings are faulty—we have no good data to rely on. We are, literally, using flawed data to point us at the wrong (human) stars.

• • •

So far, we've seen that 1) human beings can never be trained to reliably rate other human beings, that 2) ratings data derived in this way is contaminated because it reveals far more of the rater than it does of the person being rated, and that 3) the contamination cannot be removed by adding more contaminated data. And this means, in turn, that ratings-based tools, be they annual engagement surveys, performance-rating tools, 360-degree surveys, or any of the many other varieties at large, do *not* measure what they purport to measure. And *this* means, in turn, that discussions based on the data generated by these tools do *not* accurately reflect the truth of you. Faced with this sorry state of affairs, what on earth should we do?

A sensible place for us to start is by learning to tell good data from bad. As most everyone at work will tell you, we are running headlong into a big-data world in which every single process, outcome, item, personal preference, and interaction will be captured, quantified, and run through machine-learning-enabled algorithms. The promise of this world is that, with all of these data points collected in real time, we'll be able to apply artificial intelligence to examine and learn from the relationships between the points, and thereby understand which thing predicts which other thing how frequently and under what conditions.

But none of these algorithms will yield anything useful unless they're grinding on good data. If we were to discover that having your cellphone in your pocket makes thermometers go haywire (don't worry, we haven't), then we wouldn't be able to learn anything useful from studying your temperature data over time, or the relationship of your temperature to some other data point, because all of your temperature data would have been contaminated by the cellphone in your pocket—garbage data in, garbage discoveries out.

So what, precisely, is "good data"?

We can say that good data has three distinct characteristics: it is reliable, it is variable, and it is valid.

Reliable data is simply data that we are confident is measuring what it says it's measuring, in a stable and predictable way. The most obviously reliable data comes from anything that can be counted, because if a thing can be counted—whether with your fingers or with some sort of measuring tool—then no matter whose fingers or tool we are using, we'll still get the same data. Your height is reliable data, as is the amount of money in your paycheck, the number of days you missed from work last year, and the temperature outside your office on a particular spring afternoon.

If, however, we walk outside with our thermometer on that spring day and it displays a reading of 69 degrees Fahrenheit, but then ten minutes later reads 21 degrees, although it's theoretically possible that the world just got dramatically colder, it's much more likely that our thermometer is broken. If after another ten minutes it now reads 75 degrees, we can be pretty sure that it's the instrument that's gone crazy, not the world. There are various statistical tests we can do to assess the reliability of a data set, but in essence, we come to trust our data-gathering tools when the data they generate doesn't change if the thing they're measuring doesn't change. Unreliable data, on the other hand, is wobbly data—it seems to move all by itself. And any measurement tool that spits out changes in data when nothing in the real world is actually changing is, like a broken thermometer, not to be trusted.

This is why 360-degree-feedback tools are unreliable. The data they produce is supposed to measure the presence of certain competencies in the person rated, yet when we examine the data, it's clear that it wobbles about by itself, because what the tool is actually responding to is the idiosyncrasy of the rater.

Variable data is data that displays natural (unforced) range—that is, range that reflects actual range in the real world. We can judge the quality of a measurement tool by its ability to measure and display this real-world range. Sticking with our temperature example, if we had a regular, store-bought thermometer whose lowest possible reading was 10 degrees below freezing and we took it to the South Pole, then each day our thermometer would tell us that it was 10 degrees below freezing, even though, in actual fact, it was much colder than that. Our thermometer, lacking the ability to measure the full range of what we wanted it to, would fail us as a measurement tool. It wouldn't be broken; it would merely be ill-suited for the task at hand.

If you've ever taken a training course at work and then been asked to rate it, you'll be familiar with a measurement tool that produces invariable data. Ask class participants to respond to the question, "Overall, this was a good learning experience," on a five-point scale, with five being "strongly agree" and one "strongly disagree," and you'll discover that virtually all the responses are either a four or a five. Whereas our thermometer is poorly suited for its Arctic purpose, this training measurement tool is poorly designed. Nevertheless the effect is the same: the data it produces has no range, no natural variation.

Performance-rating tools are similarly poorly designed. When we ask team leaders to rate their team members on a five-point scale, the data winds up looking like it came from a tool with a three-point scale, because team leaders seldom, if ever, use the bottom two scores. (This is why so many companies feel the need to force the curve—if they didn't, the performance-rating tool simply wouldn't produce data with range.)

To produce range in our rating tools, we have to create questions that contain extreme wording. A question such as, "I feel that my job fits my abilities," produces very little range at all—pretty much everyone agrees or strongly agrees. This is why when we sought to measure the issue of strengths-role fit we chose to word the question, "I have the chance to use my strengths *every day* at work." The words *every day* are extreme, and their effect is to push respondents toward either end of the rating scale—to produce range.* Look back to each of the eight team-experience questions we described in chapter 1 and you'll see that each of them contains an extreme wording. So, for example, the question measuring mission and purpose isn't, "I believe that my company has a worthy vision," but is instead, "I am *really enthusiastic* about the mission of my company."

These may appear to be small differences, but on them rests the tool's ability to generate data that captures real-world range.

Finally, we have to ask ourselves whether this range in reliable data matters. Does a high score on the measurement tool predict a high score on something else in the real world? Does variation in the tool relate to variation in something else in the real world? This, for data geeks, is the Holy Grail, and its proper (if less than compelling) name is "criterion-related validity." We can say that a tool's data is *valid* if

---

*Strictly, to capture more of the existing range in the real world by identifying more precisely a particular experience that varies from person to person.

the range of data produced by the tool predicts range in something else—if we can prove, time and again, that it is measuring something that correlates with or predicts a different outcome measured using a different tool. For example, Amazon can say that its customer-recommendation data is *valid* (or, has "criterion-related validity") if it can prove that people who bought one item really did also buy a different item. When Amazon knows for sure that the number of clicks on one web page relates to the number of clicks on an entirely different page, then it can have confidence that it's looking at *valid* data.

Or, we can say an engagement tool's data is valid if the people who rate their engagement more positively on the tool actually wind up staying with the company longer—in this case, range in engagement scores predicts subsequent range in voluntary turnover. One piece of reliable data predicts another piece of reliable data, and so, careful step by careful step, do we add to our store of valid knowledge about the world.[8]

Reliable, *variable*, and *valid*—these are the signs of good data, and these three concepts will help you intelligently examine the quality of any data put in front of you.

For example, if someone claims his data is *valid* you might ask him, politely, whether he can prove that this data has been shown to predict something else, measured by something else, in the real world. If he can show this—*à la* Amazon and the clicks from one page driving the clicks on another—then you're probably looking at valid data.

If someone comes to you and asks you to pay attention to a data set, ask yourself if the data displays natural variation or range. Ask to see a scatter plot. If the data points on the scatter plot all cluster to one end of the scale or the other, it's probably not good data. And of course, any data in which someone has had to fake range by forcing the curve, through a calibration or consensus session, is always bad data. The consensus has contaminated the data, the range is forced, and so the data is bad.

The place to start, however, is *always* reliability. Your statistician friends will tell you that all data-based discoveries are built on reliability. When we measure things, we have to make sure that the measurement tool doesn't generate data that wobbles by itself—because if it's wobbling by itself, then we'll never be able to trust its range, and thus never be able to prove that its range can predict range in something else we're interested in in the real world. No reliability means no validity—no knowledge. On anything, ever.[9]

And, as we've seen in this chapter, the problem with almost all data relating to people—including you—is that it isn't reliable. Goals data that reports your "percent complete"; competency data comparing you to abstractions; ratings data measuring your performance and your potential through the eyes of unreliable witnesses: it wobbles by itself, and fails to measure what it says it's measuring.

One of the most bizarre implications of this systematic unreliability is that, in what is supposedly the age of big data, no organization can say what drives performance—at least, not knowledge-worker performance. We may be able to say something intelligent about what drives sales, say, or piece-work output, because both of these are inherently and reliably measurable—they can be counted. But for any other work—which means most work—we have no way of knowing what drives performance, because we have no reliable way of measuring performance. We don't know whether bigger teams drive performance more than smaller teams. We don't know whether remote workers perform better than colocated workers. We don't know whether culturally more diverse teams are higher performing than less diverse ones. We don't know whether contractors are higher performers than full-time employees, or if it's the other way around. We can't even show that our investments in the training and development of our employees lead to greater performance. We can't say anything about any of these things, precisely because we have no reliable way to measure performance.

So when you read definitive statements about these things or, for that matter, about any other aspects of performance, your data-quality alarm bells should ring in your ears. While each of these things might be true, the exact opposite might also be true. Until we come up with a reliable way to measure individual knowledge-worker performance—whether this means the performance of a nurse, or a software developer, or a teacher, or a construction worker—any claim about what drives performance is not valid. No one knows, and anyone who claims to know simply doesn't know good data from bad.

· · ·

What can you do about this? Well, you can start by asking about it. Ask where your performance or potential ratings come from. Ask what competencies you might have been rated on. Ask to see the survey questions themselves. And if you see a survey filled with questions in which the rater is being asked to rate you on your specific behaviors or competencies, ask whether this survey has taken into account the Idiosyncratic Rater Effect. You will probably get a blank stare in response, so perhaps have this chapter handy, or download one of the articles mentioned earlier. More than likely you will see no immediate change in either the tool or the process, but at least you will be aware, and you will start to gain a reputation as someone who intelligently and rigorously interrogates the data you see. That's always a good reputation to have.

The other thing you can do, if you have the influence and the intention, is to change the way that the "people stuff" in your organization is measured. Because there is a better way—a more reliable way—to capture data about people. And it is based on this truth: although we are not reliable raters of others, *people can reliably rate their own experience.*

If we ask you to rate your local representative on his political savvy, your rating is not a reliable measure of something called "political savvy"—you are not able to reach into his psyche and reliably weigh the presence or absence of this abstract quality. However, if we ask you today who you plan to vote for, your answer *is* a reliable measure of who you plan to vote for today. It is a much humbler measure since it is asking only that you tell us about how you are feeling today about your voting preference, but it is a *reliable* measure of what it says it's measuring.

Likewise, if we ask you to rate one of your team on "growth potential," then your rating is unreliable—because what is growth potential, and how can you be the judge of it? But if we ask if you plan to promote her today, your answer *is* reliable. While you may not be able to project into *her* psyche and accurately perceive her growth potential, you are able to ask *yourself* if you plan to promote her today, and the answer you get back will be a reliable one. (When we report on our own experiences, we have all the data we need—we have perfect data sufficiency—because we're with ourselves a lot!) Your answer is exactly and only what it purports to be: your subjective reaction to her, carefully measured. It is both a humbler piece of data and, at the same time, a more reliable one.

In the same vein, your rating of a team member on something called "performance" is unreliable, because your definition of *performance* is unique to you. But in contrast, your response to the question, "Do you turn to this team member when you want extraordinary results?" is entirely reliable. With this question we are not asking you to stand above her, and outside of yourself, and opine dispassionately on her performance. Instead we are asking you to look inside yourself and tell us simply whether you feel confident to go to her when you want something done excellently. You cannot be wrong about this, because there is no right or wrong, only your feeling about what you would or wouldn't do with this team member. Someone else might disagree with you, but this doesn't make that person right—it just makes his or her reaction to the team member different from yours.

Once again, the data here is humbler (it's just you rating your own experience) and at the same time more reliable (you *know* your own experience).

So as a general rule, if you're after good data, be on the lookout for questions that ask only that you rate your own experience, or intended actions. You may not know if questions such as these are valid—that is, you may not know if the responses to them predict something in the real world—but at least you'll know that these responses will be reliable. And just to be clear, *reliable* doesn't mean *accurate*. *Reliable* means something doesn't fluctuate randomly. Thus, when we say you are a reliable rater of your own experiences or intentions, we do *not* mean that you are an accurate rater of your own personality or performance. If we ask you to rate yourself on performance or on growth orientation or on learning agility, you are most definitely *not* an accurate rater of these things—if these things even exist. Instead, all we mean is that you are a reliable rater of your own internal experiences and intentions. That's it.

• • •

Looking through this lens, we can now begin to answer the thorny question of how to measure knowledge-worker performance: we can use our reliability in reporting our experience and intended actions to design a different type of question. And the trick is to invert our line of inquiry. Rather than asking whether another person has a given quality, we need to ask how we would *react* to that other person if he or she did—we need to stop asking about others, and instead ask about ourselves. Once we've designed questions like this, we could then simply ask team leaders, every quarter or at the end of every project, what their experience was like of each team member. Here's what that would look like in practice.

We could ask a question about the quality of the team member's work, such as the one from earlier: "Do you always go to this team member when you need extraordinary results?"

We could ask another about how "team-y" a person was, not by asking the team leader to rate the person on collaboration or cooperation, but instead by asking the leader about what he would do, or how he would feel, were he in the presence of someone who was highly collaborative: "Do you choose to work with this team member as much as you possibly can?"

We could ask about the team member's future prospects. And here we would again steer clear of having the team leader rate the person on potential or some other abstract characteristic. Instead we'd ask about intent, like this: "Would you promote this person today if you could?"

And finally, we'd probably want to ask the team leader if there was anything in the person's work to be concerned about, with a question such as this: "Do you think this person has a performance problem that you need to address immediately?"

Here we have four questions, each asking the team leader to tell us about the team leader's own feelings and intended actions.[10] Now, the responses to these questions are not a perfect measure of each team member's complete performance—there is no way to get at that, or even define it—but they do give us a reliable view of what every single team leader feels about every single team member, and what each intends to do with each.

We tend to think that subjectivity in data is a bug, and that the feature we're after is objectivity. Actually, however, when it comes to measurement, the pursuit of objectivity is the bug, and reliable subjectivity the feature. These questions generate reliable (and subjective) data, and while this isn't everything, it's a lot. In the same way that measuring a person's weight doesn't give a complete measure of his health but does at least give a reliable measure of something that is clearly part of health, these four items allow us to see, reliably, something that is clearly part of performance.

We might observe here, by the way, that the question "what is performance?" is exactly as abstract, and about as helpful, as the question "what is health?" We don't actually try to measure health today—we use a series of discrete measures instead. We can ask if your Body Mass Index (BMI) is too high. We can ask about your glucose levels. We can measure your recovery rate after exercise. And we can do something with the information that we gather, because its specificity leads to further helpful inquiry and action—whereas deciding that you rated a 4 on health wouldn't be much use at all. The key to understanding performance is to stop thinking of it as a broad abstraction, and instead start finding elements of it that we can measure reliably and act on usefully.

Of course, we might worry that some team leaders lack sound judgment. But we will never be able to find a valid, data-based way to identify which leaders should be trusted and which shouldn't, so the best course of action is simply to ask every team leader to answer these questions, or some like them, about every team member, every quarter. Then, at every talent review we would know that we were looking at precisely what every team leader feels about and would do with every team member. This is a humbler claim for the data to make, but because we have set our sights on what is measurable, not on what is True, we can be certain of what we have. This is what reliable performance data should look like.

Well, actually, this is what reliable performance data *does* look like. Here are the answers to the first two of our questions—the question about extraordinary results and the question about working with a team member as much as possible—from a group of team leaders at Cisco (see figure 6-1). For both of these questions, Cisco has applied an algorithm that controls for each team leader's unique rating "fingerprint"—whether he or she rates more leniently or more strictly, and whether his or her use of the scale is broad or narrow—so that this data is capturing as precisely as possible what each team leader thinks.

As you can see, beyond their reliability, these questions also create natural variation. Cisco doesn't need to force the curve, because the team leaders' answers to these carefully worded questions create unforced range.

Armed with this humble, reliable, real-world data, Cisco is now able to start answering some fun questions, and then acting on the answers. The company now has reliable, variable, and valid data at the individual level on both performance and engagement, and so can start

FIGURE 6-1

Distribution of standardized scores

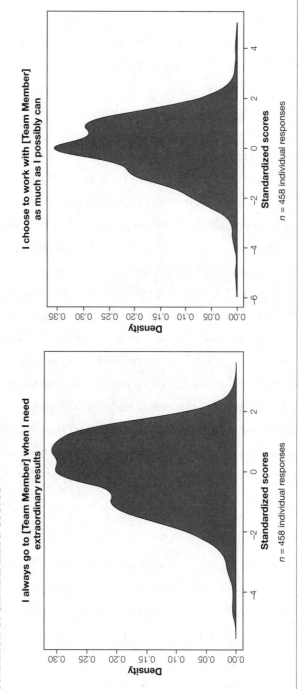

looking for connections between the two. And Cisco has discovered, for example, that when team members feel strongly that they understand what's expected of them, that they get to use their strengths frequently, that they will be recognized for great work, and that they're constantly challenged to grow (that is, when they have high scores on the "Me" engagement questions we saw in chapter 1), then their team leader, independently and without knowing their engagement scores, will tend to give them a higher score on the first performance question—will tend, in other words, to go to them more often for excellent work.

Further, when team members feel strongly that they are surrounded by people who share their values and that their teammates have their back (two of the "We" engagement questions), then their team leader, again independently and without knowing their scores, will tend to give them a higher score on the second performance question—will tend to look to work with them as often as possible. All of which might seem like research esoterica, until you're a team leader wanting to raise someone's individual contribution—in which case you should talk to him or her about expectations, strengths, recognition, and growth)—or until you're a team leader wanting to raise someone's team contribution—in which case you should talk to him or her, and the entire team, about what excellence means to all of you, and how everyone can support one another in all the things you're doing.*

• • •

We began this chapter by asking you how you can be confident that the truth of you is in the room during the talent review—how you can be confident that decisions about your pay, your next role, your promotion, and your career are being made based on a true understanding of who you are.

---

*We've included more of Cisco's and ADP's research findings in the appendixes, for those of you who want to learn more.

But actually, you don't want the truth of you in the room.

You don't want someone to be in any room pretending that they have a reliable measure of *who you are*. In the same way that you hated your singular performance rating—you were never just a 3, because you were never just a number—so you will come to despise the newer tools that now claim, ever more loudly, to capture all your essential competencies. They don't, and they never will: they simply add gasoline to the conflagration of bad data purporting to represent you. Any tool that pretends to reveal *who you are* is false.

What you want in the room is different: not the truth of you, but just the truth. You don't want to be represented by data that attempts, arrogantly, to divine who you are. Instead, you want to be represented by data that simply, reliably, and humbly captures the reaction of your team leader to you. That's not you, and it shouldn't pretend to be you. It's your leader, and what she feels, and what she would do in the future. And that's enough. Truly.

LIE #7

People have potential

Joe's an entrepreneurial sort. In the early days of the internet, he founded a pioneering yellow-pages company that integrated directory listings with mapping technology, and managed to secure backing from a venture-capital firm. The investors came in and, as is the practice of such firms, evaluated all the existing executives on their potential for guiding the future of the company. Sadly for Joe, they decided that he didn't have much of it. He had never displayed leadership in his high school or college life, he wasn't class president or captain of the lacrosse team, and now, looking at his current work and style, they determined that he lacked the potential to set the future vision and to build the right team around him. They demoted him to head programmer, and brought in a professional executive to run the company.

Joe didn't shine in this new role either. He had some software skills, but they were unpredictable, resulting in a mess of spaghetti code that other, more experienced developers had to pull apart and detangle. In fact, so messy were his creations that the entire code base of the company's product had to be rewritten. Everyone agreed that although

Joe clearly had drive, he would never become one of the company's leading software engineers. He just didn't have enough potential.

Becoming increasingly frustrated with his diminished position, and sensing that the investors didn't see much of a future for him, Joe waited for the company to be acquired and then left to start his own financial-services company. Here, he did what he'd always done—worked hard, pushed hard, challenged everything—and his new company grew large enough that an even bigger player swooped in and bought it from him.

The leaders of this new company, too, were unimpressed with his potential—or confused by it, or something—so he left once more, this time to see whether he could do interesting work in the fields of mechanical and electrical engineering. The jury is still out on his new ventures, and real profits have yet to show up on the books, but with him at the helm, his companies currently employ hundreds of people and are making truly innovative products. If he hadn't done what he did, these jobs wouldn't exist, and neither would the products. And in this sense, Joe is exactly what we want a team leader to be: a person who makes the most of his unique strengths and thereby creates a better future for all of us.

Joe's experience is relevant here because this chapter is all about the future. Specifically, it's about your future, and the future of everyone on your team—and about all the Joes out there in teams large and small, who are misunderstood by their companies, mislabeled, mismanaged, and, in the end, missed altogether.

• • •

Just for a moment, think of all the people on your team. Bring to mind each of their faces and names. Imagine what they're working on now, how they like to work, what they thrive at doing, what they struggle with, and what they aspire to. And now, if you can, answer this: Which one of them has the greatest potential?

Sooner or later in your time as a team leader, you'll be asked this exact question and told to plot your response on the *potential* axis of your nine-box grid. And as you ponder your answer, you'll pretty quickly run into some challenges. You might be quite clear that Jack is doing really well in his job today, but find yourself unsure of whether that means he has potential. And you might be equally certain that Jill is also doing well, but at the same time realize that her job is very different from Jack's job. If one of them has potential, does the other? If, as seems to be implied, potential is some sort of universal quality, then how should you gauge it in two different people doing two different jobs?

And what if Jill is in fact struggling in her current role? You might start to ask yourself whether current performance is the same as future potential or merely a clue to it, or whether, alarmingly, the two are not related at all. Perhaps you'll think to yourself that Jill might have, hidden somewhere within her, the potential to do really well at something else. You might not ponder this for long, though, because if (like Joe) she seems to lack potential in one role, and then subsequently another, it will be quite hard to convince yourself that she does indeed have potential for an entirely different role. If she's struggling now, then won't she struggle wherever she goes?

Even if she isn't struggling, if she is in fact one of your current high performers, she nonetheless wants to be challenged to grow, so you'll be forced to start thinking about other jobs on other teams, jobs she might do equally well—or even better. And when she starts asking you about her future—as she surely will—you'll quickly find yourself peering out into the fog. Since you're not nearly as familiar with those other jobs on those other teams as you are with those on your own team, how can you truly know if she has the potential to excel elsewhere? As a good team leader, you have a pretty clear sense of her present performance—what's in front of you right now—but being asked to weigh her potential requires you to project out into a world you know much less about.

This can be quite intimidating, not least because you're aware that how you weigh Jill's potential—specifically, how you rate it—will more than likely stick to her for a long time. If you rate her highly, then the received wisdom, passed on to your fellow team leaders, will be that she is now a "high potential," or "hi-po," and she will carry this quality around with her wherever she goes. She will get more attention from these other team leaders, be given more opportunities, more training, more investment, and if ever her performance falters, more benefit of the doubt. On the flip side, you realize that if you rate her poorly on potential, she'll become a proverbial "lo-po," which will be a tough label to shake off, no matter how hard she tries.

Your rating of her on potential, or more accurately, your guess about how much value she will bring to the company in the future, will, in all sorts of real ways, *create* her future. That's a lot of responsibility for you to bear.

Jill, meanwhile, perhaps aware that there's another talent review in the offing, is wondering whether she'll make the hi-po list. Like you, she isn't sure what potential is, or what a high potential is. She's just trying to do good work every day. She knows that potential is clearly a good thing to possess—it comes with all sorts of goodies and perks—but, at heart, what she really wants to know is whether she's doing well enough in her job right now, and where her career is going next. If your rating of her on potential helps her career, then wonderful—but if it doesn't, or if being branded a lo-po makes getting help with her future less likely, then she's going to be frustrated. There's a great deal at stake for her here. At some point, she will ask you what you rated her, and then you'll somehow have to justify your decision. And this will be super tricky, since, in the back of your mind, you'll know that you weren't so very clear what potential was in the first place, nor what clues might point you to it, nor what scale you should have used to rate her on it.

But that's a worry for later. Right now you'll look around and see that other team leaders on other teams seem able to announce confidently who has potential on each of their teams, so you'll put Jill's inevitable questions out of mind, pull out your nine-box grid, and do your best to do right by her. And her future.

. . .

Of course, you can't really blame your company for putting you into this sort of high-pressure situation. As with all the practices we've covered thus far in the book, assigning a "potential" rating to each employee is a product of some very good and necessary intentions. Your company is a maximization machine—it wants to make the best use of its finite resources—so it is greatly interested in identifying precisely who to invest in, and how.

The problem with this stems from the way your company executes on these good intentions. Why, for example, does it assume that it will net a good return only from certain people? Surely, the cliché that "Our people are our greatest asset" applies to *all* of the people in the company. As we've seen, every human brain retains its ability to learn and grow throughout adulthood. For sure, each brain grows at a different speed and in a different way, but this implies only that each person learns differently, not that—categorically—some people do and some don't. Therefore, the best course of action for any maximization machine worth its salt would be to figure out where and how each brain can grow the most, rather than zeroing in on only a select few brains and casting aside the others.

But sadly, somewhere along the line, companies by and large recoiled from this natural diversity, seeing it as simply too varied and too individualized to make sense of, and decided instead that the most pragmatic approach would be to invent a generic quality called "potential," rate every person on it, and then invest most in those who have lots of it, and much less in those who don't. As with all the lies we've addressed in the book so far, the lie that *people have potential* is a product of organizations' desire for control, and their impatience with individual differences.

When you think about it for a moment, the notion of a generic quality called "potential" is actually pretty odd. Look around you and you'll find hundreds of different definitions, but there's no need to look any further than *Harvard Business Review*'s very own:

> High potentials consistently and significantly outperform
> their peer groups in a variety of settings and circumstances.
> While achieving these superior levels of performance, they
> exhibit behaviors that reflect their companies' culture and
> values in an exemplary manner. Moreover, they show a
> strong capacity to grow and succeed throughout their careers
> within an organization—more quickly and effectively than
> their peer groups do.[1]

This seems like an eminently desirable quality. Who wouldn't want people who "outperform their peer groups," not just in their current role but "in a variety of settings"; who, in addition to performing with excellence, also "reflect their companies' culture and values"; and who, all the while, show "a strong capacity to grow"? We all would, of course—high-performing, culture-embodying people blessed with oodles of learning agility and lashings of successitude are the stuff of every team leader's dreams.

And yet, this definition almost immediately rings hollow for you. First, there's the feeling that, although you might want such a person on your team, you don't recognize yourself in the definition. When you think about yourself at your best, you land on specific activities you love, or skills at which you shine—whereas in contrast, this definition appears strangely vague, untethered from any actual work. And then there's the part of the description that seems to imply that you can excel anywhere, at virtually anything, "in a variety of settings and circumstances." Not only is this unlikely, but more to the point, who among us actually aspires to this sort of Jack-of-all-trades-ness? If we were to have this quality it would imply, surely, that we were not unique and distinct, but instead were empty learning vessels, blank slates waiting for our settings and circumstances to define us, adept at learning, but featureless. How depressing.

Beyond the disquieting emptiness of this definition, the most damaging inference is that this quality called "potential" is inherent in a person, and that people bring it with them from situation to situation: that no matter what "setting or circumstance" they encounter, those people with lots of it are blessed with a special power enabling them to learn faster, grow more, and achieve more. High potential is the corporate equivalent of Willy Wonka's Golden Ticket: you take it with you wherever you go, and it grants you powers and access denied to the rest of us.

In chapter 4 we drew the distinction between traits, which are inherent in a person, and states, which are changeable in the person. Using this framing, potential is clearly something we think of as a trait—it is inherent in the person, some people have more of it than others, and those who do take it everywhere with them.*

Assuming just for the moment that potential actually is a trait, the first problem we encounter is how to measure it. As we saw earlier, if we want to measure a trait, we can't ask someone to rate you on it, because it's impossible for any rater to be either perceptive enough or objective enough to reach into your psyche and assign a number to what they see inside you. And in the case of potential, the measurement challenge is orders of magnitude more difficult, since we are asking the rater to rate you not on a trait displayed in your current behavior but on a projection, a probability that you possess something

---

*Although we might question why, if it's a trait and doesn't therefore change much, we re-rate people on it every year.

that might just possibly be displayed in some future situation. It's flat-out impossible for the rater to do this reliably, so whatever data he produces about you will be the very worst kind of bad data. Yet this data will, as we saw with Jill, create the future.

But is there even anything here to measure—is potential a thing at all? Do we really think that there exists in people a trait that confers on some lucky few the ability to grow more and learn more regardless of setting or circumstance? That we could throw this hi-po into any situation and his potential would enable him to adapt, and then thrive? That this general potential will act like a turbocharger, and take any inputs from the world of work and boost them into outstanding performance?

If we do think this, then we do so in the complete absence of any evidence. Over the last hundred years we've wondered whether there was such a thing as general intelligence—the elusive *g* factor—and discovered that if it exists, we can't find it. Sure, we can build a test that reliably measures a thing called IQ, but we don't actually know much about what IQ is—it doesn't seem to independently predict educational success, career achievement, health, or happiness.[2] It's just a score on a test. The best this test can do, it appears, is tell us that, if your test score is very low, you probably have cognitive impairment and will therefore have difficulty learning. So it works as a predictor of problems but not as a predictor or descriptor of flourishing.

Likewise, evidence for the existence of general potential is nonexistent. Instead the evidence points in exactly the opposite direction. We know that each person's brain grows by adding more synaptic connections, that each person's synaptic pattern is unique, and that therefore each person's brain grows uniquely. Therefore we know a) that the ability to learn exists in us all, b) that it shows up differently in each of us, and c) that while we can all get better at anything, none of us will ever be able to rewire our brains to excel at everything. More simply, we can all get better, and we will all get better at different things, in different ways, and at different speeds.

. . .

So there is no such thing as having potential. Or rather, there is, but it doesn't mean anything. Or rather, it doesn't mean anything beyond being a human. To say that you have potential means simply that you have the capacity to learn, and grow, and get better, like every other human. Unfortunately, this won't reveal anything about precisely where you can learn, and grow, and get better, or how, or how fast, or under what conditions. Potential, like being human, doesn't tell us anything about what particular human you are, or what direction would be best for your sort of human in the future. And, of course, if having potential is just being a human, then we can't rate you on it. We can't split our company up into hi-po's and lo-po's, any more than we can rate you on your human-ness and give the most stuff to those who are most human and the least to those are who least human.

This sort of apartheid does terrible things to a company. The careless and unreliable labeling of some folks as hi-po's and others as lo-po's is deeply immoral. It explicitly stamps large numbers of people with a "less than" branding, derived not from a measure of current performance but from a rater's hopelessly unreliable rating of a thing that isn't a thing. And then this rating of a thing-that-isn't-a-thing opens doors for some, confers prestige on some, elevates some, blesses some, and sets them up for a brighter future, all while relegating others to a status less than human. How explicitly awful.

It is also unproductive. The maximization machine should make the most of every single human within it, not just a rarefied subset. This notion that some people have lots of potential, while others don't, leads us to miss the gloriously weird possibilities lying hidden in each and every team member, even the ones who, at first blush, seem to have little to offer the team's future. If we have in our head a preconceived notion—even, as in the case of the *Harvard Business Review* definition, a detailed description—of what a hi-po should do, feel like, and act like, then we will cease to be curious about the many possible futures of each idiosyncratic person on our team.

This, certainly, is what happened to Joe's employers. They had a set idea of what a high-potential CEO should look like, and what a high-potential software engineer should look like, and neither of them looked like Joe. They stopped looking at Joe, became impatient with him, diminished his role, eased him off to the sidelines, and were more than happy when he decided that his most interesting and challenging work lay elsewhere.

And that's a shame for them, because "Joe" is a pseudonym. His real name is Elon.[3] That yellow-pages company was acquired by Compaq for $307 million. The financial-services company, X.com, became better known as PayPal and sold to eBay for $15 billion. At which point you may say, "Yes, but have you seen what he's done lately?" and reference his fining by the SEC, his joint-puffing on a podcast, and any number of other transgressions that may have occurred from the time of our writing to the time of your reading. And our reply would be, "Yes, but have you seen what he's done lately?" and we'd reference his reinvention of the automobile industry, his reinvigoration of the space industry, and his counterintuitive alarm-sounding of the dangers of AI. As the *New York Times* put it immediately after the 2018 SEC action against Musk was concluded, "The Future of Electric Cars Is Brighter with Elon Musk in It."[4] Yes, he is the spikiest sort of leader, given to impulsive and imperfect actions, but to dismiss his potential is to miss pretty much everything meaningful about him. He may be a handful, and intemperate in his tweeting, but if Elon Musk wasn't a high potential, then it's time to admit that the concept serves no purpose.

• • •

Yet still you are going to be asked by your company to rate people on their potential, and by your team members to guide them toward ever-more-challenging work. So what on earth do you do? How can you honor your company's need to get the most from each person, and yet not segregate your team into artificial and demeaning categories, such as hi-po's and lo-po's?

You can start by taking a trip to the north coast of Scotland. Imagine, for a moment, that you've settled down in a small village just outside Inverness, and have opened up a hot-air-balloon sightseeing business. Your business has done well—all those lovely Scottish moors to gaze down upon—and your team has grown to five excellent hot-air-balloon pilots. One of them is named Maureen. She comes up to you one drizzly afternoon and says, "I love my current job, but I want to continue to grow. I want to stay challenged, round out my résumé, have more to offer. I think I want to become a glider pilot. Can you help me?"

What do you say?

Well, here's what you don't say. You don't say, "Maureen, do you have enough potential?" Nor do you say, "Maureen, do you have enough potential as a glider pilot?" You do not say these things because these are not things human beings say to other human beings in the real world.

Instead, whether consciously or unconsciously, you'll find yourself asking her two discrete sets of questions. And what's interesting about these two sets of questions is that they lead us away from generic potential and toward a far more useful concept for helping us understand Maureen, and for guiding her career.

The first set of questions will focus on who Maureen is as a person. You'll find yourself asking her, "What do you love most about your job right now, Maureen? What do you love most about ballooning? Do you love the piloting part, the thrill of the lift, the sensation of getting airborne; or do you love the navigating part, the movement of the light-as-air balloon through the cold northern winds, the calibration of the flame to achieve just the right altitude; or do you love the part where you show the guests the sights and get to tell them interesting facts they may not have known about this part of the world?" You'll ask her about what job she thinks she might want next, and what it is about being a glider pilot that she thinks she might enjoy. You might even ask her what her "perfect job" would look like. Each of these questions addresses who Maureen is as a person, what she loves, what she's really into, and what she yearns for in terms of her career. You're basically being curious about the specifics of what it's like to be Maureen-at-work.

The second set of things you'll ask her about will focus on how she's moved through the world thus far, and what she's picked up along the way. You'll ask her about her current performance: how many balloon trips she completes and how many guests she takes up in a month. You'll ask her about her past performance: you'll want to find out how long she's been a balloon pilot, how many hours she's logged, what her safety record has been, how often she is able to put her balloon down within the designated landing range. And then you'll get into her skills, not by asking about ratings and 360-degree scores—no one in the real world asks about such things—but instead by asking if she has her level-one, -two, and -three certifications for hot-air-balloon piloting, whether she has extended this to completing her giant-hydrogen-filled-airship certification (in your mind you might call this the Hindenburg test), and, of course, whether she has her glider-pilot's license. And with each of these questions, you'll learn more about how Maureen has moved through the world—what she has measurably achieved, and measurably learned.

From the answers to these two sets of questions, you'll have discovered, first, who Maureen is at work. These are her traits. These are things that are inherent and enduring in her—not entirely unchanging, but nonetheless resistant to change. These are the loves and aspirations that are uniquely hers, and that she carries around with her everywhere she goes, just as surely as she carries her own body. Wherever she goes, they are there. You can call these her *mass*.

And second, you'll have unearthed some things she's acquired as she's applied herself in the world to move in a particular direction: her current and past record of performance, and her tested certifications. Obviously, since she can change any and all of these things, these are states. But since they describe how she has moved through the world—how she's done it, how well she's done it, how quickly, and in what direction—you can usefully label these her *velocity*.

In the world of physics, there's a name for the discrete, measurable, definable, and directional thing that is produced when mass and velocity combine. It's called momentum. In the world of teams and team members, the same applies. Maureen has *momentum*.

By keeping these two ideas about Maureen—mass and velocity— separate, and by using *momentum* to describe their combination, we suddenly enable you, the team leader, to do all manner of useful things to help her.

First, you reject the apartheid of potential, where everyone is separated into hi-po and lo-po. "Do you or don't you have potential?" is a question that exists to serve the (well-meaning but misguided) company. But it's not helpful to you as a team leader, and it's completely uninteresting and unhelpful to Maureen. Because she knows it's not a matter of *whether* she can learn and grow, but *how*, and how efficiently, and in what direction. Only certain people have "potential"; *everyone* has momentum. One team member's might be more powerful than another's, or speedier than another's, or pointed in a different direction, but everyone has some. The question isn't whether you inherently possess a lot of it or not. Instead, when it comes to momentum, the question is how much of it you have at this very moment, right now.

Second, you convey to her something real: namely, that the speed and trajectory of her momentum at this very moment are a) knowable, b) changeable, and c) within her control. When you talk to her about her momentum, you help her to understand where she is at this moment in time, not so that she can be catalogued and categorized and put into one box instead of another, but so that she can understand what paths are possible next. Her career is moving on a particular trajectory at a particular speed, and she—with your help—can take the measure of her accomplishments, her loves and loathes, her skills and knowledge, and see where she can accelerate, or shift the path slightly, or even attempt a great leap. Where potential is assumed to be a fixed, inherent quality—she's a hi-po or a lo-po—momentum is, by definition, always in a state of change. And if Maureen wants to speed it up, or alter its direction, she can.

Third, you help her identify which parts of her current career are a function of who she is as a person—parts she will therefore likely bring with her, situation to situation—and which parts are entirely situation-dependent, and which she could change if she so chose. Given how close we all are to our own performance, and given that we are sometimes misguided in our career desires, this kind of subtle and specific insight could very well prevent her from making an ill-advised career move.

Finally, understanding Maureen's career in terms of momentum doesn't just benefit her. It frees you, as her team leader, from the awful burden of having to determine her entire future based on a fiction.

It's not true—or, indeed, useful—to think that *people have potential*. Instead, the truth is that *people have momentum*.

Potential is a one-sided evaluation. Momentum is an ongoing conversation. In a world of "potential," it's hard to imagine what, exactly, a career conversation looks like once Maureen has been shunted off into the lo-po dungeon. Momentum, on the other hand, represents the opposite of "up-or-out" thinking. And it's the best concept to address one of the key survey items that measure engagement and performance: "In my work, I am always challenged to grow." Potential doesn't do that—it doesn't challenge you to grow. It tells you that you either will, or you won't.

Addressing their potential makes people feel like they've been dealt with. Addressing their momentum makes them feel *understood*. More important, it helps them understand themselves, by encouraging them to consider where they are, right now—not as a point of stasis, but as a unique human being moving purposefully through the world.

. . .

But if this sort of straightforward conversation about the future is what is happening in the real world, we might well ask how we came to be ensnared in the bizarre apartheid-creating theory world of potential. And again, the lie that *people have potential* is another example of a specific and useful thing made generalized and useless. In this case, it's perfectly fair to ask if Maureen has the "small-p" potential to do a certain job well. But as soon as we divorce the idea of Maureen's potential from the very specific demands and rewards of a particular job—as soon, that is, as we stop asking about who Maureen is, and where she's going, and how those things mesh with what she might do next—and instead treat her potential as some abstract, mystical, and essential quality of hers that we can isolate and rate her on, then we slide down the slippery slope into untruth. And if we then institutionalize this thinking through our people-management processes and systems in the name of bringing predictability and control to our organization, we find that we have sacrificed common sense and humanity at the altar of corporate uniformity, and we shouldn't be very surprised if our people chafe at the result. We may well also find that we've created a system that codifies and amplifies our biases and projections—that the people with the most "potential" inevitably wind up looking and acting a lot like us.

Our people tools and processes can never compensate for bad team leaders. We like to think so—we figure that, even if your team leader is ignoring you, at least your crowd-sourced feedback will tell you how you're doing; or that, even if your team leader never asks about your career, at least the talent review will give you something to go on. But aside from the flaws that we've already seen with these and other common approaches, any large-scale system can never hope to replicate the very particular and specific attention that a team leader can offer. Again, teams are where we live, and team leaders can make or break that experience for us. And rather than investing in systems and processes to provide a fallback in case our managers are found wanting, it's far better to invest in helping our team leaders do what we need them to, by 1) getting rid of ratings of "potential," 2) teaching team leaders what we know about human growth, and 3) prompting them to discuss careers with their people in terms of momentum—in terms of who each team member is, and in terms of how fast each is moving through the world. This is harder, of course, than buying the latest piece of enterprise software and then imploring our people to use it, but it's the right hard thing to do.

Because when team leaders understand how careers are built in the real world, they begin to think like Andy.

Andy is a team leader at Cisco, and a little while ago he set out to help each of his team members see what their futures could look like. He started by asking them to imagine their dream jobs—in other words, to reflect on their aspirations—and then to make this practical by searching on LinkedIn. The task he set them was to split into pairs, and then to spend two hours searching on LinkedIn for jobs that came close to their ideal—with no limit on which company, or industry, or line of work these jobs were in. He asked them to work with their partner to narrow down the list to the one or two roles that excited them the most.

And then he asked them to analyze these jobs in terms of the skills and experiences and qualifications they drew on, and then to compare those lists with the skills and experiences and qualifications that each of them already had, and to figure out which new ones they wanted to go after.

He wasn't, in other words, evaluating them on their potential, and sorting them into those who could grow in some way and those who couldn't. Instead, he was helping each of them to get clear on who they were and where they wanted to go (again, *mass*), and on the measurable skills and experiences they had and wanted to acquire (again, *velocity*). His presumption was that everyone had momentum, and that it was his job to help them figure out how to direct it. "I think there's a lot of energy within our teams that isn't being used," he told us, "and I have a lot of people who, given the right circumstances, the right engagements, the right customer—whatever it is, we can find what enables them to share that energy, to bring it out."

The results were fascinating. As Andy explained to us, "We looked around the room at each other and realized that our careers were bigger than Cisco, and that we could go further down those steps to define ourselves within the market as professionals." And more than this, his team members were able, with his encouragement, to make many of the skills they wanted to learn part of their current jobs— so that their work, every day, was helping them build the skills they wanted for the future. "It changed the conversation," Andy said, "from how we could get another job outside, to how we could build our practice to be the best professionals we could be—to deliver better service internally, but also to build up our transferrable skills."

And this, surely, is what any truly people-maximizing company would want.

LIE #8

Work-life balance matters most

Work is hard. Every day, you feel the stress of performing, of delivering against your goals and objectives, of earning enough to support your family, of learning how to advocate in just the right way to advance your career and thereby earn more. And always, hanging over your head, is the threat of change as your company shifts its focus, outsources your role, or finds a particularly smart machine that can do your job better, faster, and cheaper. And then there are the other people you have to work with—an ever changing cast of characters, some of whom work across the hall, others of whom work across the world, whose collaboration you seek, but whose motives and methods remain mysterious. The commute doesn't help: the daily battle with your fellow strivers on trains, planes, and freeways, everyone rushing in and rushing out, clogging the arteries of your city, raising your stress level. Forty-five minutes, an hour, ninety minutes each way—or a two-hour flight if you work for one of the big consultancies and have to show up at the client site—all just so you can begin your daily race of life-at-work. On the way home you steal a brief moment or two to decompress, and then, once home, you have a quick dinner with the family before dragging out the phone again for the evening volley of emails and texts, hoping to catch one last request so that it won't need immediate action before your shower in the morning.

Work is hard. Particularly, it seems, if you're a physician. We might think that doctors have it better than the rest of us because at least all that frenetic dashing about is in service of something truly meaningful—if we've learned anything about what we want from our world of work, it's that we crave work with meaning and purpose. And we imagine that, while doctors have to complete forms and wade through other assorted administrivia, they nevertheless see their patients, one after another, being cured and getting back on their feet again, all by dint of the doctor's efforts and expertise. Would that we all saw so clearly and so often the point of our work. Would that we could all do what we love.

When we look at the data, however, that's not what we see: despite the purity of their purpose, physicians seem to have it harder than the rest of us; or at least, they feel it harder. According to a recent report from the Mayo Clinic, 52 percent of physicians report being burned out, and their incidence of PTSD is 15 percent, four times the levels in the regular workforce and three percentage points higher than the levels found in veterans of the wars in Iraq and Afghanistan.[1] These sky-high stress levels inevitably have quantifiable and negative effects on both patient care and physician well-being. The Mayo Clinic found not only that a 1 percent increase in measured burnout led to a 20 to 30 percent decrease in patient satisfaction but, more worryingly still, that 15 percent of all doctors have issues with substance abuse during their careers, and that their rates of depression and suicide are twice the national levels.

According to doctors, things are only getting worse. The Mayo study further revealed that 80 percent of physicians believe the medical profession is on the decline, that 60 percent of all physicians will endure a professional lawsuit during their career, and most tellingly of all, that 73 percent of doctors would *not* recommend the medical profession to their children. As a result, if current trends continue, by the year 2025 the United States will experience a shortfall of more than twenty thousand physicians.

The only job harder than being a doctor—so the data tells us—is being an emergency-room nurse, which comes with higher levels of burnout and depression and (at 19 percent) almost twice the level of PTSD seen in combat veterans.

The health-care profession is taking this data seriously, and is devoting significant time and money to conferences, research, and practical experiments, all to figure out what's making work so demoralizing, and what can be done.

The prevailing approach will not surprise you. Though each health system differs in its methods and priorities, the basic assumption in most of these efforts is that these days being a doctor or a nurse is unavoidably hard, and that therefore the enlightened hospital should do whatever it can to help health-care professionals recover from the stress of work, and should also find ways to limit the work week to fewer than sixty hours—to provide some barrier against the ever rising tide of stress. Some health systems offer meditation rooms just off the ER, others provide support with all that electronic record keeping, still others pay for monthly meals out with colleagues and family.

With its stress levels and stress-related problems, the world of doctors and nurses serves as an extreme example of the rest of the working world. Work, our experience teaches us, is toil—a stressor, a drainer of our energy—and if we are not careful, it can lead to physical exhaustion, emotional emptiness, depression, and burnout. It's a transaction—we sell our time and our talent so that we can earn enough money to buy the things we love, and to provide for those we love. Indeed, the term we use for the money we earn in this transaction is *compensation*, the same word we use for what we get when we're injured or wronged in the eyes of the law. Our wages are not just money, then: they are money to make up for the inherent badness of work—a bribe, if you will, to tough it out.

Work is even a distraction from work. When we need to get something important done, we recognize that it will be hard to do unless we can somehow make our escape from the daily grind, and so we go on a leadership *retreat* to get away from the noise and stress of work, to better focus on other work.

And because the effects of work are so potentially toxic, the obvious and sensible precaution to take, so that we don't all expire at our desks, is to balance it out with something else, with something better. With *life*.

We lose ourselves in work, and rediscover ourselves in life. We *survive* work, but *live* life. When work empties us out, life fills us back up. When work depletes us, life restores us.

The answer to the problem of work, the world seems to say, is to balance it with life.

Of course, we are simplifying things here. Some people succeed in finding great satisfaction in their work, while others have hugely stressful lives outside of work. We know, too, that some jobs seem to be inherently difficult, or even inherently boring. No one's work, or life, is ever completely joyous, or completely controllable.

Yet still, the assumption that pervades our working world is that "work is bad" and "life is good," and therefore *work-life balance matters most.* "Does the company support work-life balance?" is right up there with "What's the company culture like?" in the list of questions candidates inevitably ask during the interviewing process—which explains why, in these tight labor markets, companies highlight their on-site dry-cleaning, banking, and child-care services, their quiet rooms, in-chair massages, sleep pods, and luxury shuttle buses. These perks are tremendously well intended and are often highly valued by employees—and at the same time are rooted in the idea that work is a heavy weight on the scales, and that the enlightened organization is one that does everything it can to lessen that weight, and thereby tip the scales back toward life.

· · ·

Good intentions aside, the problems with all this begin with the concept of *balance*—and it's a concept with a long history.

If you visit the Presidio of Santa Barbara—the fort the Spanish explorers built to support the Mission of Santa Barbara—you will see on the wall a list of the provisions the captain of the fort requested of his superiors in Mexico City. The date of the requisition list is 1793, and along with "Two pounds of gold musketeer braid, fine for epaulets," and "Two beaver hats; one black and one white," you'll find "Four pounds of rose oil, three ounces of Galapa powder, two ounces of sweet mercury, and one little box with twelve cupping glasses, filled with seedless cotton wool."

While some of these might have been used for making dessert, or drinking tea, their primary purpose was something else. From the time of the ancient Greek physician Hippocrates until the advent of modern medicine in the mid-nineteenth century, our concept of physical health was founded on the idea of balance. Hippocrates posited that each of us contained four humors—black bile, yellow bile, blood, and phlegm. Even though each of our bodies held slightly different amounts of each, which in turn created our different personalities (the phlegmatic person had an abundance of phlegm, the calm or "sanguine" person contained more blood), the healthy person was he or she who maintained the perfect balance between all four.

If your humors were out of whack, you fell ill, and so you were told to take sweet mercury to purge you of phlegm, or to use cupping glasses to draw out your blood. With your humors back in balance, your sickness would be cured and you would be well again. The requisition list on the wall of the fort was, then, a list of supplies for the pharmacy.

Over time, this emphasis on finding physical balance took on psychological overtones—if you were too short-tempered, it was because your yellow bile was out of balance; if you were lazy, you had a body overloaded with phlegm—and from there grew to become an explanation for the entire physical universe. The metaphysical extrapolation of the four humors was the four elements—earth, fire, water, air—each of which was believed to balance out the others in the harmony of creation.

All of which is to say that we humans appear to have had a thing for balance for a long, long while. To us it has always seemed like the right, the noble, the wise, and the healthy state for which we should all strive. And we can speculate that the difficulty of achieving it has added in some way to its allure—it's another of those things, like working to remedy our faults, that's always a work in progress, that's fantastically hard to achieve in practice. You've striven for it, haven't you? You've tried to find that delicate balance between the needs of yourself, your family, your friends, your work colleagues, your boss, and your community. You're aware that each of these constituencies places different and often conflicting demands on you, and you've struggled to give due attention to each one, satisfying their differing needs while still attending to your own. You've sat on a conference call in the car-pool line and mouthed "Sorry!" to the kids in the back. You've rationalized a missed Presidents' Day outing with the family because, well, it's a Monday, your other team members appear to be online, and besides, Presidents' Day isn't a proper holiday anyway, not really.

You've taken on a "stretch" assignment because it might—just might!—come with a raise, or at least a bonus, and so enable you to afford a better house for your family. But because you now have more work to do, and more resting on it, you've found that you can't attend that school-board meeting, or your cousin's wedding, or that online management course, because life is about trade-offs and this one is yours.

You've found yourself spinning plates, or juggling balls, or plugging gaps—whatever the metaphor, you've known too often the feeling of too many requests from too many quarters and not enough hours in the day. You've told yourself that if you can just keep the plates spinning, the balls in the air, the gaps plugged, then perhaps you can parcel out your attention and energy so that no one, in your work or your life, will feel too neglected—so that, although you can't be all things to all people, your unflagging efforts will at least achieve some sort of equitable distribution.

But in the real world does anyone, anywhere, man or woman, young or old, affluent or barely solvent, ever actually find balance?

If any have, we haven't met them yet. And this is why balance is more bane than benefit. In practice, striving for it feels like triage, like trying to erect some sort of barricade against the endless encroachments on our time and the relentless ratcheting of expectations to work more, all while worrying that someone else has figured out how to do this better than we have. Obviously, triage can be necessary in life, but it surely is not enough—it keeps things at bay, but it takes us away from ourselves. And in the end, balance is an unachievable goal anyway, because it asks us to aim for momentary stasis in a world that is ever changing. Supposing we ever get things just exactly in balance, we know for sure that something will come along and unbalance them and that we'll be back to pushing our balance rock up the hill again. Balance as an ideal erases our humanity— the essence of who each of us is and aspires to be—and replaces it with a Sisyphean coping strategy.

So what then should we do? Work can be hard. So can life. And there's too much of both, too much of the time. If balancing everything out isn't the answer, then what is?

We need a new way of thinking. About work. About life.

• • •

Throughout this book we've found our answers by trying to examine the world as it really is, rather than as we wish it were. While initially it might seem that certain elements need to be in balance (acidity or insulin levels in the body, for example), when we look more closely what we find is flow. Today we know that all matter is made up of infinitely more particles than four, and that the balance between these millions of particles is far less important than the ongoing relationship between them all and the biological, chemical, and physical processes that these relationships create. Something can be said to be "healthy" only when its process allows it to take inputs from the world, and first, metabolize them to produce something useful, and second, do so in such a way that it can keep doing it. Health is less balance than it is motion.

You are one such process. Neither you nor your life are in balance, nor will you ever be. Instead you are a unique creature who takes inputs from the world, metabolizes them in some way, produces something useful, and does so in such a way that you can keep doing it. At least, you are when you're healthy, when you're at your best, when you are contributing all that your talents allow you to. When you're flourishing you are acting on the world and it on you. Your world offers up to you raw material—activities, situations, outcomes—in all parts of your life, and some of this raw material invigorates you and gives you energy. You are at your healthiest when you find this particular kind of raw material, draw it in, allow it to feed you, and use it to contribute something—and when that contribution actually seems to leave you with more energy, not less.

This state, not balance, is what we should strive for. What should we call it?

The Greeks called it *eudaimonia*, which sounds like a cleaning product but which actually means "the fullest and purest expression of you in your most elevated state." Their idea was that each of us had a spirit, or *daimon*, that embodied our greatest and most unique possibilities—our natural strengths or talents—and that the state we should all seek was one where, because of the happy intersection of our role, our skills, our team, and our context, we turned these possibilities into contribution, and thus liberated our good spirit.

We could stick with the Greeks and *eudaimonia*, but while the word captures the meaning quite well, it's a bit of a mouthful. So let's play out what this state actually looks like in the real world, a world so busy and distracted that it doesn't seem much concerned with your particular *daimon*, and see if that helps us find something a little more down-to-earth.

Miles is a physician. More specifically he's an anesthesiologist, the chap who puts you to sleep and wakes you up again. He lives in the United Kingdom, where anesthesiologists are called anesthetists. He loves what he does and has been at it for twenty years. Tens of thousands of his colleagues may be struggling with burnout, but he seems to revel in his work.

We were interviewing him the other day, trying to figure out how a regular doctor working in a regular ward of a regular National Health Service teaching hospital could find a state of mind and heart that has eluded so many other physicians, when we made a rude discovery: Miles doesn't like sick people. To be more specific, he doesn't seem to get much of a kick out of helping sick people get better.

Here's what this discovery sounded like in our interview:

Marcus and Ashley: So, Miles, is there anything about your role that brings you down, or frustrates you?

Miles: Other than the hours?

Us: Yes. Anything in the work itself?

Miles: Well, I really don't like the follow-up.

Us: Pardon?

Miles: Yeah, I really don't like meeting up with the patients after the operation, seeing how they're doing, checking up on their recovery, giving them a few things they can do at home to alleviate their symptoms, and then meeting up again after a bit to track their progress. Don't like any of that at all.

Us: [*pause*] But isn't that what being a doctor is?

Miles: Not for me it's not.

Us: What don't you like about that?

Miles: The pressure.

Us: Pressure?

Miles: Yes, the pressure to make them get well. I mean, what if they don't? The body is a complex and individualized organism, so many variables, and then you combine that with a patient's lifestyle, environment, psychology, luck, and who knows if they are really going to get better. It's just too much pressure for me.

Us: Oh.

So that's what it sounded like: a very successful, truly happy doctor revealing to us that the thing he is most stressed about at work is seeing whether his patients actually recover. Since this flew in the face of pretty much everything we'd read on physician satisfaction—namely that doctors, like people in all professions, should "start with why" and should derive most of their joy at work from seeing their true purpose come to life—we pressed on.

Us: Then can you tell us what you do truly enjoy about what you do?

Miles: Sure. Well, first off, I love the stress.

Us: What? Didn't you just say you didn't like stress?

Miles: No, I said I didn't like the pressure of making a patient get better over time. I absolutely love the stress of keeping a patient hovering between life and death. We still know so little about how anesthesia actually works. When I first started, we used mostly thiopental. Nowadays everyone goes with that new drug propofol—the one that Michael Jackson took, which is actually a far better drug. And yet no one really knows how it all works. Both drugs seem to slow down the flow of minerals through the blood system, and so put you to sleep without stopping your heart, but we still don't know much about how either one actually does that. The whole challenge of putting someone to sleep, and keeping them hovering there, caught between life and death, for sometimes sixteen hours at a time, all the while not quite knowing how or why it's working—man, I love that!

Us: Have you always loved that part of it?

Miles: Yep, right from the start. Some people freak out when you have to put someone under and then gradually ease them back to life, but I always leaned into that. I'm something of an adrenaline junkie—swim with sharks, jump out of planes, that kind of thing—so this part of it really wakes me up, makes me feel alive.

Us: Anything else you love?

Miles: Well, yeah. Frankly, it's the responsibility of the role. In the UK—less in the US and Canada—but in the UK the person who is supposed to understand the entire body of each patient is the anesthetist. The surgeon can fix the heart valves. The neurologist can tease apart the brain. The general surgeon can maneuver the bowels—all critical stuff, but all very focused and specialized. The doc who needs to understand the entire body—the entire respiratory, cardiovascular system, gastrointestinal, everything—is the anesthetist. All of those systems feed into how a patient will respond to the drugs and how he or she will hover asleep. Because when you're under, you're never just under. You're always moving up or moving down, and my job is to be finely attuned to the entire person, and to understand their entire body so well I can hold them just so. Being an anesthetist is rather like flying a plane—one wrong move and you can start to spiral down, and then another slight mistake, and then the spirals speed up, and in an instant you can find your patient spiraling down, down and away from you. I love that kind of responsibility—twelve people in the OR and all of them relying on you to know the whole person, and hold the whole person.

Us: It sounds terrifying.

Miles: No, really, it's amazing. Every day. Just love it.

We don't know what you make of all this, but we did what we always do in interviews with people who thrive at work: we listened in the moment, wrote it all down, and then pondered it later.

And where we landed was that, as ever, the theoretical models of what people are supposed to feel about their work rarely, if ever, match up to what a particular person truly does feel. Miles is a brilliant and successful doctor who hates the pressure of helping someone get well, and yet loves the life-and-death stress of holding a patient just outside death's door, all while not fully understanding precisely how he's doing it. Some might judge Miles and say, "Well, all doctors should love seeing patients get healthy. That, after all, is the purpose of being a doctor." And yet what use is that judgment? Miles is Miles. He knows not only why he became a doctor, and why he became an anesthetist, but also what specific aspects of being an anesthetist he loves most. Others can judge all they want, but we know which doctor we would want putting us under. We'd want a doctor who derived great joy from what he did, who was fascinated by the subtle complexity of his responsibilities, and who got his kicks from keeping us just this side of the river Styx. We'd want Miles.

And so, doubtless, would you.

We wish you could have been there to actually hear him talk, because when he does, his whole tone and demeanor shift and lift, and when he starts diving into what he loves about what he does, you sense you're in the presence of a special state of mind, a truly happy heart, a "good spirit." Would that all doctors could feel this way.

And would that *you* felt this way about your work. You know you want to. You listen to folks such as Miles and you wish that one day you could feel what he feels about his work. Not that he skips to work every day—some days are hard, some are exhausting, and some are probably deeply sad and difficult. But you feel his joy, and you want a part of it. You want this in your working life. You want to find love in what you do.

However, the moment you start thinking this to yourself, you almost immediately dismiss it as sappy or unrealistic. Watch any famous commencement address on YouTube, or take a long lunch with a mentor, and it's almost guaranteed that at some point you'll hear the advice to "Do what you love, and you'll never work a day in your life again." And when you hear that, your heart sinks. On the one hand, the thought seems to make perfect sense—wouldn't it be great if we could all do what we love?—but on the other, it seems, in this day and age, to be something of a luxury. It invites the response that it's all very well for you, lucky person, to have made your way doing what you love, but for the rest of us work is very much a requirement, and love an added— and rare—bonus.

Linger on it for a moment, though. We're going to take a longer look at love; not to drag you away from the hard realities of the world of work, or to dismiss the demands and discoveries of reliable data, but instead to dive deeper into both. In doing so, we'd like to share the truth that—more than striving for balance between work and life— *love-in-work matters most.*

Love-in-work is less of a mouthful than *eudaimonia*, for sure, but it might also sound soft, idealistic, and far removed from the real-world pragmatism of the freethinking leader. If it does, then bear with us. Because love—specifically, the skill of finding love in what you do, rather than simply "doing what you love"—leads us directly to a place that is the epitome of pragmatism.

• • •

On the face of it, though, organizations don't appear greatly concerned with love. Southwest Airlines can stick a heart on its planes, and Facebook can claim that its mission is to "ship love," but in these two cases, as in most others, the love refers to the customers, not the employees. Most organizations are much more worried about the meaty stuff: performance, goals, achievement, discipline, execution, and rigor. Get all this done, meet all the deadlines with the necessary levels of quality, and maybe then you can sprinkle a little dusting of love on it at the end.

If this is your view of your organization, then you—and it, if it shares this view—are missing the mark. Because the truth is that even the most hard-nosed, performance-oriented organizations desperately want you to find great love in what you do. They just don't call it that.

Have you ever been deeply in love? Cast your mind back to when that was—when you were so in love with someone that you couldn't wait to see that person, when time flew by quickly when you were together, and when, after parting, you ached to see your love again.

When you're in love, you're a different person. Looking at the world through the rosy lens of love, everyone seems wonderful, people are beautiful, the world is happy and kind, and spring is in the air. Love lifts you up. It elevates you to a new plane, where you're at your most productive, creative, generous, resilient, innovative, collaborative, open, and powerful. When you're in love, you are simply magnificent.

Look at those adjectives again: *productive, creative, generous, resilient, innovative, collaborative, open, powerful.* Not only are they a pretty good description of how you hope to be in your life, or how your spouse or family wants you to be, but they're also, surely, the exact qualities your organization's CEO is looking for in every team member. Put the list of you-in-love qualities next to your CEO's list of ideal-employee-at-work qualities and you'll see that the list is the same.

But you don't get to feel any of these things by writing them down, just as your organization won't create any of these in you merely by discussing them with you in a training class. You—and your organization—get them only if you create them, and you create them only through love. The poet Pablo Neruda, in love, wrote "I want to do with you what Spring does with the cherry trees." That's the power of love. With it, you blossom. You flourish. You look forward to what you're about to do. Time flies by while you're doing it. And when you're done with it, you feel an urge to start right back up again. You experience *eudaimonia*, your spirit manifesting its fullest and most beautiful expression. That's what your organization wants, that's what you want for yourself, and that's what you want for your people. You want love.

Most organizations shy away from the word *love*, preferring more business-appropriate terms such as *committed* or *motivated* or *discretionary effort*. (Maybe, about now, you're privately wishing that we would shy away from it, too.) But in the real world we have to engage with what really is, not some watered-down version of how we'd like people to be or to feel. If we want our people to flourish, if we want them to be creative and intrigued and generous and resilient, then we've got to help them find what Miles found. There's love in work, and we should use the word. We should be curious about how each of us can find it. We should honor the truth that our organization can never find it for us, can never define it for us. For too long we've allowed our organizations to appropriate human words—*love, passion, excitement, thrill*—and persuade themselves that, by invoking these words, they've created genuine human feelings. They haven't, and they never will. The organization is a fiction, an "intersubjective reality," to use the term from chapter 1, and it's simply not real enough or human enough to know which activities at work you love. Only you can know that. Only you are close enough to yourself to know where you find love and where you don't, at the level of detail that Miles did. He said, in essence, "I love this specific thing, not that specific thing." And no one, before or after he was hired, would have known this about him. This was a transcendent part of him that only he had access to.

The same is true for you. There's a little bit of you that your organization can never touch, never know, never see, and certainly never feel. And yet it's this part of you—the loving, feeling part of you—that makes you feel alive at work, able to do things that surprise and delight you, things that are ridiculously good, unexpectedly made, astonishing to your team, and that light you up from the inside.

Organizations are not powerless, but their power (and their name) comes from their ability to organize what is already there in plain view. Your organization, if it is careless, can crush your spirit, can diminish or ignore your *daimon*. But only you can animate it. Only you can bring love into your world at work.

And when you do all sorts of good things happen. The Mayo Clinic actually managed to quantify the power of love-in-work. It asked physicians how much of their time at work they spent doing those activities they loved the most. Those who reported that they spent at least 20 percent of their time doing things they loved had dramatically lower risk of burnout. Each percentage point reduction below this 20 percent level resulted in a commensurate and almost linear increase in burnout risk. Remove the love from a physician's work, and the work grates, and grates some more, until it hurts.

• • •

The big question, then, is how to make this happen. Whether we call it love-in-work or *eudaimonia* or anything else, the fact remains that work is called work for a reason, and your work is not only busy and sometimes repetitive but—more to the point—is not always of your own making. You have a particular job, in which certain outcomes are expected, and your responsibilities are what they are. What's love got to do with that?

Well, the Mayo Clinic research reveals that love actually has a great deal to do with it. You can, and should, weave love into your work, no matter what role you're in. And in case you're wondering, the data reveals that, for most of us, the problem of loveless work lies less in the fact that our job is too constricted and more in the fact that we can't figure out how to weave. The ADP Research Institute's global engagement study revealed that only 16–17 percent of workers say they have a chance to play to their strengths every day, whereas their surveys of a representative sample of the US working population reveal that 72 percent of workers say, "I have the freedom to modify my role to fit my strengths better." In psychology we refer to this as an attitude-behavior consistency problem—we know we *can* modify our roles to fit ourselves better, but most of us simply don't.

So, here's a way to remove the problem—here's how to intentionally and responsibly weave love into your work.

Think about the most successful person you know. Not in terms of money, necessarily, but in terms of her contributions to her team, and her organization—someone enormously productive, creative, resilient, and seemingly at one with her work. More than likely, as you think of this person, you're thinking she got lucky. "How," you're asking yourself, "did she *find* that role, how did she *find* that work, how did she *find* that life? I wish I could find something that fits me as well as her work fits her."

If you are indeed thinking this, then first, good for you for recognizing something special and precious, and second, you've landed on the wrong verb. This person didn't *find* this work—she didn't happen upon it, fully-formed and waiting for her. Instead, she *made* it. She took a generic job, with a generic job description, and then, within that job, she took her loves seriously, and gradually, little by little and a lot over time, she turned the best of her job into most of her job. Not the entirety of it, maybe, but certainly an awful lot of it, until it became a manifestation of who she is. She tweaked and tweaked the role until, in all the most important ways, it came to resemble her—it became an expression of her.

You can do the same.

Twice a year, spend a week in love with your work. Select a regular week at work and take a pad around with you for the entire week. Down the middle of this pad draw a vertical line to make two columns, and write "Loved It" at the top of one column and "Loathed It" at the top of the other.* During the week, any time you find yourself feeling one of the signs of love—before you do something, you actively look forward to it; while you're doing it, time speeds up and you find yourself in flow; after you've done it, there's part of you looking forward to when you can do it again—scribble down exactly what that something was in the "Loved It" column.

And any time you find yourself feeling the inverse—before you do something, you procrastinate, perhaps handing it off to the new person because it will be "developmental"; while you do it, time drags on and ten minutes feels like a hard-fought hour; and when you're done with it, you hope you never have to do it again—scribble down exactly what *that* something was in the "Loathed It" column.

Obviously, there'll be plenty of activities in your week that don't make either list, but if you spend a week in love with your work, by the end of the week you will see a list of activities in your "Loved It" column that feel different to you than the rest of your work. They'll have a different emotional valence, creating in you a distinct and distinctly positive feeling, one that draws you in and lifts you up.

---

*As we've shared this exercise around the world, we've learned that not all languages and cultures use the words "love" and "loathe" in the same way—in the Netherlands, for example, there is no single word for "love." So to be clear: the key idea here is to capture your strong positive and negative reactions to your work, so pick whatever words mean that to you—you're after the extremes of your experience, not the "meh" in the middle.

Think of these activities as your "red threads." Your work is made up of many activities, many threads, but some of them feel as though they're made of particularly powerful material. These red threads are the activities you love, and your challenge is to pinpoint them so you can ensure that, next week, you'll be able to recreate them, refine them, and add to them. You are weaving red threads into the fabric of your work, one thread at a time. Now, you do not have to end up with an entirely red quilt. The Mayo Clinic researchers found that when the physicians spent *more* than 20 percent of their time on activities they loved, there was no corresponding reduction in burnout risk. The 20 percent number was a threshold, which is to say that a little love goes an awfully long way: when you can deliberately weave your red threads throughout the fabric of your work you'll feel stronger, perform better, and bounce back faster.

These red threads are your strengths. Typically we think of our strengths as what we're good at and our weaknesses as what we're bad at, and that our team leaders, or our colleagues, are therefore the best judges of both. But as we saw in chapter 4, this is not the best definition of either strengths or weaknesses. A strength is any activity that strengthens you (for Miles the anesthetist, keeping a patient hovering between life and death), and a weakness is any activity that weakens you, even if you're good at it (for Miles, helping patients recover). "Performance" is what you have done well or poorly, and your team leader can be the judge of that. Team leaders and colleagues, however, can't judge what strengthens or weakens you.

If you spend a week in love with your work and realize that you love finding patterns in data, then your team leader can legitimately tell you, in regard to your *performance*, "Well, you're not explaining the patterns well enough," or "Well, you're not finding patterns that are useful," or, "You're not putting them on a PowerPoint slide properly." Your team leader can say all these things. But what she cannot say is, "No, you don't love finding patterns in data," just as we can't say to

Miles, "No, you don't love holding people between life and death." She can't say that your red thread isn't a red thread. You are the one and only judge of that.

And don't imagine that your teammates in the same role as you share the same red threads as you. They don't. Think back again to Miles. We have interviewed other anesthetists—indeed, other anesthetists who are the same age as Miles and who work in the same health-care system as he does—who don't sound anything like Miles when they describe what they love. One loves the bedside conversations before the operation, and the calm sensitivity required to bring a sedated patient gently back to consciousness without the panic that afflicts many patients. Another is drawn mostly to the intricacies of the anesthetic mechanism, and has dedicated herself to defining precisely how each drug does what it does—get her on the subject of what exactly "consciousness" is, and you'll hear the same passion as Miles displayed when he described the thrill of the stress.

And yet, looking at Miles, you would never have known what his red threads were. He looks and acts no differently from any other middle-aged British doctor. His red threads have nothing to do with his race, his gender, his age, or his religion. They are simply and only an artifact of his uniqueness. For no good reason other than the clash of the chromosomes, Miles loves certain aspects of his work and loathes other aspects. It is therefore his responsibility to identify these red threads, see them for what they are, and then deliberately weave them into the rest of his work. No one can do this for him—neither the identification, nor the weaving. Only he, with discipline and intelligence and intention, can bring love into his work.

The same is true for you, of course. You have a unique relationship with the world, a relationship that reveals to you things that only you can see. It offers thread-weaving opportunities all the time, but the only person who knows if those threads are red is *you*. The world won't do your weaving for you—it doesn't care about your red threads. The only person who can stop and be attentive enough to identify these threads, and weave them intelligently into the fabric of your work, is you.*

This is true not only in your work life but in your life in general. Despite how it might feel a lot of the time, you do not have many different compartments of your life, each of which must be carefully balanced. Instead, you have one life, one whole cloth, one fabric for you to weave your red threads into. It's up to you to know what you love about work, what you love about hobbies, what you love about friends, and what you love about family, and those things will be different from everyone else's things. So when people say, "Well, as a father/friend/colleague I think you should do this or that," remember that they do not know you like you know you, that they are well intended yet blind. Your world has an n of 1, and that 1 is you.

Should you work fifteen hours a day? Should you have three kids before the age of thirty? Should you devote all your time to your career until you can afford the day care you will need? Should you take six weeks of vacation a year, or none? Should you quit your job and go surfing or van-ing? These are all choices that only you can make, and the only way to make them wisely is to honor the truth that your life will give you strength if you can but pay attention to your emotional reactions to the events and activities and responsibilities you choose to fill it with.

And what of the list of "Loathed It" things? Obviously these are your fraying, weak threads, and your aim is to incorporate as few of them as possible in your life's fabric—either by stopping these activities altogether, by partnering with someone to get them done as painlessly as possible, or by seeing if, in being combined with an activity you love (by being braided with one of your red threads), they can become less draining for you. When you start to think about your life in this way,

---

*You're often told, by the way, to "take ownership of your career." This is what it actually means—it means taking ownership of the weaving of your red threads.

you'll quickly realize not only that "balance" is an unhelpful idea but that we have the categories wrong. What we all wrestle with every day in the real world is not so much *work* and *life* as it is *love* and *loathe*.

Watch for your red threads. Take them seriously. They are light, they are strong, they are true, and they are yours. And when you feel run down, or burned out, or at risk, or that everything is coming apart at the seams, cling to them tightly. They will hold fast until you have the strength to begin weaving something new. This new thing you make, this new idea, or project, or job, or relationship, or life, will not necessarily be balanced as others see it. It will not necessarily be a life that others would have made or would even approve of. Nor will it necessarily be easy. But it will be yours. It will be crafted from sources of strength felt only by you, and so it will be strong. It will flourish. It will not wither, and neither will you.

• • •

Wouldn't it be wonderful if work were *for* love—if the point of work were to discover that which each of us loves? Obviously, today we don't think of it that way. We think of it as a transaction: you get things done, and then we pay you to buy things you love. But what if we flipped that all around? What if we made the purpose of work to help people discover that which they love; if we changed the American Management Association slogan from *Get work done through people* to *Get people done through work*? We'd fail, of course, because people are complicated, and so is work, and so is life. And besides, no person is ever "done." But what if we made the attempt the entire point of work: To teach our kids and our college graduates, our workers young and old, our people in the second decade of their first career and our people in the first year of their third career, how to use the raw material of work to find their very own red threads and then to take responsibility for weaving them into something fine and strong?

We wouldn't net any less productivity. We would net more, and as the Mayo data shows, this productivity would be healthy—underpinned by resilience and fulfillment. In the end, shouldn't that be what work is for?

• • •

About twenty years ago, a thirteen-year-old gymnast named Sergei Polunin was plucked from his depressed Ukrainian town and brought over to White Lodge, the junior Royal Ballet School in the middle of Richmond Park, London. For the rest of his childhood he was trained in the Royal Ballet techniques, and he displayed such extraordinary natural talent that, at nineteen, he became the youngest principal male soloist in the history of the Royal Ballet Company. Everyone in London agreed that he was better than Baryshnikov, better than Nureyev, better even than Nijinsky, the most technically perfect dancer in a century. London was proud to have found and nurtured him.

But no one truly knew him, and no one truly cared to. He was a passionate, lyrical dancer, strong but fluid, soulful but angry, his tattooed body merely the most obvious sign of his need to push the boundaries. The powers that be at the Royal Ballet Company ignored all this, and instead did what they always do with their prodigies: they made him follow the strictures of the Royal Ballet Way. He would dance the classical ballet repertoire, in the classical ballet form and mold, and they would make him do it again and again, to glorify the company and delight the London crowds. And so he danced, and he danced, and he delighted and amazed, until one day, at the age of twenty-one and only two years after he ascended to principal, he quit.

There was a pattern for the perfect Royal Ballet dancer, and this pattern didn't care what Sergei Polunin loved. It didn't care about whatever his red threads as a dancer might be, and sadly he wasn't strong enough to believe that holding fast to these threads was vital for him. He was forced to conform to this pattern and he let his threads slip away, and soon, quite soon, he fell apart. Ballet, as you know, is an unremittingly technical and demanding craft, but if you build technical craft on a loveless foundation, you net only burnout, because technical mastery absent love *always* equals burnout. Burnout isn't the absence of balance but the absence of love.

The Royal Ballet Company had won the talent war. It had found the most technically and lyrically gifted dancer in a century, and then, blind to his loves, it had torn him up. And we, the world, suffered for it. He had nothing left to contribute. Sergei flailed around for a few years, no longer at home in either London or the Ukraine, lost without his passion, and, after his parents divorced, alone and unmoored.

And then he did what you might have done if you've ever found yourself similarly untethered: he found one thing he knew he loved—one frayed strand of a red thread—and he followed where it led. He asked a choreographer friend of his to create one dance that he would truly love, a choreography as lyrical as it was technical, equally precise and passionate. He would practice the piece, dance and film it twice during one muggy afternoon in Hawaii, post the video on YouTube for his close friends and family to see, and then—well, he had no idea what would happen next. He was simply taking hold of one strong thread, weaving it into something that was, at the very least, authentic, and then hoping it would have enough power to pull him back onto his life's path.

On the day after Valentine's Day in 2015 he published, to very little fanfare, his version of Hozier's "Take Me to Church."

If you've never seen it, take a moment now to log onto YouTube and watch—it's four minutes and eight seconds that you'll never forget. Whether you're a fan of ballet or not, you'll recognize it not only as the work of a man at the end of his tether, but also as a pure expression of technical craft and unabashed joy. You see here a man who is taking his loves seriously, interlacing them with craft and discipline, and contributing to us something passionate, rare, and pure. You will see, from the inside out, that this is the fullest, most authentic, and richest expression of this unique person. If the people coming to work on your team could feel more like this, if you could help them take their red threads this seriously—not to make your people feel good about themselves, although that helps, but so they could share more with the world—what a beautiful and lasting contribution you and your team would make.

Since it was posted, Sergei's video has been viewed more than twenty-three million times. He's danced the piece on stages as diverse as Covent Garden, the Hollywood Bowl, and *The Ellen DeGeneres Show*, and has rediscovered his love for his craft as a guest principal at Europe's most prestigious ballet companies. No longer tied down to the classical Royal repertoire, he's rediscovered his love-in-work, and all of us are the beneficiaries.

We ask the same of you. Spend a week in love with your work. Hold tightly to your red threads. Yes, so you can blossom. But mostly, so you can figure out ways to share what's unique about you with the rest of us.

The power of human nature is that each human's nature is unique. This is a feature, not a bug. So your responsibility is to take seriously the uniqueness of your uniqueness, and design the most intelligent, the most honest, and the most effective ways to volunteer it to the rest of us. We—your teammates, your family, your community, your company—are waiting for you to share with us your unique loves. We're here for but a few short years. Please don't make us wait too long.

Leadership is a thing

Memphis, Tennessee, is the home of the National Civil Rights Museum. We visited the museum a couple of years ago, and spent two or three hours there learning about the civil-rights movement and the long struggle of African Americans to end institutionalized discrimination and achieve some measure of equality.

The layout of the museum—really, the layout of the experience of a visitor—is arresting. Rather than comprising a series of rooms that you might visit in turn, the main exhibit is laid out as a winding path across the floor of a large room—making a sort of high-walled maze—so as you walk you encounter the various displays and artifacts in chronological order. You begin with the conclusion of the Civil War, and see the hopes and possibilities of that brief moment in time quickly pushed aside by Jim Crow laws. You see the struggles over segregation leading up to the *Brown* v. *Board of Education* decision in 1954. And then, rounding a corner, you see a full-scale replica of a bus—an entire city bus, not gleaming and new and modern, but old, banged-up, hard-working, and hard-worked, the sort of vehicle that shuttles anonymously to and fro in our lives, moving us from one place to another while we think of other things. This particular bus, however, serves to remind us of one of those moments in history that cleave time into before and after, because in 1955, on a bus like this one, Rosa Parks, after another long day at work, refused to give up her seat to a white person when instructed to do so by the driver. The ensuing Montgomery bus boycott, carried forward by a young minister from a local church, became one of the early flashpoints in the civil-rights struggle.

. . .

This is not a chapter about leadership.

It's become something of a cliché, in the business literature, to bemoan the vast volume of writing on the topic; to list the number of books on leadership that come up if you search on Amazon; to point to the great library of articles and blog posts and videos and inspirational speeches as evidence that leadership is either a Really Important Subject or else a Really Over-Analyzed Subject. If it's possible to distill the essence of what all these written and spoken words have to tell us, it would be something like this: that leadership is enduringly fascinating to us and that we believe it to be critically important at work.

And we can say a little more. We can say that there appears to be broad agreement that certain people exhibit a definable, consistent, and meaningful quality called leadership. That there are some characteristics of a person that are in some way above and different from that person's technical skills (whether he or she can write good code, for example, or good English) and that also transcend that person's interpersonal or "soft" skills (whether he or she can make the sale, or negotiate a deal) and that make the person a leader.

We can also say that we tend to agree that all the best leaders possess this quality, or set of qualities—so, leadership is something that lives, specially, in those who lead and is in some way responsible for their ability to do so. And we can say that, as a consequence, most of us would agree that if you want to be a leader, you have to have this set of qualities.

There is a frustrating circularity to this argument—that there's a thing called leadership, and we know it's a thing because leaders have it, otherwise they wouldn't be leaders. It's like saying your cat has cat-ness because he's a cat: it might be true, but it's hardly helpful to your hamster if he dreams, someday, of being a cat. This know-it-when-we-see-it vagueness explains, in part, why we can talk about leadership so much without usefully advancing our understanding of it, or getting much better at it.

Perhaps to combat this vagueness, some go further and begin to try to specify some of the qualities that make up leadership. Being inspirational seems to be important. Being able to create and articulate a vision matters a lot. The ability to formulate strategy is good, as is the ability to distinguish a good strategy from a bad one. Sometimes mastery of execution makes the list—the art of getting stuff done. Setting a direction for an organization is important, and, in concert with this, bringing people into alignment with that direction and motivating them to move ahead. Decision making is high on the list, together with managing conflict. Innovation and disruption usually put in an appearance. Communications skills also rank highly, and having what's commonly referred to as "executive presence" is also felt to be critical.

To this collection of long-limbed characteristics are added some personal traits. Leadership requires authenticity (the ability to come across as a "real" person) and often, too, vulnerability (the courage to be imperfect in public, to relinquish the need to be right or to be the smartest person in the room). These things, and a few others, are said to be needed so that our leaders can build effective relationships with others.

And yet these characteristics are curiously circumscribed: authenticity is important, right up until the point when the leader, authentically, says that he has no idea what to do, which then fractures his vision. Likewise, vulnerability is important until the moment when the leader's comfort with her own flaws causes us to doubt her, and to question whether she is sufficiently inspirational. Apparently, we require authentic sureness and reassuring vulnerability, however contradictory those things may be. The personal qualities that make the list are Goldilocks qualities—they must be neither too hot, nor too cold, but just right.

These little inconsistencies, however, melt away in the face of our conviction that leadership is a great good at work—it is *always* better for a person to have more of it, and the more leaders an organization has, the better. This much, at least, appears settled—and as a result you will be told that the most important thing you can do to advance your career is to "grow your leadership."

Now, some might choose other attributes for their lists, but those above are a reasonable summary of the theory-world view of leadership. And the reason that this isn't a chapter on leadership is not that the qualities listed aren't useful (they are) or that this topic has been done to death (it's close) but, rather, that when we look critically, we realize that we may well have misunderstood leadership altogether.

Indeed, the final lie that we encounter at work is that *leadership is a thing*.

• • •

In June 2004, while tidying a basement, a sheriff's deputy in Montgomery, Alabama, came upon several books of mug shots. The books were clearly old, and the photos inside them had been carefully sorted by gender and by race. In a volume titled "Negro Male" was a page showing photographs of some of the eighty-nine people arrested on February 22, 1956, during the Montgomery bus boycott.

As we look at that page today, twelve men look back. Some are dressed informally; some formally. Some are younger; some older.

Some seem worried; some resigned; some defiant. Each has an arrest number in front of him: some are holding it; some have it hanging from their necks on a chain. As it turns out, we know the names of all twelve men on this page, although we know little else about them beyond that. And we know their names because of something they did together, and something that invites us to think about leadership differently.

The thing that the men in the mug-shot book have in common is explained by the identity of one of them in particular. On the top row of the page, the man bearing number 7089 stares back at the lens, his light-colored suit coat buttoned, his tie straight, his hands resting on his knees. At the time this photograph was taken, he was twenty-seven years old, and was the pastor of the Dexter Avenue Baptist Church in Montgomery. In the days following Rosa Parks's arrest, he had been asked to lead the boycott, which, beginning in December 1955, saw widespread participation and created significant economic problems for the city's transit system. In early 1956 a county grand jury returned indictments against several of the boycott participants for violations of the Alabama Anti-Boycott Act, and the pastor, together with eighty-eight others, was arrested.

His name, of course, was Martin Luther King Jr. But the story these pictures have to tell us is not, in the first instance, a story about him, about Number 7089. It's a story about the other eleven men on the page, and it's a story that—in all the theorizing about leadership, in all the competing lists and competencies, in all the articles and surveys and assessments and books, in all the dissection and analysis and categorization—is sadly lost. For leadership does not live in the abstract, does not live in the average. It lives, instead, in the real world.

And if we look at that world, this is what we see.

First, the ability to lead is rare. It was not inevitable that Martin Luther King Jr. would emerge from the Montgomery bus boycott as a national leader whom millions would follow—there were other good people guiding the Montgomery Improvement Association, just as there were other, earlier bus boycotts, such as the one in Baton Rouge, Louisiana, a couple of years before. But something about King in Montgomery was special. The fact that we lionize those who have this special ability; the fact that we spend so much time looking for it and trying to get more of it; and the fact that it plays such a prominent role in how we think about our organizations: these point not to its ubiquity but to its scarcity—and this scarcity, in turn, belies the supposed ease with which we're all meant to be able to get better at it. If leading were easy, there would be more good leaders. If there were more good leaders, we might be just a little less focused on it.

Second, leaders have shortcomings. Their skill set is incomplete. We don't need J. Edgar Hoover's surveillance files to reveal that King was not in possession of every quality the perfect leader should possess. And this is confounding, because it challenges the notion that there is in fact a list of leadership qualities, each of which is essential. For every quality on the list, we can think of a respected leader in the real world who lacks it. If leadership is about being inspirational or visionary, then what should we make of Warren Buffett, whose principal activities as a leader seem to consist of sitting in an office in Omaha, Nebraska, drinking Cherry Coke, and finding companies to buy? If leadership is about creating a winning strategy, then what should we make of Winston Churchill, whose disastrous policies in the 1920s and 1930s led to his exile from government? If leadership is about execution and communication, then what should we make of King George VI of Great Britain, who was revered for his leadership of that nation during the Second World War, but who could barely speak in public, and who wasn't in a position to execute anything? If leadership is about building a winning coalition, then what should we make of Susan B. Anthony, whose falling-out with her fellow women's-suffrage leaders created a split in that movement that lasted twenty years?

If it's about ethics, what do we make of Steve Jobs's buying a new car every six months to avoid registering it, so as to be able to park in handicapped spots whenever he wanted to? If it's about caring for those in your charge, what do we make of General George Patton and his physically assaulting soldiers with PTSD? If it's about authenticity, where does that leave John F. Kennedy and his hidden illnesses and affairs?

What does it mean for all the models and lists if the things on them are optional? The lesson from the real world is not that there is any particular collection of qualities that every leader has, but rather that every leader we can think of has obvious shortcomings—that leaders aren't perfect people, not by a long way.

And finally, it follows that leadership is not about being the most well-rounded of the well-rounded people. As we saw in chapter 4, the best people aren't well-rounded. The same is true for the leaders we see in the real world—and even more so. As with some of the great performers we met earlier—think Lionel Messi and his amazing left foot—we don't see the most respected leaders spending much time trying to round themselves out, trying to develop abilities in areas where they have none. Instead, we see them trying to make the best use of what they already have, with the result that whenever we look closely, we see them going about the task of leading in very different ways. In this way, leading is the same as all other fields of human endeavor—high performance is idiosyncratic, and the higher the level of performance the greater the level of idiosyncrasy.

King, too, had a very particular approach to leading, and his genius and his effectiveness lay not in trying to round himself out and acquire the skills of, say, a Rosa Parks, a Malcolm X, or a Ralph Abernathy, but instead in starting from, cultivating, and, in moments of crisis, falling back on his very particular gifts as a leader—which we'll try to describe shortly.

This is why the idea that *leadership is a thing* is a lie. When you take any of our definitions of that thing, and then try to locate it in the real world, you encounter exception upon exception upon exception. The very least we can conclude is that if there is some magical set of attributes, we haven't yet figured out what they are, and that plenty of leaders are doing plenty of leading without many of them. And if that's the case, then the things that supposedly make up leadership neither add to our understanding of it nor help us be better at it.

• • •

But if the real world shows us what leadership *isn't*, does it give us any clues at all that we can learn from? Can we say nothing more than that leading is a free-for-all, a grab bag of different skills and attributes and states and traits that will remain ever mysterious? Or is there a different way to understand what's going on?

What's most remarkable about the events in Montgomery in 1956 is not that one individual took a stand and was imprisoned as a result—it is not what this one man said or did. It is rather that others chose to follow him. What is truly before us on the page of mug shots is a picture of a leader *and his followers*—and it is because, on that day, the eleven chose to follow that sixty years later we know their names. In the midst of physical attacks and intimidation and firebombings, the eleven saw something special in King, something that they chose to follow, and because of what they did, and then because of what countless thousands and millions did in the ensuing years, we recognize him as a leader.

This is the true lesson in leading from the real world: a leader is someone who has followers, plain and simple. The only determinant of whether anyone is leading is whether anyone else is following.

This might seem like an obvious statement, until we recall how easily we overlook its implications. Followers—their needs, their feelings, their fears and hopes—are strangely absent when we speak of leaders as exemplars of strategy, execution, vision, oratory, relationships, charisma, and so on. The idea of leadership is missing the idea of followers. It's missing the idea that our subject here is, at heart, a question of a particularly human relationship—namely, why anyone would choose to devote his or her energies to, and to take risks on behalf of, someone else. And, in that, it's missing the entire point.[1]

This notion—that a leader is a person with followers—does not emerge from a list of skills, or tactics, or competencies; it doesn't coincide with a person's level within a hierarchy; and it doesn't actually tell us very much about the nature of the leader him- or herself. But it does capture a condition, a litmus test if you like, for leading. And that condition is precise—it's about the presence, or absence, of followers.

So the question we should really be asking ourselves is this one: Why do we follow? What is it that makes us work hard late into the night—to go beyond what's expected of us? What makes us move someone to the front of our queue? What makes us voluntarily place some part of our destiny in the hands of another human being? What makes us give our breath to another?

What made those eleven men entrust their well-being and their hopes to Number 7089?

• • •

We can see some part of the answer in those eight items with which we began the book. We know that the feelings measured by those eight items exist disproportionately on high-performing teams, so we know something of what followers need from their team leader.

Broadly speaking, we want to feel part of something bigger than ourselves—the "Best of We"—while, at the same time, feeling that our leader knows and values us for who we are as a unique individual—the "Best of Me."

More specifically, we follow leaders who connect us to a mission we believe in, who clarify what's expected of us, who surround us with people who define excellence the same way we do, who value us for our strengths, who show us that our teammates will always be there for us, who diligently replay our winning plays, who challenge us to keep getting better, and who give us confidence in the future.

This is not a list of qualities in a leader, but rather a set of feelings in a follower. When we say to ourselves that leadership is indeed a thing, because we know it when we see it, we're not really seeing any definable characteristic of another human. What we are "seeing" is in fact our own feelings as a follower. As such, while we should not expect every good leader to share the same qualities or competencies, we *can* hold all good leaders accountable for creating these same feelings of followership in their teams. Indeed, we can use these feelings to help any particular leader know whether or not she is any good. Those eight items introduced in chapter 1 are a valid measure of a leader's effectiveness. We need not dictate how each leader should behave, but we can define what all good leaders must create in their followers. And since we measure this by asking the followers to rate their own experiences, rather than rating the leader on a long list of abstract leader qualities, this measure of leader effectiveness is reliable.

Leadership isn't a thing, because it cannot be measured reliably. Followership is a thing, because it can.

And it's a lie that *leadership is a thing* because no two leaders create followers in quite the same way. What's true in the real world is that leading is many different things. Your challenge as a leader is not to try to acquire the complete set of abstract leader competencies—you will fail, not least because the first hurdle you will fall at is authenticity. Instead, your challenge is to find and refine your own idiosyncratic way of creating in your team these eight emotional outcomes. Do this well and you will lead well.

Interestingly—and happily—a close study of the real world reveals that these two are linked. Your ability to create the outcomes you want in your followers is tied directly to how seriously and intelligently you cultivate your own idiosyncrasy, and to what end. The deeper and more extreme your idiosyncrasy becomes, the more passionately your followers follow—and while this is frustrating to us when we happen to disagree with the ends of a particular leader, it is so nonetheless.

• • •

We leave the Montgomery bus behind us and continue our walk through the exhibition. We see the student sit-ins of 1960, and we follow the Freedom Riders of 1961. We learn about efforts to organize resistance and protests in Mississippi and in Albany, Georgia. And then we arrive at a replica of a jail cell in Birmingham, Alabama.

In the 1960s, Birmingham was known as the most segregated city in America. In early 1963 the Alabama Christian Movement for Human Rights, together with Martin Luther King Jr.'s Southern Christian Leadership Conference, began a nonviolent campaign against the segregation. A local justice issued an injunction against the protest. The civil-rights leaders duly announced they would disobey this order, and on April 12, 1963, King and other marchers were arrested and incarcerated. That same day, eight white Alabama clergymen published an open letter in which they criticized King and his methods, and a copy of the newspaper in which it was printed was smuggled in to King in his cell. King, on reading it, began writing. At first, he wrote in the margins of the newspaper. Then, when those were covered, he wrote on the toilet paper in his cell, and then on scraps of paper given him by a friendly fellow inmate, and then, finally, on a writing pad brought in by his lawyers. When King finally set down his pencil, he had written what is now known as the Letter from Birmingham Jail. We read a copy of it on the wall outside the jail cell.

It's a long letter—an impassioned letter. It's a plea against settling, against compromise, against the path of least resistance. And in it, King talks about extremism. "The question," he says "is not whether we will be extremist, but what kind of extremists we will be."

Warren Buffett, the uninspiring Coke-drinker from Omaha, is an extremist. He's exceptional at finding and buying companies. Winston Churchill, while he might have been a poor policy maker, was exceptional at inspiring uncompromising resistance. Susan B. Anthony was really good at focusing her energies, and those of the people around her, on a specific goal. Steve Jobs was really good at creating hardware and software that was delightful to use. George Patton was really good at fighting, with his whole being, whatever was in front of him on any given day. And John F. Kennedy was really good at making the future feel universal and morally uplifting. What each of these leaders had in common was that they were really good at something—each was, in their different way, an extremist.

We have seen, already, that the best people aren't well-rounded, but are instead *spiky*—they have honed one or two distinctive abilities that they use to make their mark on the world. What we see in the best leaders is a similar extremism—a few signal abilities refined over time. But now, these abilities are so pronounced, and the leaders so adept at transmitting them to the world, that they stand out to all of us. And so this truth: *we follow spikes.*

We do this not merely because a leader who has deep mastery in something will be able to excel at it, but because these spikes change the way we feel about the future. There aren't many human universals—the anthropologist Donald Brown's book *Human Universals* lists sixty-seven of them—but one of them is that every human society ever studied ritualizes death.[2] Each society does this differently, but we all do it. Death is the great unknown, and these rituals serve to lessen our fear and give us some illusion of control. These death rituals are merely the most obvious sign of something common to us all: we humans fear the unknown. The past is what it is, the present is where we stand, yet the future is a scarily uncertain place. This uncertainty leads us to seek reassurance, and in particular, reassurance through the ritualization of that most uncertain certainty of all—our ultimate demise.

This particularly human characteristic presents a challenge for you, the modern day leader. You are charged with rallying your team toward a better future, yet many on your team are fearful of this future. And this fear isn't unjustified. It's adaptive. Those of our forebears who lacked it, who paddled their little rafts toward the horizon, asking themselves "Ooh, I wonder where the sun goes to sleep?" often didn't return to pass on their genes. Being a bit cautious can be a sensible thing.

As a leader, you can't be dismissive of this fear. You can't tell your people to "embrace change" and to "get comfortable with ambiguity." Well you can, but you will then get them thinking ever more deeply about change and ambiguity, which will, in turn, *increase* their anxiety and lessen your effectiveness as a leader. It's an irony that while consultants wax lyrical about change, real-world leaders hardly use the word at all, realizing that their followers want instead an increasingly vivid picture of the future, not another reminder of its inherent uncertainty.

Your greatest challenge as a leader, then, is to honor each person's legitimate fear of the unknown and, at the same time, to turn that fear into spiritedness. We, your followers, like the comfort of where we stand, yet know that the flow of events is pulling us inexorably into the unknown. So when we find something, anything, however slight, that lessens our uncertainty, we cling on for dear life.

The final characteristic of the best teams, as we saw in chapter 1, is the feeling that, for each team member, "I have great confidence in my company's future." This confidence in the future, it seems, is the antidote to our universal uncertainty. And it explains why we follow. The act of following is a barter—we entrust some part of our future to a leader *only* when we get something in return.

That "something in return" is confidence.

And what gives us confidence in the future is seeing, in a leader, some great and pronounced level of ability in something we care about.

We follow people who are really good at something that matters to us. *We follow the spikes.*

It's as if the spikes give us something to hook on to. We're well aware of our own shortcomings, and we know that what lies ahead of us in life is unknowable. We're aware, also, that our journey will be easier if we can do it in partnership with others. And when we see, in those others, some ability that offsets our own deficits, and that removes for us, even if only slightly, some of the mist of the future, then we hold on. We don't necessarily follow vision, or strategy, or execution, or relationship building, or any of the other leadership things. Instead we follow mastery. And it doesn't much matter how this mastery manifests itself, as long as we, the followers, find it relevant. John F. Kennedy was a master at getting us to see and engage with the near-term future in a way that made it morally enlarging—even during the Cuban Missile Crisis he ended his address to the nation by reaching out to the Cubans themselves, saying, "I have no doubt that most Cubans today look forward to the time when they will be truly free—free from foreign domination, free to choose their own leaders, free to select their own system, free to own their own land, free to speak and write and worship without fear or degradation." His brother Robert didn't share this spike. Robert F. Kennedy's spike was urgent, present-day righteousness. Whether he was rooting out Communists under Joe McCarthy, or attacking the Teamsters boss Jimmy Hoffa, or aggressively pushing forward the Civil Rights Act in spite of his brother's caution, RFK's focus was on making things right, right now.

Each truly effective leader cultivates his or her mastery in a way that communicates to us something certain and vivid. It's as if we trust leaders only when they've proven to us that they've opened more doors than we have, seen round more corners than we have, dived deeper than we have, taken themselves more seriously than we have. We trust the seriousness of this. We trust its predictability. We are drawn to its specialness. We sense its authenticity. We are attracted to the beautiful clarity of great ability, the brief moments of awe. We ignore everything else.

. . .

One of the lessons of the Nine Lies is that when we blind ourselves to what's around us, and instead theorize about how the world ought to be (or how we'd like it to be if only it were tidier), our people vanish. We stop seeing them. We mute our curiosity, and we replace it with dogma and dictum. The same happens with the people we call leaders—the moment we start theorizing, they vanish, too.

And here are the truths that vanish along with them.

The truth that no two leaders do the same job in the same way.

The truth that as much as we follow the spikes, they can also antagonize us.

The truth that no leader is perfect—and that the best of them have learned how to work around their imperfections.

The truth that leaders are frustrating—they don't have all the abilities we'd like them to have.

The truth that following is in part an act of forgiveness—it is to give our attention and efforts to someone despite what we can see of their flaws.

The truth that not everyone should be, or wants to be, a leader—the world needs followers, and great followers at that.

The truth that a person who might be a great leader for me might not be a great leader for you.

The truth that a person who might be a great leader for one team, or team of teams, or company, might not be a great leader for another.

The truth that leaders are not necessarily a force for good in the world—they are simply people with followers. They aren't saints, and sometimes their having followers leads to hubris and arrogance, or worse.

The truth that leaders are not good or bad—they are just people who have figured out how to be their most defined selves in the world, and who do so in such a way that they inspire genuine confidence in their followers. This isn't necessarily good or bad. It just is.

The truth that leading isn't a set of characteristics but a series of experiences seen through the eyes of the followers.

The truth that, despite all this, we reserve a special place in our world for those who make our experience of it better and more hopeful.

And the truth that, through it all, we follow your spikes.

• • •

We spend vast sums of money, in the corporate world, on training and developing our leaders—in the United States alone, a jaw-dropping $14 billion every year.[3] The usual leadership course goes something like this: there's a video, either of people talking about leaders, or else of a real leader in the real world. It's intriguing, provocative, and moving. We learn about the impact leaders have had on the various interview subjects, or we feel it ourselves as we see the real leader on-screen. While watching, we feel inspired, curious, energized—that we are going to learn about something important, and that we have just, in a small way, felt that important thing for ourselves.

Then a facilitator steps to the front of the room and explains *the model*. The model takes whatever we've just seen and experienced and makes it boring. The model is usually a two-by-two grid of little boxes, and in each of the boxes is written some sort of abstract word: *empathy, authenticity, vision,* and so forth. And then the facilitator explains that for the next several hours of our lives, we will take each little box in turn, and learn about the abstract thing written in it, and how each of us can have more of that thing. Sometimes the course has been preceded by an assessment that we've all taken, and partway through the course we get to see our results, and how we compare with the things in the boxes. Sometimes we get to give one another feedback in real time at our tables on how we're doing at the things in the boxes. Sometimes we build action plans and write down in our notebooks well-meaning commitments about how we'll do more of the things in the boxes, knowing as we do so that the moment the course finishes, these commitments will join "floss more often" in the *Big Lifetime Pile Of Things Not Done.*

We're told, as we do all these things, that at the end of this process, we will all be more like the leader we saw at the beginning. But our experience, as we go along, is one of increasing frustration. None of the things in the boxes helps us locate the feeling we had, in the opening video, about a particular leader. Indeed, the things in the boxes seem to have nothing on earth to do with the actual leader we've seen, or any actual leaders we've seen. We encounter leaders, in life, emotionally. In our leadership training, the first thing we do—in our attempt to understand leadership—is to wring the emotional life out of the thing.

Because what never, ever happens in any of these courses is our starting with the question: Who are you? Not, who are you in comparison with some model involving abstract words in little boxes, but who are you as a living, breathing, growing, worrying, joyous, uncertain, loving, striving, messy, and yes, spiky human being? We never ask why, given your particular jumble of characteristics, anyone would follow you. We never ask how—given that one-of-a-kind mixture of states and traits that makes you who you are—you would use those things to create an experience for the people around you, and use what you have to help them feel better about the world you're all walking through together, and, while we're at it, how we might give you some measure of that so you can adjust your course as you go.

So we need to stop with the models. Stop with the 360-degree assessments. Stop with the minute and meaningless parsing of how to move your "effective communications" score from a 3.8 to a 3.9, while also figuring out why your peers gave you a 4.1 on "strategy" yet your boss gave you a 3.0. Stop with the endless lists of abstractions. Stop debating whether it's authenticity or tribal leadership or situational leadership or level-five leadership or whatever the latest leadership-nirvana thing is. Stop with the one-size-fits-all.

Instead, let's get humble—the experience of the people on our teams and in our organizations is a true thing, and we don't simply get to choose what it is.

Let's get curious about that experience and how our actions shape it.

And let's follow our own reactions to real people in the real world. When we feel uplifted by what someone does or says, we need to stop and ask why. When we feel a fresh rush of energy after talking with someone, we need to stop and ask why. When we feel, in response to another human being, that mysterious attraction tugging on us—like a fish on a line, or like a needle twitching in a compass, an attraction that says Here, something is happening, something true and visceral and substantial, something that will change, however slightly, the arc of our future—we need to stop and ask why.

We need to get to know real leaders in the real world, and we need to come to know them as followers ourselves. Then we can start learning.

• • •

Our walk continues. Now we come to a representation of the Edmund Pettus Bridge, at Selma, across which King led marchers in 1965 after the horrors of Bloody Sunday. As we walk, imagining as best we can the hundreds upon thousands of determined footsteps that the bridge has come to represent, we notice that the ground is rising beneath us—that we are ascending. Our pathway doubles back on itself. We see murals of the Selma marchers, and we hear the sound of marching feet. We hear King's words—"How Long, Not Long"—as they were delivered at the Alabama State Capitol steps in March of that year. And then, all at once, quiet. We have ascended a full floor, and turning once again, we can see down on the exhibition, and the path that we have traveled.

Now, King's journey is clear to us. Now, looking down from above on each of the protests, and marches, and arrests, and setbacks, and turning points, and triumphs, we can see, neatly laid out on the exhibition floor, the voyage he took. How Montgomery led to Albany, and Birmingham led to Washington, and thence to Selma. How, "This movement will not stop, because God is with the movement," was followed by, "We . . . will not be satisfied until justice rolls down like waters and righteousness like a mighty stream," and then, "The arc of the moral universe is long, but it bends toward justice." And through and across these places and words, we see King harness the nonviolent protest methods of Gandhi to his own particular brand of persistence. We see him fuse his personal bravery and sacrifice to his prose, borrowing as it did the rhythms and cadence of the pulpit and transforming them into a universal poetry of hope.

But let us go back, for a moment, to somewhere near the beginning of this journey, to the meeting of a few dozen local ministers at King's church in Montgomery at which he was asked to lead the boycott, and imagine what might happen if that meeting were instead to take place in a business organization today—if we were, say, selecting a leader for a key corporate initiative. We would first ask the assembled group to identify what qualities were necessary in the leader. We'd present the ministers with a list—results orientation, strategic orientation, collaboration and influence, team leadership, developing organizational capabilities, change leadership, and market understanding, say—and ask them to gauge just how much of these would be needed for the leader to succeed.[4] We'd then ask the group to rate Dr. King and any other candidates on each of these, both in terms of his current level of ability and his potential for growth in each, and we'd compare those with the required levels of ability. Then we'd use this to predict his chance of success, and weigh that in our decision of whether to ask him to lead. And then, if we went ahead and decided King was the man for the job, we'd suggest development opportunities for him to grow in the areas we'd decided mattered most. We'd do this because this is our theory of leadership in action. And the point is not that we wouldn't choose Dr. King but that we wouldn't in any meaningful sense see him at all.

But now look down with us again to the exhibition floor, and now think of the followers without which the journey would not have been. These theoretical things would have meant exactly nothing to them. What they saw was not a perfectly balanced set of abstract qualities. What they saw resembles in no way our tidy, hindsight-blinded models. What they saw was an imperfect man who understood very well what sort of an extremist he should be. For Dr. King, leading meant defining, vividly, the goal, and then taking advantage of any opportunity to press toward that goal. There was no detailed plan of execution—first this, then this, then that. Rather, there was a clarion vision—"let freedom ring"—and then an unswerving commitment to intervene whenever and wherever progress toward that vision could be made, and to do so regardless of the personal or physical risks that any such action entailed. His approach was contingent, opportunistic, and incremental. It focused on imagined change, not on predictable execution. Its focus was at once broad, in terms of vision, and narrow, in terms of what must be done in the here and now—but its focus was not in between those two, in any kind of roadmap to success. It relinquished certainty on how the goal might be met, and substituted trust that the right actions done now and repeated at every future opportunity would ultimately prevail.

As we stand and survey the exhibition, our perspective, looking down from above and at the same time looking back from the future, offers us a certain clarity. King's followers, however, were not afforded that luxury. What confronted African Americans in the 1950s and 1960s who sought to claim those rights that the Constitution had promised them was not a tidy journey with well-defined steps. It was, rather, massive and pervasive uncertainty. King, the spiky extremist, helped them see into that future; helped them perceive, however dimly, what its contours might be, and how they might be a part of it.

• • •

In the spring of 1968, Memphis is a troubled city. In February the city's sanitation workers, frustrated by years of poor pay and poor working conditions, and angered by the deaths of two of their number in a garbage-crushing machine, go out on strike. A march to support the strike, with King in attendance, degenerates into violence, and one young protester is killed. A second march is organized for the following week, and again, King plans to attend.

His staff and close friends don't want him to go. He's tired, depressed, not sleeping, and drinking heavily. He's being criticized, constantly, by the press, by local leaders in Memphis, and even by some within his own movement. He's watched wherever he goes. He has even, a couple of weeks earlier, sent his wife synthetic red carnations instead of real ones, because he wants her to have something that will outlast him.[5]

He knows, however, that unless he can lead a nonviolent protest in Memphis—unless he can reclaim the moral high ground—the future of all he has worked for will be at risk. So he goes. His flight to Memphis is delayed by a bomb threat. When the plane finally makes it to Tennessee, it's met, unexpectedly, by a police detail, which seems to be there less to protect him than to monitor him. During his first meeting of the day, word comes in that the city has issued an injunction against the march. His second meeting of the day is with a group of black activists who are believed to have been responsible for the violence in the first march, and whom King is trying to persuade to act peacefully if the second march goes ahead. He's pulled away from this meeting to confer with his lawyers about their strategy to remove the injunction. Then, it's back to the activists. Outside, the skies darken—a storm is on the way.

Exhausted and battling laryngitis, he tells his colleagues that he won't be able to speak at a rally planned for that evening, and asks Ralph Abernathy to give an address in his place. He lies down on the bed in his room and tries to rest. Before very long, Abernathy calls. There's a huge crowd at the rally, and they want to see King. Can he come after all?

King often speaks without preparation, and the speech he gives this evening is no exception. He begins by imagining that he's been given the choice of which era of human history he would like to live in, and his answer becomes a sort of journey. From ancient Egypt, to ancient Greece, to Rome, and then to the Renaissance, King tells us what momentous events he would be able to witness in each place, before rejecting each in turn, declaring, "But I wouldn't stop there." He keeps going, past Lincoln's Emancipation Proclamation, and past Roosevelt's New Deal, until he arrives in the second half of the twentieth century. It's a familiar rhetorical device, of course—not this . . . not this . . . but *this*—and here it serves to locate the present moment in the arc of history. This is the moment in all of history he would choose, because now matters most, at least to this man.

Next he is practical and directive. Unity is critical—division will lead to defeat—and it is important to "keep the issues where they are":

> The issue is the refusal of Memphis to be fair and honest in
> its dealings with its public servants, who happen to be sani-
> tation workers. Now, we've got to keep attention on that . . .
> we've got to march again, in order to put the issue where it
> is supposed to be—and force everybody to see that there are
> thirteen hundred of God's children here suffering, sometimes
> going hungry, going through dark and dreary nights won-
> dering how this thing is going to come out. That's the issue.

He emphasizes the importance of economic protest, reminding his listeners of their collective economic power and encouraging them to use it to hold corporations to account. He goes so far as to list names of particular brands of bread to avoid (Wonder Bread and Hart's Bread), and tells his audience to encourage their neighbors, too, to boycott these brands. He advocates for black-owned banking and insurance companies. All this, he says, is in the name of intensifying the protest: "Up to now, only the garbage men have been feeling pain; now we must kind of redistribute the pain."

He tells the story of the Good Samaritan, and uses it to make a very specific point. He asks his audience to imagine why the Levite and the priest did not stop to help the injured man, and wonders if it was because they were afraid of what might happen to them. He describes the road between Jerusalem and Jericho where the events of the parable took place—he has driven down it—and tells his audience how remote and dangerous ("really conducive for ambushing") it is. And he makes the question that faced the Samaritan the question that faces his listeners, as they consider, perhaps fearfully, whether to join the upcoming march:

> That's the question before you tonight. Not, "If I stop to help the sanitation workers, what will happen to my job." Not, "If I stop to help the sanitation workers what will happen to all of the hours that I usually spend in my office every day and every week as a pastor?" The question is not, "If I stop to help this man in need, what will happen to me?" The question is, "If I do *not* stop to help the sanitation workers, what will happen to them?" That's the question.

Then he begins his ending. In both an echo and a continuation of his opening tour of history, he tells the audience of being stabbed by a deranged woman years before, and learning that the knife had come so close to his aorta that had he sneezed, he would have died. And now this—"If I had sneezed"—becomes a refrain as he recounts what he has witnessed in a few years in the second half of the twentieth century. If he had sneezed, he wouldn't have seen the sit-ins of the 1960s. If he had sneezed, he wouldn't have seen the Freedom Riders. If he had sneezed, he wouldn't have seen the Montgomery bus boycott, or the protests in Birmingham, or the "great movement" in Selma. And finally:

> If I had sneezed, I wouldn't have been in Memphis to see a community rally around those brothers and sisters who are suffering.
>
> I'm so happy that I didn't sneeze.

He ends where he began: Now is the most important time. Here, Memphis, is the most important place.

What connects all these things? What connects a tired man, coming to Memphis against the advice of his team, to this same man giving a speech when all he wants to do is to stay in his hotel; to the opening rejection, in that speech, of every period in history in favor of now; to the advice to stay together; to the injunction to keep the issues where they are; to the reminders and instructions on the power of economic action; to the tale of the Samaritan, used to encourage people to march in support of the sanitation workers; to his final words, locating Memphis in this moment at the apex of a journey without peer in history?

We follow a leader because he is deep in something, and he knows what that something is. His knowledge of it, and the evidence of his knowledge of it, gives us both certainty in the present and confidence in the future. And the something that we see when we look at Dr. Martin Luther King Jr. is not, ultimately, the oratory, magnificent though that is, or the self-sacrifice, inspiring though that is, or the ideology of non-violence, uplifting though that is, or even the indefatigable persistence, humbling though that is—but rather the end to which all these are deployed, time and time again. Martin Luther King Jr. was a crucible maker. He brought issues to a head, deliberately and relentlessly. His brilliance was the brilliance of not letting go, of creating intensity and focus and a concentration of time and place, and then adding more fuel and urgency and energy until, out of the white heat that he had made, something happened. That was his spike.

We see this in the structure of his speech that night in Memphis—in the opening, using the repetition of "but I wouldn't stop there" to intensify our focus on *now*, and in the closing, using the repetition of "if I had sneezed" to point us to *here*—and we can speculate whether the tension-building techniques of the orator, which he learned at a young age, were in fact the germ of this ability.

We see it when he says, directly:

> . . . we have been forced to a point where we are going to
> have to grapple with the problems that men have been trying
> to grapple with through history, but the demands didn't force
> them to do it. Survival demands that we grapple with them
> . . . It is no longer a choice between violence and nonviolence
> in this world; it's nonviolence or nonexistence. That is where
> we are today.

It's not violence or nonviolence, because that's not a crucible. It's nonviolence or nonexistence, because that is.

We see it in the contours of his life, laid out for us in his final speech and laid out before us on the exhibition floor in Memphis. He didn't always know what the next point of friction would be, but he could seize a moment and make it a crucible, time and time again. This was his way to get people to see his truth—that the current day was not the Promised Land. And it was his way to recognize, honor, and alleviate the uncertainty his followers felt. This was not the totality of King, of course; it is, however, what we see as most distinctive about him, and it is what we hook on to and follow.

And the uniqueness of this ability to force the issue becomes clearer still when we think about what his contemporary leaders were doing. When John F. Kennedy said, "The torch has been passed to a new generation of Americans," it was inspiring and future-is-now-ing, because that was his spike—but it wasn't crucible making. When Malcolm X said, "There's no such thing as a nonviolent revolution," it was raising the temperature, because that was his spike, but it wasn't raising the intensity—it wasn't crucible making. And when Robert Kennedy said, "Let us dedicate ourselves to what the Greeks wrote so many years ago: to tame the savageness of man and make gentle the life of this world," it was to focus his listeners on a noble and righteous cause in his own spiky way, but it wasn't crucible making.

Crucible making was the pattern and the technique of King's life. And the compulsion to do this was what led him to ignore his advisers and return to Memphis, because going back was the only way to force the issue.

As he nears the end of his speech that night, he's well aware of the dangers facing him. He knows that he's such a good crucible maker that sooner or later something bad is bound to happen; that he is such a good crucible maker that sooner or later he will get caught up in the fire; that, moreover, his putting his own life repeatedly at risk is an essential element of his ability to continually force the issue. He knows, therefore, that as the noise surrounding him becomes louder—as it has been doing for weeks—he needs to anticipate what will happen if he is no longer there. And he knows that he wants his movement—his series of crucibles, each leading to a breakthrough, and each creating the possibility of the next—to continue after him, and that for this to happen, he must subordinate himself to it, and yet imbue it with such energy that it is unstoppable. He does this as only he can:

> Well, I don't know what will happen now. We've got some difficult days ahead. But it really doesn't matter with me now, because I've been to the mountaintop.

And I don't mind.

Like anybody, I would like to live a long life. Longevity has its place. But I'm not concerned about that now. I just want to do God's will. And He's allowed me to go up to the mountain. And I've looked over. And I've seen the Promised Land. I may not get there with you. But I want you to know tonight, that we, as a people, will get to the Promised Land!

And so I'm happy, tonight.

I'm not worried about anything.

I'm not fearing any man!

Mine eyes have seen the glory of the coming of the Lord!

· · ·

And now the reason for our ascent is clear, because now we are looking into a motel room, and it is the motel room, on the second floor of the Lorraine Motel, where Martin Luther King Jr. spent his last day. After his sermon the evening before, King spent most of April 4, 1968, in this room, joking with his brother, who was also there, calling his parents, and even, at one point, starting a pillow fight with a fellow minister. It's a modest room—meager, even. Two queen beds with thin coverings; a nightstand with a phone and a lamp; a small TV attached to the wall on a bracket; the bedclothes brown, the curtains holding back the bright light also orange-brown; the carpet brown, too. And a door leading to the balcony. A few moments after six o'clock that evening, King stepped through the door, onto the balcony, and it was there that the assassin's bullet found him.

As we write, we are days away from the fiftieth anniversary of King's death. Our journey to the Promised Land is further along now, and yet still incomplete and still contested. And across five decades the force of what this man stood for is still strong, even to those of us who were born after his death, and who know him only through the sermons, and speeches, and memorials. It is strong not because of the breadth of his abilities, but because of their narrowness and their focus, and consequently their distinctiveness and their power. This is what drew followers to him in their millions during his life, and this is what outlives him and draws us to his cause to this day.

Leading and following are not abstractions. They are human interactions; human relationships. And their currency is the currency of all human relationships—the currency of emotional bonds, of trust, and of love. If you, as a leader, forget these things, and yet master everything that theory world tells you matters, you will find yourself alone. But if you understand who you are, at your core, and hone that understanding into a few special abilities, each of which refracts and magnifies your intent, your essence, and your humanity, then, in the real world, we will see you.

And we will follow.

Truths

TRUTH #1 People care which team they're on

(Because that's where work actually happens.)

TRUTH #2 The best intelligence wins

(Because the world moves too fast for plans.)

TRUTH #3 The best companies cascade meaning

(Because people want to know what they all share.)

TRUTH #4 The best people are spiky

(Because uniqueness is a feature, not a bug.)

TRUTH #5 People need attention

(Because we all want to be seen for who we are at our best.)

TRUTH #6 People can reliably rate their own experience

(Because that's all we have.)

TRUTH #7 People have momentum

(Because we all move through the world differently.)

TRUTH #8 Love-in-work matters most

(Because that's what work is really for.)

TRUTH #9 We follow spikes

(Because spikes bring us certainty.)

The ADPRI's Global Study of Engagement

Dr. Mary Hayes, Dr. Frances Chumney
Dr. Corinne Wright, Marcus Buckingham

In July 2018 the ADP Research Institute (ADPRI) conducted a nineteen-country study of the world's workforce. The aim of the study was to measure the relative levels of engagement of each country, and to identify the conditions at work that are most likely to attract and keep talented employees. This study repeated and amplified a similar global study conducted in 2015 that involved thirteen countries.

In each country we identified a random sample of 1,000 full-time and part-time employees, stratified by various demographics, such as age, gender, and education level, and broken out by various industries and work types. With oversampling, a total of 19,346 employees were selected and surveyed.

The survey asked about many aspects of respondents' attitudes to work, but at its core was a reliable and valid measure of engagement, developed over the last decade, and comprising eight questions. Extensive previous research has shown that those who answer these eight questions positively are more likely to be seen as highly productive, and less likely to leave, and these predictive relationships between high scores on the questions and higher performance and retention are statistically significant and stable across industries and roles.

Using this survey we are able to calculate the percentage of workers who are Fully Engaged in any team, company, or country; and to examine which conditions are most likely to lead to being Fully Engaged at work.

- The percentage of Fully Engaged workers is calculated using a formula that captures the extreme positives on each question, and then weights each question's responses according to its relative power, giving more weight to those questions with the greatest explanatory power.

- Those workers who are not Fully Engaged fall into a category we call, simply, "Coming to Work." These workers are not necessarily actively disengaged—the survey was built to measure positive functioning, not pathology. They are instead merely workers who are not contributing all that they possibly could.

In 2018 we used the same survey and same sampling methodology, and applied the same country-specific corrections (to take into account how different nationalities respond differently to survey scales), as we did in 2015. As far as we are aware, this 2018 study is the largest and most reliable study of global worker engagement yet undertaken. The ten principal questions that we explored, together with our findings, are as follows.

1. Has global engagement increased or decreased in the last three years?

Global engagement remains at almost exactly the same level as it was in the thirteen original countries.

- 16.2 percent Fully Engaged in 2015, as compared with 15.9 percent in 2018. This means that, globally, fully 84 percent of workers are merely Coming to Work, and are not contributing all they could to their organizations.

Clearly, organizations have not yet solved the challenge of getting most workers to see work as a place where they can give of themselves, and be recognized and valued for their best.

There are obviously many entrenched reasons for this—macroeconomic forces; the difficult, dangerous, and monotonous nature of some kinds of work; and the labor policies of certain countries, for example. However, as we will see below, the data suggests that there are nonetheless some actions that organizations can take to be more intentional and systematic in the way they seek to engage their workers.

Though the overall level of engagement remained stable from 2015 to 2018, we found significant variation in the percentage of Fully Engaged workers by country.

- In eight countries the percentage of those Fully Engaged increased (Argentina, Australia, Canada, France, India, Italy, Spain, and the United Kingdom).

- In four countries the percentage of those Fully Engaged decreased (Brazil, China, Mexico, and the United States).

India showed the largest increase in the percentage of Fully Engaged workers, up 5 points to 22 percent, and China showed the largest decrease, with a 13-point drop to 6 percent.

2. Which are the most and least engaged countries in the world?

In 2018 we surveyed an additional six countries to those surveyed in 2015: Egypt, the Netherlands, Saudi Arabia, Singapore, South Africa, and the United Arab Emirates. The UAE has the highest percentage of Fully Engaged workers, at 26 percent, while China has the lowest percentage of Fully Engaged workers, at 6 percent.

3. What factors contribute most to a worker's feeling Fully Engaged?

We examined many variables that could possibly contribute to a feeling of engagement at work, such as industry, position title, education level, gender, part-time versus full-time, and gig versus nongig.

Although each of these revealed interesting relationships (which we reference below), one factor trumped all others in its ability to explain a worker being Fully Engaged: whether or not the worker was on a team.

- Workers who say they are on a team are 2.3 times more likely to be Fully Engaged than those who say they are not.

This finding holds true within all countries in the study, and in many countries the disparity between nonteam and team workers is even greater.

- For example, in Brazil 5 percent of nonteam workers are Fully Engaged, whereas 15 percent of team workers are Fully Engaged. Likewise, in Singapore 4 percent of nonteam workers are Fully Engaged as compared with 22 percent of team workers.

Across the world, the data reveals that it is extremely difficult to engage workers who do not feel part of a team. The challenge for almost all organizations today, however, is that they are not set up to know very much about their teams. Current human resource systems are extensions of financial systems and so are able to show only who-reports-to-whom boxes on an organizational chart. The challenge with this, of course, is that most work does not happen in these structured boxes.

- Of those who say they work in teams, 64 percent of them report that they work on more than one team, and that this team is not represented in the org chart.

Clearly, there are many reasons why engagement levels remain relatively low across the world, some of those reasons relating to the nature of work itself, some to macroeconomic conditions in the region or country, and some to the specifics of the industry or company. However, it appears that one of the reasons that engagement remains relatively low across the world is that organizations do not understand, or act on, the vital power of teams.

- Organizations do not know how many teams they have, who is on them, or which are their best and most engaged teams.

- When organizations make great teams their primary focus—what creates them, what can fracture them—we may well see significant rises in global engagement.

4. What factors create a highly engaged team?

Eighty-three percent of workers report that they are on a team. Some of these teams, though, are more engaging than others. When we examined the most engaged teams we found that by far the best explainer of engagement levels was whether or not the team members trusted their team leader.

- Of those who strongly agreed that they trusted their team leader 45 percent were Fully Engaged. Of those who didn't strongly agree only 6 percent were Fully Engaged. A worker is twelve times more likely to be Fully Engaged if she trusts her team leader.

Across countries, industries, and positions a trusted team leader is the foundation for building highly engaged teams.

5. Which factors create trust in a team leader?

Two questions in the survey showed the strongest relationship to a worker's feeling of trust in his team leader:

- Do I know clearly what is expected of me at work?

- Do I have the chance to use my strengths every day?

This data suggests that these two conditions—knowing what is expected, and being able to play to one's strengths—are the foundations of trust. When a team leader, despite the ambiguities and the fluid and fast pace of the world of work, can help team members feel clarity about expectations and a sense that their best is recognized and utilized frequently, then trust is built, and a Fully Engaged team becomes more likely.

6. Is it more engaging to be a full-time worker, a part-time worker, a virtual worker, or a gig worker?

According to the study, the most engaging work status is to have one full-time job and one part-time job.

- Of those who have this status, 25 percent are Fully Engaged, compared to 16 percent for those whose status is captured in only one of the other categories.

- A possible explanation is that this status brings the best of both worlds—the full-time job brings stability and benefits, while the part-time role brings not only some additional earnings but also flexibility and the chance to do something the worker truly enjoys.

Gig-only workers who are part of a team are also highly engaged.

- Of gig-only workers on teams, 21 percent are Fully Engaged, as compared with 15 percent of traditional workers.

The two most common reasons for taking gig work are flexibility of schedule and the chance to do something the worker loves, suggesting that, as we saw with part-time work, these two factors may well be one of the sources of the worker's higher level of engagement.

- The most common title of gig-only workers is president, suggesting that many people take gig work because they like to see themselves as their own boss.

When we examine all of the eight engagement questions closely we see that gig-only workers score more positively on six of the eight, but significantly lower on the remaining two. The two questions where the gig-only workers scored lower than traditional workers were:

- "In my team, I am surrounded by people who share my values."

- "My teammates have my back."

This suggests that, as other researchers have noted, gig-only workers may well feel more isolated than other sorts of workers. However, when we examined gig-only workers who were also on a team, the differences on these two questions disappeared. This implies that gig work does not necessarily have to be isolating, and that if a gig worker can work in a team then she will net all the benefits of gig work (greater flexibility, higher chance of doing work she enjoys, being her own boss) while at the same time feeling the benefits of traditional work (the safety and support of her teammates). One implication for companies is that, if they choose to use contractors or gig workers—and today many do—the faster and more genuinely they can introduce these workers into teams, the more engagement, more productivity, and higher retention they will see from these workers. The inverse is also true: that the more companies can make traditional full-time work similar to gig work—as in, greater flexibility and ownership for team members, and a greater chance to do what they love—the more engagement, productivity, and higher retention they will see from their full-time workers.

In all countries and industries, virtual workers—so long as these workers are also team workers—are more likely to be Fully Engaged than those who do their work in an office:

- Of virtual workers, 29 percent are Fully Engaged, versus 17 percent for traditional office workers.

This suggests both that physical proximity is not required to create a sense of team and that the flexibility and ease inherent in working virtually are appealing to all workers (as long as they feel part of a team).

Working virtually is not the same as traveling for work. Those workers who reported that they traveled for work displayed the lowest levels of engagement.

- Of those who travel for work, 11 percent are Fully Engaged, versus 16 percent for those who don't travel for work.

7. Are workers with more education generally more engaged at work?

Yes they are.

- Of those with an advanced degree, 19 percent are Fully Engaged, compared with 12 percent for those with no college education.

8. Are higher-level workers more engaged than entry-level workers?

Yes they are.

- Of C-suite/VP-level workers, 24 percent are Fully Engaged.

- Of mid-level and first-level team leaders, 14 percent are Fully Engaged.

- Of individual contributors, 8 percent are Fully Engaged.

9. Are millennials less engaged than boomers?

Slightly. But contrary to our initial hypotheses, we found very little difference in engagement by generation.

- Of millennials, 16 percent are Fully Engaged, as compared with 18 percent of boomers.

10. Are men more engaged than women?

No. The data actually points slightly in the other direction.

- Globally, 17 percent of women are Fully Engaged, compared with 15 percent of men. Given the large sample sizes these differences are statistically significant, but a two-point difference such as this is not practically significant.

Seven Things We Know for Sure at Cisco

Roxanne Bisby Davis
Ashley Goodall

Four years ago, the human resources team at Cisco set out to measure the world of work as carefully and reliably as possible. Since then, we have led a group of a dozen researchers and data scientists in exploring the characteristics of Cisco's best teams, the relationship between attention and performance, the relative importance of team and company in our experience of work, and much more. Here are some highlights of what we've discovered so far.

1. The best teams are built on strengths.

We began by seeking to understand in detail what the best teams at Cisco look like. Our study, which we called the Best Teams Study, replicated studies done over the last twenty years by Gallup, Deloitte, and others, and began with the hypothesis that the experience of working on a high-performance team is measurably different from that of working on a non-high-performance team.

To test this, in late 2015 we identified a study group of ninety-seven high-performing teams by asking leaders across the company to give us the names of teams they wished they had more of—the teams they would clone if they could. We then defined a control group, which was a stratified random sample of 3,600 individuals across Cisco designed to represent the average team member's experience of his or her team. We deployed a confidential eight-item survey to both groups with identical messaging.

Once the survey responses were received we assessed content validity (assessed by item correlation), construct validity (established by confirmatory factor analysis, item-to-total correlations, and regression analysis), and criterion-related validity (measured through the strength of the connection of the survey items to the concurrent criterion of study- or control-group membership). Taken together, these tests told us that:

- The eight items were measuring a single factor ("engagement"), which is associated differentially with the best teams at Cisco.

- The item "I have the chance to use my strengths every day at work" exhibited the strongest connection to overall engagement and the strongest connection to other items in the survey. The item "My teammates have my back" showed the second-strongest connection, and the item "In my team, I am surrounded by people who share my values" had the third-strongest connection.

- The study group (i.e., "the best" teams) outpaced the control group (i.e., "the rest") on six of the eight items at the aggregate (whole-company) level. The two items that did not differentiate between the groups were both scored the same. (See "3. There are three distinct sources of engagement" for our further investigation of this result.)

Our study did show a statistically significant and meaningful difference between the best and the rest, suggesting that, at Cisco, the best teams harness the individual excellence of each team member, unlock the collective excellence of the team, and do so in an environment of safety and trust.

2. More-frequent check-ins are associated with increased use of strengths.

Wanting to understand more about what differentiated our best teams, we wondered if the simple act of a leader's checking in on a frequent basis with his or her team members influenced the team members' engagement level.

After completing the Best Teams Study described above, we gave every team leader at Cisco the ability to measure his or her own team on the eight engagement items we had used. While the data for a particular team was visible only to that team's leader—it was intended to help leaders understand how they were doing, not to evaluate them— we were able to use anonymized data for research purposes. We called our measure the Engagement Pulse.

To investigate the relationship between check-in and engagement, we selected as our sample team members who had responded to at least one Engagement Pulse over the course of two fiscal quarters. This gave us a research sample of 16,485 team members from the first quarter and 18,816 team members from the second quarter. We then determined for each quarter whether a team member was checking in frequently (80 percent of the time or more) or infrequently (less than 80 percent of the time).

We examined, for each quarter, the average response scores for all eight Engagement Pulse items, and looked for any differences between the group that was checking in frequently and the group that was not. In both quarters, we found that the team members who checked in frequently had statistically significantly higher scores for three of the eight items:

- Scores for the item "I have the chance to use my strengths every day at work" exhibited the largest difference between those who were checking in frequently and those who were not. Scores for the item "In my work, I am always challenged to grow" showed the second-largest difference, and those for the item "I know I will be recognized for excellent work" showed the third-largest difference.

This suggests that team members who check in with their leader frequently have an enhanced sense of being able to use their strengths every day, of being recognized for excellent work, and of having opportunities to grow. Although this study did not distinguish between correlation and causation (we could not tell whether the increased frequency of conversation led to increased engagement or vice versa), subsequent research, a portion of which is described in the final section of this appendix, indicated that it was in fact the increased attention, via frequent conversation, that led to the increased levels of engagement.

3. There are three distinct sources of engagement.

Our next piece of research set out to shed light on who has the biggest impact on a team member's engagement. To do this, we needed first to understand our engagement construct further and then to explore the difference, if any, between a team member's engagement across multiple teams.

As described in chapter 1 of this book, the eight items which most effectively capture team performance—and which are the same as those in the Engagement Pulse—can be divided into four "we" items, which capture team environment and company experience, and four "me" items, which capture each individual's experience of work. To further explore our engagement construct, we collected responses from 33,018 individuals who completed at least one Engagement Pulse survey over a six-month period, and performed two studies.

First, using a split sample exploratory and confirmatory factor analysis, we discovered that (at least at Cisco) there are two factors of engagement within the Engagement Pulse. The first factor comprises all four "me" items together with the two "we" items that ask about team environment, and so consisted of:

- At work, I clearly understand what is expected of me. (Me)

- I have the chance to use my strengths every day at work. (Me)

- I know I will be recognized for excellent work. (Me)

- In my work, I am always challenged to grow. (Me)

- In my team, I am surrounded by people who share my values. (We)

- My teammates have my back. (We)

We chose to call this factor *team engagement*. The other factor comprised the remaining two "we" items:

- I am really enthusiastic about the mission of my company. (We)

- I have great confidence in my company's future. (We)

We chose to call this factor *company engagement*.*

Our second study looked at how these two factors either varied for individuals who were part of more than one team, or changed as an individual moved from team to team. We found that changes in different parts of the engagement construct had different sources. In particular, we found that as someone moved from team to team,

---

*This is the discovery described in chapter 3.

company engagement varied least, whereas the items "In my team, I am surrounded by people who share my values" and "My teammates have my back" varied most.

Drawing together this study and the Best Teams Study described earlier, we have greater insight into the relationships between engagement, teams, and team leaders, namely:

1. All eight engagement items are scored more highly on the highest-performing teams, and there is strong evidence (in our studies and others') that higher engagement causes higher performance.

2. Of the eight items, the two constituting the company engagement factor are least sensitive to the particular team an individual belongs to.

3. Of the eight items, "In my team, I am surrounded by people who share my values" and "My teammates have my back" are most sensitive to the particular team an individual belongs to.

4. Of the eight items, the "me" items (addressing expectations, use of strengths, recognition, and growth challenge) are most sensitive to an individual's relationship with his or her team leader.

One way to think of these results is to imagine a team leader having three distinct jobs. Her first is to ensure her team members feel connected to the purpose and future of the company, even though she may not directly define those. Her second is to ensure that her team members, *as a group*, understand and support one another. And her third is to ensure that her team members, *individually*, understand what's expected of them and how they can do their best work now and in the future, all while feeling recognized for who they are.

4. Decreasing engagement leads to voluntary attrition.

Voluntary attrition is generally high on the list of concerns for organizational leaders, so in this study we sought to explore the connection between a team member's engagement and his or her likelihood to choose to leave Cisco. More specifically, we wanted to identify which of the Engagement Pulse items influenced a team member's decision to leave voluntarily.

We used both termination and Engagement Pulse results from a fiscal year, and from this constructed a population for those who completed an Engagement Pulse survey and either remained at Cisco or voluntarily left in the same fiscal year. Using a range of methodologies, including Pearson's correlation between predictors and outcome variables, a variety of regression models, and the bootstrap method to ensure the stability of our findings, we discovered that four Engagement Pulse items are significant predictors of voluntary attrition. They are, from most to least predictive power:

- "I have a chance to use my strengths every day at work."

- "In my work, I am always challenged to grow."

- "I am really enthusiastic about the mission of my company."

- "I have great confidence in my company's future."

This finding validates that there is a connection between a team member's engagement and the likelihood of his or her subsequent decision to resign. It further demonstrates that the more positively people feel about their strengths, now and in the future (the first two items above), and about their company's mission and future prospects (the second two items above), the more likely they are to stay with that company. The subtlety here is that, as we saw above, the feeling of enthusiasm about a company's mission, and confidence in its future, *still vary team to team*. In other words, our experience of our company is significantly mediated by our experience of our team.

The implication of this study is that, above all else, a focus by team leaders on helping each team member play to his or her strengths helps insulate the team against attrition.

5. Attending company events is associated with higher purpose and confidence.

Since 2015, Cisco has held a monthly all-hands meeting—led by our executive leadership team—that we call the Cisco Beat. The intended outcome of this monthly ritual is that our people gain a stronger collective understanding of our purpose as a company and a stronger sense of confidence in Cisco's future.

To measure if this was happening we investigated the relationship between the following:

- The number of Cisco Beats a team member attended.

- The average Engagement Pulse responses for that team member for items relating to the company engagement factor (collective purpose and confidence in the future).

Using data from 52,819 team members who responded to an Engagement Pulse over three quarters, we then identified how many Cisco Beats each team member had attended out of the eight that had been held in that period. Attendance was defined as attending the event in person, watching the event live via Cisco's broadcasting technology, or watching the event replay within two weeks of the event. We then segmented the team members by attendance—those who had attended no Beats, those who had attended from one to three, those who had attended from four to six, and those who had attended either seven or eight. We took this segmentation and looked at the average Engagement Pulse response for team members in each segment for the items "I am really enthusiastic about the mission of my company" and "I have great confidence in my company's future" (the two items constituting the company engagement factor identified previously).

Our analysis revealed that the more Cisco Beats a team member attends, the higher his or her average item response.

- Scores for "I am really enthusiastic about the mission of my company" increased from 4.37 for the team members who did not attend any Cisco Beats to 4.48 for those who attended all Cisco Beats or all but one Cisco Beat. This increase was statistically significant.

- Scores for "I have great confidence in my company's future" increased from 4.25 for those who attended no Cisco Beats to 4.35 for those who attended all Cisco Beats or all but one Cisco Beat. This increase was also statistically significant.

Those team members who are regularly attending Cisco Beats are more enthusiastic about our collective purpose and more confident in our future as a company. We have not yet explored whether attendance at these events subsequently increases engagement in this way, or whether those who are more engaged in the first place subsequently attend more Cisco Beats.

6. Highly engaged people talk about work differently.

We have found in the course of our research that it is helpful to distinguish between those team members with a particularly high level of engagement and everyone else. We refer to those individuals in the high-engagement group as Fully Engaged and everyone else as Not Fully Engaged. Our research has led us to a good understanding of the quantitative differences between these two groups. However, we were curious about the difference in the way Fully Engaged team members talked about work versus the way their less engaged counterparts did.

We investigated open-text survey responses to answer the following:

- What was the sentiment of each group overall?

- What topics did each group discuss?

- Were there differences in sentiment and discussion topics between the two groups?

To do this, we used our Real Deal survey. This Cisco-developed survey is sent to a representative sample of our population each quarter, and includes open-text response items. We isolated responses from team members who responded to the Real Deal's open-text item "What would you tell your functional leader about life in your function?" and who also completed an Engagement Pulse survey during a given quarter. In all, 1,275 team members met both criteria.

Using both natural-language processing technology and our own analytical approach, we were able to investigate the differences in the sentiment of the Fully Engaged and Not Fully Engaged groups. We used each group's Emotional Promoter Score (a measure of sentiment ranging from −100 to 100, calculated using a third-party algorithm) and the distinct words chosen in each group's text responses to spot differences in discussion topics and to automatically sort comments into themes. This allowed us to see how often each group discussed certain predefined topics.

Taken together, these data sets revealed clear differences between the two groups:

- Those who were Fully Engaged had, on average, an Emotional Promoter Score of 26 and discussed excellence on a team and/ or hopes for the future in their comments. The following comment is representative of this group: "It is very rewarding to see how the managers are willing to incorporate new ideas and new members to the team to improve and achieve sales goals. It is a very creative and productive way of working. If the teams are productive and happy, customers also perceive it."

- Those who were Not Fully Engaged had, on average, an Emotional Promoter Score of −16 and were more negative when describing their experiences on their teams. Comments from these team members reflected uncertainty about the future and frustration with internal bureaucracy. The following comment is representative of this group: "I think we need some sort of 'offsite' so we can help build trust across the next level of the organization. There's still a lot of silo-based behavior a couple levels deep and it would be great to show how we're trying to break that down."

As we continue to explore the natural-language processing of open-text responses, our next major focus will be the words team members use to describe their careers and career aspirations.

7. Some forms of attention are better than others in creating engagement.

Beyond understanding which things in the world of work are related to which other things (that event attendance is related to confidence in the future, for example, or that high engagement is related to specific text responses in a survey), we are of course most interested in what causes what. This last summary is an example of this type of research.

We wanted to understand whether the different ways a leader chooses to pay attention to a check-in influences his or her team member's engagement over time. Could we discern that team members who received frequent attention from their team leaders had higher levels of engagement than those who did not, and that a live conversation between a leader and team member was the best type of attention for a leader to provide to a team member?

To do this we investigated the following:

- How often team members were receiving attention from their leader, in the form of responses to check-ins entered in our team technology.

- Whether any methods of giving attention (viewing a check-in in the technology, commenting on it in the technology, or having a live discussion) were better than others.

- Which patterns of attention over time were most common (no attention, some attention, constant attention).

- How team-member engagement changed over time given the type and frequency of attention.

Looking at data from early 2018, we identified 6,726 team members who had responded to two or more Engagement Pulse surveys. We then used the first and last surveys for these team members to identify if they were Fully Engaged (FE) or Not Fully Engaged (NFE) at Time 1 and Time 2, respectively. This allowed us to identify those whose engagement, over the course of the study period, had increased (NFE at Time 1 to FE at Time 2), had decreased (FE at Time 1 to NFE at Time 2), or had stayed the same (either FE or NFE at both Time 1 and Time 2).

We then looked at check-in behavior and the different types of attention that can occur:

- For team members, we looked at whether they requested attention (by submitting at least one online check-in during this time period) or not.

- For team leaders, we looked at the four possible responses to a team member's request for attention: viewing a check-in online, entering a comment on a check-in online, having a live discussion with the team member (as subsequently confirmed by the team member), or providing no attention at all by not responding in any of the first three ways. After analyzing the data we grouped these possible responses into three segments: "no attention," "any type of attention," and "attention that included a conversation."

We were now able to examine the changes in engagement between Time 1 and Time 2 as a function of the most frequent type of attention received by each person. Since most team members respond to an Engagement Pulse survey every three months, these changes reflect the effects of different amounts and types of attention over the course of three months.

- For team members who did not ask for attention by submitting a check-in, the proportion that were Fully Engaged decreased 13 percent and had the lowest absolute level.

- For team members who consistently or near-consistently checked in but did not receive any sort of attention in return, the proportion that were Fully Engaged decreased 2 percent. We have found that check-in frequency drops significantly when team leaders do not respond, so we imagine that this group will, over time, come to resemble the group above—not checking in at all—with a commensurately larger engagement decrease

- For team members who always received some type of attention from their leader, the proportion that were Fully Engaged increased by 2 percent.

- For team members who consistently received attention in the form of a conversation, the proportion that were Fully Engaged increased by 3 percent.

We can conclude that any attention is better than no attention, that frequent attention is better than infrequent attention, and that the type of attention a leader gives matters. When the type of attention a leader gives to his or her team members includes a live discussion, we see the highest levels of team-member engagement and the biggest positive change in team-member engagement over time, irrespective of the conversational skill of the team leader or the quality of the conversation.

Research Contributors

John Lagonigro, Madison Beard, Mary Williams, Hanqi Zhu, and Thomas Payne

Notes

INTRODUCTION

1. "23 Economic Experts Weigh In: Why Is Productivity Growth So Low?" *Focus Economics*, accessed November 10, 2018, https://www.focus-economics.com/blog/why-is-productivity-growth-so-low-23-economic-experts-weigh-in.

LIE #1

1. To offer just one example, a recent article in *Harvard Business Review* suggests that culture comes in eight flavors (Learning, Purpose, Caring, Order, Safety, Authority, Results, and Enjoyment); that each of these is measurable across a company as a whole; that companies can combine several of these into their overall culture; and that an important part of selecting senior leaders is to assess the degree of correspondence between their intrinsic characteristics and the desired corporate culture. Boris Groysberg et al., "The Leader's Guide to Corporate Culture," *Harvard Business Review*, January–February 2018.

2. Edmund Burke, *Reflections on the Revolution in France* (London: James Dodsley, 1790).

3. Yuval Noah Harari, *Sapiens: A Brief History of Humankind* (London: Harvill Secker, 2014).

4. Yuval Noah Harari, *Homo Deus: A Brief History of Tomorrow* (London: Harvill Secker, 2016).

LIE #2

1. Stanley McChrystal et al., *Team of Teams: New Rules of Engagement for a Complex World* (New York: Penguin, 2015).

2. *The Battle of Britain, August–October 1940: An Air Ministry Record of the Great Days from 8th August–31st October, 1940* (London: H.M. Stationery Office, 1941).

3. McChrystal, *Team of Teams*, 216.

4. Ibid., 217.

5. Cisco data, as presented at the annual conference of the Society for Industrial and Organizational Psychology (SIOP), 2017.

LIE #3

1. Lisa D. Ordoñez et al., "Goals Gone Wild: The Systematic Side Effects of Overprescribing Goal Setting," *Academy of Management Perspectives* 23, no. 1 (2009): 6.

2. Teresa Amabile and Steven Kramer, *The Progress Principle: Using Small Wins to Ignite Joy, Engagement, and Creativity at Work* (Boston: Harvard Business Review Press, 2011).

3. Mark Zuckerberg, Facebook post, January 11, 2018, https://www.facebook.com/zuck/posts/10104413015393571.

4. Cammie McGovern, "Looking into the Future for a Child with Autism," *New York Times*, August 31, 2017.

LIE #4

1. See https://www.youtube.com/watch?v=ch-vWyK2yJs.

2. Stephen Pile, *The Ultimate Book of Heroic Failures* (London: Faber and Faber, 2011), 115.

3. Stated during an appearance in the 2017 documentary *George Michael: Freedom*, directed by David Austin.

4. "IBM Kenexa Core (Foundational) Skills and Competencies: A Framework with Core Skills Required for General Job Roles," IBM Corporation, 2015.

5. See https://performancemanager4.successfactors.com/doc/roboHelp/12-Getting_Familiar_With_PA_Forms/ph_wa_use.htm (retrieved 8/25/18).

6. See, for example, Dr. Robert Kegan's talk at the 2016 NeuroLeadership Summit, available here: https://neuroleadership.com/bob-kegan-feedback/.

7. Walter Isaacson, *Steve Jobs* (New York: Simon & Schuster, 2011), 42.

8. This story is told in more detail by Todd Rose in his wonderful book *The End of Average: How We Succeed in a World That Values Sameness* (New York: HarperCollins, 2016). We're grateful to him for his permission to summarize it here.

9. Stated precisely, there was no evidence that the average characteristics of a group applied to any individual in that group.

LIE #5

1. See https://www.youtube.com/watch?v=EqVyHMtSvFE.

2. Ray Dalio, *Principles* (New York: Simon & Schuster, 2017).

3. Adam Grant, "Billionaire Ray Dalio Had an Amazing Reaction to an Employee Calling Him Out on a Mistake," *Business Insider*, February 2, 2016.

4. Brian Brim and Jim Asplund, "Driving Engagement by Focusing on Strengths," *Gallup Business Journal*, November 12, 2009.

5. Joseph LeDoux, *Synaptic Self: How Our Brains Become Who We Are* (New York: Viking Adult, 2002).

6. Richard Boyatzis, "Neuroscience and Leadership: The Promise of Insights," *Ivey Business Journal*, January/February 2011.

7. Ibid.

8. Rick Hanson, "Take in the Good," https://www.rickhanson.net/take-in-the-good/.

9. Including, according to one recent piece of research, by looking for a less critical social network so as to avoid hearing the negative feedback in the first place. See Scott Berinato, "Negative Feedback Rarely Leads to Improvement," *Harvard Business Review*, January–February 2018.

10. David Cooperrider and Associates, "What Is Appreciative Inquiry?" http://www.davidcooperrider.com/ai-process/.

11. John M. Gottman and Nan Silver, *The Seven Principles for Making Marriage Work: A Practical Guide from the Country's Foremost Relationship Expert* (New York: Crown Publishers, 1999); and Barbara L. Fredrickson, "The Broaden-and-Build Theory of Positive Emotions," *Philosophical Transactions of the Royal Society B: Biological Sciences* 359, no. 1449 (2004): 1367.

12. See https://www.chronicle.com/blogs/percolator/the-magic-ratio-that-wasnt/33279.

13. Barbara L. Fredrickson, "The Role of Positive Emotions in Positive Psychology: The Broaden-and-Build Theory of Positive Emotions," *The American Psychologist* 56, no. 3 (2001): 218.

LIE #6

1. Robert J. Wherry Sr. and C. J. Bartlett, "The Control of Bias in Ratings: A Theory of Rating," *Personnel Psychology* 35, no. 3 (1982): 521; Michael K. Mount et al., "Trait, Rater and Level Effects in 360-Degree Performance Ratings," *Personnel Psychology* 51, no. 3 (2006): 557; and Brian Hoffman et al., "Rater Source Effects Are Alive and Well after All," *Personnel Psychology* 63, no. 1 (2010): 119.

2. Steven E. Scullen, Michael K. Mount, and Maynard Goff, "Understanding the Latent Structure of Job Performance Ratings," *Journal of Applied Psychology* 85, no. 6 (2000): 956.

3. More precisely, according to the researchers' determination of how much of the ratings variance could be tied directly to someone's individual performance, the person being rated is 16 percent there and 84 percent not there.

4. Hoffman et al., "Rater Source Effects Are Alive and Well after All."

5. This definition is from the *Financial Times*, and can be found at http://lexicon.ft.com/Term?term=business-acumen (retrieved 2/17/18).

6. James Surowiecki, *The Wisdom of Crowds* (New York: Anchor Books, 2005).

7. See Galton's original letter sharing his findings at "Vox Populi—Sir Francis Galton," The Wisdom of Crowds blog, http://wisdomofcrowds.blogspot.com/2009/12/vox-populi-sir-francis-galton.html.

8. This might be a little inside baseball for you, but please watch out for anything calling itself "driver analysis." This describes an approach in which the creator of a survey includes many questions about a subject, such as employee

engagement, and then at the end of the survey adds a short list of summary questions, such as, "I am proud to work for my company," or, "I plan to work for my company a year from now." The survey creator then runs a driver analysis to examine which of the questions in the body of the survey "drive" the summary items, and winds up pronouncing that certain items are the drivers of employee engagement because people who scored higher on them also scored higher on the summary items. Superficially this appears to be a conclusion based on valid data, but it isn't terribly helpful. One-off driver analysis doesn't tell you what drives behavior in the real world: it simply reveals that people who rated certain items more highly earlier in the survey also rated other items highly later in the survey; that people who were happy early in the survey were still happy later. Technically, this conclusion is valid. It just doesn't matter very much.

9. Lord Kelvin (né William Thomson)—the British scientist who, among other things, determined the value of absolute zero and who therefore knew a thing or two about measurement (and thermometers)—once said, "In physical science a first essential step in the direction of learning any subject is to find principles of numerical reckoning and methods for practicably measuring some quality connected with it. I often say that when you can measure what you are speaking about, and express it in numbers, you know something about it; but when you cannot measure it, when you cannot express it in numbers, your knowledge is of a meagre and unsatisfactory kind: it may be the beginning of knowledge, but you have scarcely, in your thoughts, advanced to the stage of *science*, whatever the matter may be." Sir William Thomson, "Electrical Units of Measurement," a lecture delivered at the Institution of Civil Engineers on May 3, 1883, published in *Popular Lectures and Addresses*, vol. 1, *Constitution of Matter* (London: Macmillan and Co., 1889), 73.

10. We could also, by the way, use this type of approach to design a better 360-degree-feedback tool—if we wanted to understand what someone's peers felt about his or her performance. In doing do, we'd have to be sure the questions asked each peer to rate him- or herself, as we've seen. But we'd also need to solve for two data-sufficiency issues: First, who makes up the right set of people to rate you, and how many of them do we need to respond to our survey? Second, how do we know that they know your work well enough to provide good data? These are tricky questions to solve.

LIE #7

1. Douglas A. Ready, Jay A. Conger, and Linda A. Hill, "Are You a High Potential?" *Harvard Business Review*, June 2010.

2. For a good discussion of this, see Ken Richardson and Sarah H. Norgate, "Does IQ Really Predict Job Performance?" *Applied Developmental Science* 19, no. 3 (2015): 153.

3. See https://www.britannica.com/biography/Elon-Musk.

4. John Paul MacDuffie, "The Future of Electric Cars Is Brighter with Elon Musk in It," *New York Times*, October 1, 2018.

LIE #8

1. Kristine D. Olson, "Physician Burnout—A Leading Indicator of Health System Performance?" *Mayo Clinic Proceedings* 92, no. 11 (2017): 1608.

LIE #9

1. We are not the first to make this point. But those who have arrived at it before us then continue by trying to identify the set of traits that all leaders should acquire in order to attract followers—bringing us right back to the idea that *leadership is a thing*. Our line of inquiry has taken us in a different direction.

2. Donald E. Brown, *Human Universals* (New York: McGraw Hill, 1991).

3. Pierre Gurdjian, Thomas Halbeisen, and Kevin Lane, "Why Leadership-Development Programs Fail," *McKinsey Quarterly*, January 2014.

4. This list is taken from Claudio Fernández-Aráoz, Andrew Roscoe, and Kentaro Aramaki, "Turning Potential into Success: The Missing Link in Leadership Development," *Harvard Business Review*, November–December 2017, 88.

5. Joseph Rosenbloom, "Martin Luther King's Last 31 Hours: The Story of His Final Prophetic Speech," *The Guardian*, April 4, 2018.

Index

Acknowledgments

There's one other pattern in the eight engagement items that we haven't explored yet. The first two

1. I am really enthusiastic about the mission of my company.

2. At work, I clearly understand what is expected of me.

address how we experience *purpose*, collectively and individually, at work. The next two

3. On my team, I am surrounded by people who share my values.

4. I have the chance to use my strengths every day at work.

capture how those around us help us achieve *excellence*, again collectively and individually. The next two

5. My teammates have my back.

6. I know I will be recognized for excellent work.

are all about *support*, and how we get that from our team and from the individuals around us. And the last two

7. I have great confidence in my company's future.

8. In my work, I am always challenged to grow.

capture how those around us help us see our collective and individual *future*.

So we thought it only appropriate to thank all those who've helped us write *Nine Lies About Work* in these categories—as each of their contributions has helped make the two of us a stronger team.

For helping us understand more clearly our own purpose in writing this book, thanks to our wonderful editor, Jeff Kehoe, to Adi Ignatius for his calm and compelling support, and to our incomparable agent, Jennifer Rudolph Walsh. For the questions, and for the challenges to hone our message and serve our true reader, thanks to Fran Katsoudas, Tracy Hutton, and Amy Leschke-Kahle.

For pushing us to be better in every chapter, every paragraph, and every turn of phrase, and for helping us glimpse what excellence could be, thanks to Adrienne Fretz, Yosi Kossowsky, Adam Grant, Alli Walton, and Katie Flores. For sharing with us their reactions to the manuscript, thanks to Jen Waring, Ania Wieckowski, Amy Bernstein, and the entire HBR editorial and production team. For living out our shared commitment to rigorous research methodology and the definitive data-driven discoveries to which it leads, our thanks to Drs. Mary Hayes, Fran Chumney, and Corinne Wright at the ADP Research Institute and to Roxanne Bisby Davis and the Team Analytics and Research squad at Cisco. And to Lisa and Andy and Miles and many unnamed others, thank you for allowing us to share your stories of what excellence looks like and feels like in the real world of work.

For supporting us on what has been an immensely rewarding journey from idea to proposal to manuscript to book, thanks to, at Cisco, Chuck Robbins, Megan Barba, Gianpaolo Barozzi, Christine Bastian, Megan Bazan, Madison Beard, El Cavanagh-Lomas, Jen Dudeck, Shannon Fryhoff, Dan Gibbs, Leslie Gordon, Scott Herpolsheimer, Charlie Johnston, Jean Kerr, Robert Kovach, John Lagonigro, Alicia Lopez, Amy Manning, Elaine Mason, Dolores Nichols, Jason Phillips, Oliver Roll, Rachel Samitt, Shari Slate, Tschudy Smith, Gaby Thompson, Mary Williams, and Tae Yoo. All of you know how messy the real world of work can be, and by dint of your efforts, each day you're making it better and more human.

At ADP, thanks to Carlos Rodriguez, Don Weinstein, Dermot O'Brien, Sreeni Kutam, Joe Sullivan, Charlotte Saulny, and the entire StandOut team; to Meredith Bohling for your prose and your community building, to Kevyn Horton for your web building, to Darren Raymond for your "potential," and to Christian Gomez for the power of your persuasion.

At HBR, thanks to our designer, Stephani Finks, and to our publicity and marketing team, Julie Devoll and Erika Heilman.

And for giving us the confidence to keep hammering away at the keyboard, for challenging us to put as much of ourselves into this as we possibly could, and for pushing us to write something that might actually make the future world of work meaningfully better, thanks to our families—Chris, Jenny, William, Graeme, Jo, Jack, Lilia, Marshy, Fitz, and Mojo.

From Ashley to Tina: I knew when I married you twenty years ago that you would be a better partner and friend than I had ever dreamed of finding on this earth, and that has proven to be so in more ways than I could have imagined. And although I also knew back then that you were a wonderful word-wrangler, and the most magical idea-honer I have ever known, the thought that one day my words would be the beneficiary of your keen attention never entered my mind. How lucky I am.

And, finally, from Marcus to Myshel: from "Who do these lies serve?" to "What does Picasso say about creation and destruction?" to "What can the freethinking leader teach the rest of us?" your questions have given voice to how our reader thinks and feels. And more, your patience in the process, your wit in the face of my writer's block, and your joy—love even—in the words we chose, all are red threads we have woven into the fabric of this book. Thank you for these, and, above all, for the passion.

One lesson of this book is that no one fits perfectly in any category we can think up, and of course the same is true for all the wonderful people we've listed in the categories above—so many of you have helped us in so many ways. We thank you all from the bottom of our hearts.

About the Authors

Marcus Buckingham is a bestselling author and global researcher focusing on all aspects of people and performance at work. During his years at the Gallup Organization, he worked with Dr. Donald O. Clifton to develop the StrengthsFinder program, and coauthored the seminal business books *First, Break All The Rules* and *Now, Discover Your Strengths*. He designed the StandOut strengths assessment completed by over one million people to date, and authored the accompanying book, *StandOut: Find Your Edge, Win at Work*. He currently heads all people and performance research at the ADP Research Institute. *Nine Lies About Work* is his ninth book.

Ashley Goodall is the Senior Vice President of Leadership and Team Intelligence at Cisco Systems. In this role he has built a new organization focused entirely on serving teams and team leaders—an organization that combines learning and talent management, people planning, organization design, executive talent and succession planning, coaching, assessment, team development, research and analytics, and performance technology. Prior to joining Cisco, he spent fourteen years at Deloitte, where he was responsible for Leader Development and Performance Management.